THE MOVES
THAT MATTER

THE MOVES THAT MATTER

A Chess Grandmaster on the Game of Life

JONATHAN ROWSON

BLOOMSBURY PUBLISHING

NEW YORK · LONDON · OXFORD · NEW DELHI · SYDNEY

BLOOMSBURY PUBLISHING
BLOOMSBURY PUBLISHING
Bloomsbury Publishing Inc.
1385 Broadway, New York, NY 10018, USA

BLOOMSBURY, BLOOMSBURY PUBLISHING, and the Diana logo
are trademarks of Bloomsbury Publishing Plc

First published in 2019 in Great Britain
First published in the United States 2019

Copyright © Jonathan Rowson, 2019

For legal purposes the Acknowledgements on p. 287
constitute an extension of this copyright page

ISBN: HB: 978-1-63557-332-9; eBook: 978-1-63557-333-6

Library of Congress Cataloging-in-Publication Data is available.

2 4 6 8 10 9 7 5 3 1

Typeset by Newgen KnowledgeWorks Pvt., Ltd, Chennai, India
Printed and bound in the U.S.A. by Berryville Graphics Inc., Berryville, Virginia

To find out more about our authors and books visit
www.bloomsbury.com and sign up for our newsletters.

Bloomsbury books may be purchased for business or promotional use.
For information on bulk purchases please contact
Macmillan Corporate and Premium Sales Department at specialmarkets@macmillan.com.

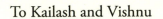

To Kailash and Vishnu

It is a very plain and elementary truth that the life, the fortune, and the happiness of every one of us depends upon our knowing something of the rules of a game infinitely more difficult and complicated than chess. It is a game which has been played for untold ages, every man and woman of us being one of the two players in a game of his or her own. The chessboard is the world, the pieces are the phenomena of the universe, the rules of the game are what we call the laws of Nature. The player on the other side is hidden from us.

Thomas Henry Huxley, *A Liberal Education*, 1876

Contents

Prologue

A wayward young man sought guidance in a temple on the outskirts of his city. He was weary, tired of pretending that he knew what life was for.

The resident master looked him over. 'What have you studied?' he asked.

'The only thing that ever really captivated me was chess.'

The master fetched his nearby assistant and reminded him of his vows of trust and obedience. He instructed him to fetch a chess set and a sharp sword.

He returned to the young man. 'You will now play a game of chess with my assistant, and I will behead whoever loses. If chess is really the only thing you feel is worth mentioning, and you can't beat someone who barely knows the rules, your life is not worth saving.'

On sitting down to play, the young man noticed he was beginning to tremble; the prospect of death bringing him to life for the first time in months. Suddenly something mattered. After a few familiar moves he rediscovered the bliss of concentration, the beauty of ideas, and his superior understanding became obvious.

On realising that he would soon deliver checkmate, he looked up at his opponent. The master's assistant was so unlike him. On the chessboard he was floundering, but he looked disciplined, dignified and full of the goodness of life.

The significance of the next few moves would live on and the young man was no longer sure what he wanted from the game. He maintained his advantage, but started to make small mistakes to keep the game going. The master noticed the change in perspective and swept the pieces from the board.

'No one needs to die here today!' he said. 'Only two things matter on life's path: complete concentration and complete compassion. You have learned them both today.'

But the master did not fully convince. The players knew the game might have ended differently. The young man stayed a while in the temple and the opponents became lifelong friends. It is not known whether they ever played chess again.

Introduction

Chess is just a game in the way that the heart is just a muscle. There is a muscle that pumps blood around the body, but it is the heart that sustains life, signifies love and situates courage. There is a game with sixty-four squares, thirty-two pieces and some rules, but it is chess that has become a metaphor for human battles big and small, an enchanting mirror for the psyche, and an icon for all that is deep and difficult.

Chess is not the meaning of life, but it does simulate conditions for a life of meaning. Whether through work or love or art, life becomes more meaningful whenever we take responsibility for something or someone. Responsibility is not always pleasurable or even positive, but it is purposeful – it adds significance and direction to life and helps answer the perennial human question: what should I do? And while our lives are characterised by many things, they are defined most profoundly by the open secret of our inevitable deaths. Chess simulates the meaning of life because it is a ritual encounter with death in disguise, where we experience the responsibility to stay alive one move at a time.

The game is sublimated warfare and chess players are compelled to kill, but unlike the gruesome horror of war, the martial conceit of chess allows us to experience aesthetic liberation. Every battle is a unique geometric story where two protagonists seek to destroy each other, but the underlying logic feels beautiful and true. The more intense the battle and the more sublime the ideas, the more we experience power and freedom.

No wonder chess has long served as the touchstone of choice for the competitive tension that defines business, sport and politics. The themes of planning ahead, knowing the opponent, anticipating responses and sacrificing for future gains are adaptable, and meaningful for anybody familiar with the symbolism of chess, even if they have never pushed a pawn.

However, the connection between chess and life is usually assumed to be almost exclusively about the application of strategic thinking. Too little has been written about how chess evokes and illustrates emotional and existential issues. There is more to be said, for instance, about the anguish of defeat, the craving for status, the joy of reaching beyond our grasp, and the sublime beauty of an unexpected winning idea.

This book is a philosophical offering on chess as a metaphor for life as a whole. The question that drives my inquiry is, simply: what has chess taught me about life? I attempt to answer that question through sixty-four vignettes over eight chapters. The narrative proceeds from psyche to community to world; encompassing cognition, competition, education, culture, technology, politics, aesthetics and beyond.

The psychotherapist Carl Rogers said that what is most personal is most universal, and I seek to be personal in that sense. The ideas that follow have been fashioned from the experience of dedicating myself to chess as a confused child, building a resilient teenage identity through the game, becoming a Grandmaster at twenty-two, travelling around the world as a professional player, teacher and writer for much of my twenties and early thirties, becoming British champion three times and regularly competing with world-class players, and then doing something that most Grandmasters never do: enduring a maturational process of detaching from the game and building a professional and family life outside it.

In a *New Yorker* essay on the famous Bobby Fischer–Boris Spassky match in 1972, the polymath George Steiner muses on the curious quality of 'trivial depth' that characterises the game. He describes chess as 'ultimately insignificant though enormously meaningful'.

The same description applies to many activities, and perhaps even life itself, and yet, Steiner notes, 'we have no logical-philosophical rubric for this strange amalgam'.[1]

As a chess Grandmaster who once lived for the game, and who now lives with the memory of that intensity as a father and a philosopher, I have come to know 'this strange amalgam' of meaningful insignificance or insignificant meaningfulness well. I have learned that it is precisely because chess is both something that doesn't really matter *and* something that matters enormously that the game is something else too: a gateway to the enigma of life. This book is about the challenge of living well in the context of that enigma.

Chess has been a silent witness to at least 1,500 years of human history, changing only very gradually as the world around it continually transformed. The notion that the game popped into existence at a single place and time doesn't ring true. Chess *emerged* from diverse influences and *evolved* to its current state.

There are some alternative histories out there about chess-like games appearing initially in China, Uzbekistan, Afghanistan and even Ireland, but the conventional wisdom is that the precursor to the modern game flowered in northern India at some point in the period between AD 531 and 579. Historians believe the game was invented for the particular purpose of illustrating the four 'limbs' of the Indian army at the time. Infantry (pawns), cavalry (knights), chariots (rooks) and elephants (latterly bishops) formed a game called *chaturanga*, which in classical Sanskrit means 'composed of four armies'. A king and his commanding officer (latterly the queen) were added, and the forces placed opposite each other on a tessellated board of sixty-four squares. The game evolved through Persian, Arabic and European influences, with subtle changes to the names of the pieces and how they moved until about 1640, when the castling rule was added and the modern version of chess settled into its final equilibrium.

Since then, for almost 400 years, chess has spread throughout the world and become an integral part of civilisation. The combination of global heritage, beguiling depth, strategic resonance and aesthetic charm makes it a game that amounts to much more than a game. To play chess is not to be an artist or scientist or sportsperson as such, but rather to know life through a singular combination of these major cultural touchstones.

In his 2006 BBC Reith Lectures the pianist and conductor Daniel Barenboim spoke of music's wider resonance in a way that also applies to chess:

> Why is music something more than something very agreeable or exciting to listen to? Something that, through its sheer power, and eloquence, gives us formidable weapons to forget our existence and the chores of daily life. My contention is that this is of course possible [...] but music has another weapon that it delivers to us, if we want to take it, and that is one through which we can learn a lot about ourselves, about our society, about the human being, about politics, about society, about anything that you choose to do. I can only speak from that point of view in a very personal way, because I learn more about living from music than about how to make a living out of music.

Barenboim's point is not that a particular piece of music evokes a particular feeling or feature of life, but something subtler; the phrase 'if we want to take it' is key. When a cultural phenomenon like music or chess has co-evolved with human society it contains meaning that is implicit in the way that most culture is implicit; as water is implicit for a fish, or the sky for a bird. We are surrounded by patterns of significance that shape our shared sense of what matters and why, and chess is one such pattern. The meaning of the game is sensed rather than grasped, which makes it all the more resonant and generative.

In his classic text of cultural analysis *Mythologies*, Roland Barthes writes that all meaning is in some sense warlike. No wonder snapshots of chess battles in motion can feel meaningful even when we don't know what is technically going on. In life we are always caught up in some kind of battle; sometimes for survival, sometimes for status, sometimes just to return home safely and get to bed. Those battles define us, shaping our identity, perception and priorities. As the Indian spiritual teacher Jiddu Krishnamurti puts it: 'Look at that battle you are involved in; you are caught in it. You are it.'

Each chess battle is a series of power struggles. The ultimate goal is checkmate, but the path to getting there involves positioning our forces such that we increase the aggregate power of our own pieces while reducing the power of our opponent's. If we succeed in gaining that kind of positional supremacy, our forces are likely to have superior scope and coordination and tactical opportunities will begin to arise; we are likely to win 'material', for instance picking off a pawn that has become weak or rounding up a knight that has been trapped. Then, all else being equal, we will be able to use our superior force to overpower the opponent, or to exchange pieces so that we are eventually the only side with any power left at all. There is usually scope to reverse the change in power dynamics, but both players know they can fall into an inexorable downward spiral at any moment. Set against that context, there is also a struggle within ourselves to replenish willpower and concentration, to fight ferociously while remaining calm and objective; a strenuous and dissonant combination of mindsets that very few can pull together consistently. There is also a subtle psychological power struggle between the players. Outright gamesmanship is rare – wearing a curly pink wig and sunglasses, eating loudly, or slamming the pieces on the board is more likely to distract the perpetrator than the opponent, because self-consciousness is more harmful to concentration than mere distraction. Nonetheless, we do try to silently impose our wills on each other through the nature of the decisions we take – our aggression and ambition – and how quickly and confidently we take them.

When struggling for power, details matter. Strategically critical squares can *infatuate* us because they determine who controls the position, we sometimes *crave* pawn structures because they help to clarify purpose, and we can *yearn* for beautiful tactical sequences to work even when, maddeningly, they go against the logic of the position. The experience is intense and captivating, but it is more about a sense of emergence than emergency. Thinking is sometimes something we do, but it is also something that discloses itself. As we mull over the position, ideas cross-pollinate and become systems of harmony and purpose, only to relapse into disparate moves because of annoyingly prosaic details. Then the clusters start forming again and we feel our way towards a decision. This welter of meaning is not on the board as such, but in the liminal space that emerges between our minds and possible worlds on the board. Most of this meaning remains implicit, and lives and dies within the duration of the game, as it must. As with life in general, we need our filters. Too much meaning is worse than none at all.

Chess is abundantly meaningful for those who play it; but the exposition of its meaning for the public at large remains vexing. Since the meaning of chess is mostly implicit, the relationship between chess and life is not captured in simplistic parallels to be merely noted – about thinking ahead or knowing your opponent. Instead, the challenge is to uncover a set of subtle, embedded, encoded associations that have to be filtered through technical expertise and professional experience. That means the inquiry has to be profoundly personal. I say this as someone who has lived deeply in two overlapping worlds; gladly lost in the sixty-four squares, but also searching for himself in the circles beyond. The main bridge between those worlds is metaphor, and the metaphorical significance of chess has been the story of my life.

In many ways I owe chess everything. I learned the game through family osmosis in Aberdeen, Scotland, when I was five. My mother taught me the rules and made sure I kept to them. There was always a chessboard at home, and my brother Mark beat me consistently and gleefully – I didn't think to mind. My Grandad Rae, Uncle Philip and two Uncle Michaels would offer to play against me regularly. I inferred from them that chess was not just one game among many like Scrabble or Monopoly. I couldn't articulate the experience as such at the time, but chess was as much a ritual as a game, as if every contest was not merely a playful activity to be shared but also a cultural rite to be enacted. That experience ripened over the years. With support and serendipity, chess became a *notion*: an enchanted social practice characterised by rituals, words, feelings and people that made me feel like I was growing.

On the week of my sixth birthday I was diagnosed with type 1 diabetes. Good medical care and my mother's encouragement gave me the lifelong conviction that this was just an irritation that needed to be managed rather than a chronic disease and incipient disaster. Against that supportive backdrop, chess gave me a felt sense for rules and consequences, an 'if this, then that' mentality, but more generally diabetes taught me that cognition is embodied. If chess can seem abstract, a hypoglycaemic attack, in which blood sugar can plunge to levels where you struggle to talk and walk and lose consciousness, is not. I do not know how many games I have lost over the years from blood-sugar levels that were too high – where you become sluggish – or too low – when you lose the capacity to focus – but I know that being diabetic gave me forms of self-knowledge that are otherwise hard to acquire. For instance, the kind of physiological introspection required to gauge one's approximate blood-sugar level when no means to test it are available is similar in spirit to metacognition – thinking about thinking – which is required to learn how to make better decisions on and off the board. You cannot really know your mind until you know your body; they are part of the same system, which is itself part of other systems. It is through paying heed to the interaction of mind and body and world that we begin to know not so much who we are but what we are. Our minds are embedded in their environments, encultured by the world around them and extended through technologies, but above all they are embodied. If your heart stops, you stop.

Chess also gifted me the knowledge of benign explorable worlds beyond my own, and how we need them. I was an unremarkable eight-year-old, but through chess I knew the giddy excitement of playing in the same primary school team as my older brother three years ahead, and soon afterwards I experienced the pride

of representing my city and latterly my country. These benign
explorable worlds are sometimes thought of as 'hobbies', but
the underlying desire is often not so much for the activity as for
periodic exile from our ordinary lives, with the promise of safe
return.

Building my life around chess as a bewildered ten-year-old gave
me a way to postpone confronting the reality that my father had
something called *schizophrenia* and that my family had gradually
and peacefully fallen apart. I grew up thinking this was OK.
Domestically and financially my mother heroically managed to
keep the show on the road. Emotionally everything was presented
as being more or less normal, and I was well enough cared for
and too young to have any need to think otherwise. My mother
began a new relationship and took me and my brother to Whitton
in Middlesex, just outside London, but things didn't work out.
The new father figure I had hoped to attach to turned out to be
controlling, narcissistic and domineering. However, the silver
lining in that brief interlude was that we lived on the same street as
the celebrated chess teacher Richard James, author of *The Complete
Chess Addict*, who ran the Richmond Junior Chess Club. His was
the first 'chess library' I had seen, and he introduced me to the
pivotal idea that chess can be studied. Chess thereby became not
just a game to play but a world I could visit alone and make sense
of on my own terms, and a thing to do that at least wouldn't make
matters worse.

But I was unhappy and homesick, and I came back to Aberdeen
to live with my grandfather in a maisonette in an urban valley
surrounded by two parks. My brother followed a few months
later, my mother a few months after that, but I suspect that brief
initial time of relative solitude and self-reliance was essential for the
person I became. The family's wooden chess set was propped on
top of three pine drawers stacked in the bay window enclave in my
bedroom on the first floor, overlooking our neighbour's garden. For
several years I sat on a round wooden chair with a red leather cover
studded with gold upholstery tacks. It didn't occur to me to ask
for a desk rather than drawers, and there was no legroom, so I sat

sideways to the board, or with knees on the reversed chair, or else I simply stood. That's the place I would eat bran flakes and raisins and flirt with new opening variations while listening to U2 albums, hoping my skin would look clearer the next day. Chess was part of the room, part of the home, part of the experience of growing up.

That same space was soon surrounded by games collections, tactical puzzles, endgame strategy books and manuals on opening theory, and I read them, in a manner of speaking. I played out book contents on the board, typically with the left hand holding the book open, the right hand moving the pieces, and the eyes shifting between book and board, as if watching a very slow tennis match of my own staging. That inconspicuous square metre of space changed my life. That is the place where I 'got good'.

Chess achievement gave me intellectual confidence that I might otherwise not have had. More precisely it gave a wayward twelve-year-old the will to heal and grow through autonomy and mastery; through outcomes and narratives I could control and get better at controlling. At that point this confidence did not translate into good school results, but more importantly it gave me the inner strength not to be defined by teachers' assessments.

As I became a young teenager, chess fostered a will to learn, despite the fact that schoolwork felt irrelevant. National exams began when I was fifteen, and the taste I had acquired for disciplined victory kicked back in, just in time to surprise my teachers and friends. Many teachers had long told me: 'If you are good at chess, you should be able to do this.' I had rejected this idea for years, partly because it is based on a stereotype but mostly because it meant I had to try harder. Yet I decided they might be right after all. I vividly remember the moment I put my chessboard away under the bed and did what we had been advised to do at school, namely to create a 'study timetable'. An ambitious weekly schedule stipulating what I would study and when was pinned to the bedroom wall. This practice had felt far too regimented to me – a constraint on freedom – but I was beginning to understand that the best kinds of freedom involve choosing your constraints wisely and claiming them as your own.

It became clear that I might have some academic aptitude. I began to love reading and learning and thinking and writing and speaking. The confidence gained through chess achievement fostered a desire for clarity of thought more generally, and an intellectual disposition that would later lead to Oxford, Harvard and a Ph.D., but there was nothing inevitable about this development. I was not a particularly promising pupil and could just as well have remained callow and adrift; messing up at school and taking refuge in chess, or leaving them both behind for drugs, sex and rock and roll. That might sound absurd, but it is more or less what happened to my brother, who began showing signs of psychosis around this time.

Maturing into a viable adulthood is partly about discipline, but it is also about luck. Aldous Huxley famously wrote that 'experience is not what happens to you, it is what you do with what happens to you'. That is profoundly correct – our life experience is not one event after the other, but a series of opportunities to grow by making sense of what is meaningful and what isn't – some do that better than others. Still, what happens to you in life is a matter of luck, before we even have the luxury of choice to shape character. I feel lucky to have escaped mental illness, to have lived a full life, and I feel the foundation for that was the confluence of people, place and priorities coalescing for me in the right way at the right time when I was about sixteen. Through chess and then exam success some kind of resolve emerged that was generative; I decided to be less defined by my circumstances and more capable of shaping them. Before then I was just an adolescent who was good at chess.

Several months later, on the week of my eighteenth birthday, my maternal grandfather died after enduring several months of bladder cancer. He had relocated to my bedroom to avoid climbing stairs and be closer to our bathroom, and so he spent his last few days in the same room as my chessboard and books. That is indicative of how chess formed me – it was part of the context in which life told its story as I tried to tell mine. Grandad had lived with us for years, and looked after me alone for months, often feeding me stovies – assorted leftovers emboldened by their status as a national Scottish delicacy, typically featuring potatoes, onions, vegetables and beef gravy. He drove me around Aberdeen on the back of his basic Honda scooter; his helmet was blue, mine was white; the uniform of our micro-platoon. I remember enjoying breezy streams of consciousness on the back of the bike, thinking not so much of chess positions but of social contexts where I might have conversations about chess positions, sharing my grasp of recently acquired chess lingo or opening theory. It felt good to simulate the sense of acceptance and delight we feel when seen and heard by like-minded people, and it was all in my head, under my helmet.

I can't say that chess helped me cope directly with my grandad's death, but at times like that an awareness of a world beyond my own emotional life offered some inner stability when so much else was still in flux. I remember sitting next to my brother in the car on the way to the funeral; he looked cadaverously handsome but completely disengaged. He had long been growing distant and was increasingly eccentric – at least that's what we all hoped. But at some point Mark, my former chess idol among other things, was sectioned under the Mental Health Act. The law exists to protect vulnerable people from themselves and others in theory, but being 'sectioned' is also a euphemism for being locked up and injected with medication against your will. I remember visiting the psychiatric ward, which was only a few minutes from home. Somehow we broke through the electronic gate and escaped outside – the closest thing I have known to a prison break. Although we were going nowhere in particular and were only two minutes away, a police car was called automatically. The officers insisted that Mark be driven back, despite my plea to let him walk back with me for the sake of his dignity. They said it was the law, and he had to get in the car for the sake of his safety. I got in with him, defeated but not humiliated, and consoled by the notion that we held the moral high ground.

I share these details here not because I went home after such incidents and frantically played chess to recover. Chess's role in coping with trauma is as much about being part of the setting as being part of the plot. Chess was always there in a way a listening friend or attentive pet is always there, and it felt solid and valid and reliable enough to confer distraction and security. I couldn't discuss my emotions with the game, but I could channel and act them out without harming anybody or being harmed. There was plenty of pain to sublimate, but my childhood was not generally unhappy and chess wasn't all about survival. There was childish fun and simple ego gratification along the way, and chess achievement made my transition to adulthood relatively painless. This emotional resonance is part of the metaphorical significance of chess. The game is never just about itself. Steeped in history and the accumulated wisdom of centuries of human experience, chess and its symbols can take on almost any character the player needs at that time; an encounter where we can express, discover, create and enjoy ourselves.

Chess is associated with intelligence mostly because the game involves logically working through complex problems, but I have come to believe that the power of chess as a symbol of intelligence also lies elsewhere: in the tacit recognition that metaphors are at the heart of creative intelligence and that chess is a particularly important kind of metaphor. We associate chess with intelligence not just because the game requires us to think several moves ahead, but because its relationship to culture discloses our mind's relationship to the world.

Intractable political negotiations are regularly described as stalemates, unwitting characters in movies are often described as pawns, and sporting commentators often announce disconcertingly that the tennis or cricket match you thought you were watching is now 'a chess game'. When I hear chess metaphors like these I feel bemused, not because they don't work but because they invariably do, and yet we rarely ask why. We think with and through metaphors all the time, but rarely notice we are doing it because our appreciation of metaphor is underdeveloped. We learn about metaphor in school alongside similes and analogies, but metaphor is more than just a way of comparing things.

I think of metaphor as the creative device we use more or less consciously to construct meaning through shifts in context, relationship and perspective. The poet Mary Ruefle calls metaphor 'an exchange of energy, an event, [that] unites the world by its very premise – that things connect and exchange energy'. Metaphors anchor the sense-making process by relating subjective and objective features of the world. I am with the physicist Robert Shaw when he says: 'You don't see something until you have the right metaphor to let you perceive it.' One famous example of metaphor as insight comes from Einstein when he was just sixteen, when he grasped the essence of his later theory of special relativity by imagining himself trying to chase a beam of light. Metaphor is less like a comparison to think about, and more like the psychoactive lens through which we see, creating patterns that shape how we feel and think.[2]

If metaphors help to disclose life, chess helps to disclose metaphorical thinking, and it is no accident that chess plays this role of metaphorical touchstone. There are deep and extensively explored cultural and historical reasons for the magnificent fit between chess and the human condition.[3] Chess is international and transcultural, recognised and played throughout the world in part because it represents so many elements of human experience and endeavour – work and play, hope and fear, science and art, truth and beauty, life and death. Chess is a symbol, and as the American social philosopher Norman O. Brown puts it: 'Symbolism is not the apprehension of another world, but the transfiguration of this world.'

Chess is therefore not merely one metaphor but several – in fact, we can think of it as a meta-metaphor. Just as it is said that the Bible is more like a library than a book, and the Iliad not one story but several, chess has enough historical, symbolic and psychological richness to be an abundant source of scientific, artistic and competitive metaphors. Moreover, there is a sense in which the metaphor of chess has greater reality and resonance than the game itself. People are more familiar with what the game means as a cultural trope than they are with what the moves of the game mean. When people speak of chess metaphorically they are not really speaking about the game but about the metaphor of the game. In terms of its wider influence and resonance, the metaphor of chess is more influential than the game of chess, and subsumes it. Chess reveals that metaphor is sometimes the pre-eminent reality, or at the very least an existential toy that allows mind and reality to play with each other in a contest where no one can predict the result.[4]

Metaphors matter because they give conceptual shape to life, and we live within the dimensions of those shapes as if they were real. The cognitive scientists George Lakoff and Mark Johnson suggest: 'Our ordinary conceptual system, in terms of which we both think and act, is fundamentally metaphorical in nature.' Life really is 'a journey', 'big' things really are significant, sophisticated ideas really are 'deep'. Such conceptual shapes are real because we make them so. It helps to wake up to the fact that we are to some extent free to create new conceptual shapes, indeed that this may offer our only hope for a genuinely new world. It is for this reason that the mythologist Joseph Campbell says: 'Every religion is true when understood metaphorically. But when it gets stuck to its own metaphors, interpreting them as facts, then you are in trouble.'[5]

Metaphors help us perceive truth, beauty and goodness because they ground our thoughts and feelings in things beyond our current context while helping us undertake the inner work to generate imagery, association and our own felt sense of the 'fit' between the metaphor and the reality it relates to. We can learn to feel a metaphor's legitimacy at a visceral level, sizing it up for its appropriateness. We tap metaphors against what we already know to test their fidelity to the apparently real world.

For instance, a wise business might ask itself: Is this organisation more like a machine or an organism, and what does the answer imply for how we take decisions? If it is an organism, how might we propagate, and are we vulnerable to infection? If it is a machine, what kind of fuel is it running on and how might it break down? If it is both an organism and a machine, is it a cyborg? If not, why not? And so on. The point is not to find the right answer but to feel that your subjective experience of the metaphor is beginning to tally with objective feedback that arises from the world. Does this fit? Does it work? Why exactly doesn't it feel right?

Through exploring questions like these, metaphors draw upon a much wider range of cognitive and emotional processes than most forms of thinking, and we rely on them to make sense of the world. Not everyone agrees that metaphors are quite so primary, but understanding our relationship to metaphor better matters. Our culture is full of bad metaphors and, as the anthropologist Mary Catherine Bateson puts it: 'There are few things as toxic as a bad metaphor.' We very rarely hear politicians asked about why they are rendering their argument in particular metaphorical terms, terms that are often used to obscure rather than illuminate, and interviewers rarely suggest competing metaphors to move the discussion to a new register. I believe a more reflexive relationship to metaphor is critical to the next phase of our cultural evolution and that chess has things to tell us about how we get there. Enriching and expanding our range of images and ideas associated with chess therefore matters socially and culturally, and even politically.[6]

Everything is embarrassingly interconnected, not least our ideas of metaphor, mind and chess. Chess is often used to illustrate qualities of mind, but a mind is often tacitly assumed to be a computer, or like a computer, and it is nothing of the sort. And yet our language is full of this implicit association. As the psychologist Robert Epstein puts it:

> We don't store words or the rules that tell us how to manipulate them. We don't create representations of visual stimuli, store them in a short-term memory buffer, and then transfer the representation into a long-term memory device. We don't retrieve information or images or words from memory registers. Computers do all of these things, but organisms do not.[7]

Living as an organism is an experience in a way that living 'as a computer' cannot be. However, it is precisely because your mind is not a computer that it can entertain the notion that it might be, and use that notion to think further about better metaphors for the nature of the mind. That kind of metaphorical inflexion is the cutting edge of understanding. When we think not merely with metaphors or through them, but *about* them, we move beyond conventional analogies and unconscious frames towards forms of subtle knowing that define our relationship to life as a whole.

For instance, chess is not really *like* mathematics – metaphors are more than similes – but it does contain and reflect mathematics and is therefore often used to illustrate mathematical concepts like exponential growth and infinity. The most famous example is the medieval story of the wise man who was offered a gift by a king he had advised. The so-called wise man, who actually sounds slightly twisted, asked for the gift of a single grain of rice to be placed on a square of a chessboard, and then doubled repeatedly square by square. To the uninitiated that sounds like it might add up a bit, perhaps to a modest heap, but the scheme plays on the limitations of our intuitions. The perpetual doubling process means that the operative number is two to the power of 63. That means 1 becomes 2 becomes 4, 8, 16, 32, 64, 128 and eventually that grows to 18,446,744,070,000,000,000. If you were to place those pieces of rice alongside each other they would stretch for about 60,000,000,000,000 miles, which is further than the distance between Earth and the nearest star Alpha Centauri, and back again.

And that's just rice. When you factor in the relationships between different kinds of pieces that can move in different ways the numbers quickly run further out of control, and so chess acts as a metaphor for hidden depth. I can make 20 possible moves on the first move, and for each of those my opponent can make 20 in return, and these already growing numbers increase as the forces become integrated and the variations get longer. It may sound like the kind of exaggeration made by advertising agencies, but there really are more possible chess games than atoms in the known universe (*games* yield a far higher number than mere positions, because games include positions in a range of different sequences). And yet chess is not infinite, but rather an illustration of the conceptual difference between an enormous and functionally indefinite number of possibilities that is still theoretically constrained by rules (e.g. checkmate) and boundaries (e.g. 8x8 board) and the esoteric mathematical idea of a series that never ends. Chess is perhaps as close to infinite as a finite thing can be.[8]

The vastness of possibilities that are nonetheless finite makes the game feel inexhaustible and mysterious rather than completely beyond us. One of my favourite moments in Vladimir Nabokov's celebrated novel *The Luzhin Defense* features the main character Luzhin lighting a match for a cigarette during an important game. He is so deeply concentrated on the myriad variations that he forgets to extinguish the flame and burns himself. Nabokov writes that at that moment Luzhin experienced 'the full horror of the abysmal depths of chess'.

And the game is dark as well as deep. It seems fitting that just before the most popular Everyman character of the last few decades, Harry Potter, first encounters the quintessentially evil dark lord Voldemort, his final obstacle is a chessboard, in a game that nearly kills Ron, his closest friend. Chess simulates a truth that we tend to suppress, namely that life is hazardous and we are always at risk. The game is fun, but it's not an entirely innocent fun, which is why we tend to reach for chess metaphors in tense situations with high stakes.

Love, for instance, is a tense situation with high stakes, or at least it can be. Historically, various works of art and literature associate chess with courtly love and by extension with love in general. However, chess is a metaphor for love not because the players long for each other or want to knock down the pieces and make out on the board, though there is of course a time and a place for that. The link between chess and love is much more oblique.

The spirit of Eros permeates the game in the forms of suffering and passion that characterise unrequited and unconsummated romantic love; most of the time we are not merely thinking at the board, but also craving in a state of low-level anguish that we nonetheless enjoy. And shared attention over any process of co-creation is a rare and profoundly intimate process. In fact the intimacy we feel through shared attention may be an unconscious emotional driver that keeps us coming back to the game. Moreover, chess thinking in some ways entails compassion, because it is about cultivating order from chaos through caring about the felt significance of particular pieces and squares and ideas and outcomes.[9] The philosopher Martin Heidegger argued that caring is a fundamental feature of 'being-in-the-world', and a famous piece of research in gerontology helps to reinforce this point – in an old people's home, controlling for all other variables, those who were given a potted plant to look after consistently lived longer that those who were not.[10] So in the case of love, chess is about the experience of passion, intimacy and caring, but not in the way we typically use these terms – the game reveals implicit meanings in the idea of love by offering a shift in perspective and context.

The point is that metaphors don't function merely as comparisons but more like translations, re-creations or re-presentations. The theoretical biologist Diego Rasskin Gutman pushes this point further with reference to the role of the opponent as a source of thought and desire and will at odds with our own. He examines how the human mind has evolved to its present state through complex social interaction and highlights the non-trivial value of chess in that socio-biological context: 'What could be more human than a state of permanent doubt when facing the thoughts and actions of our fellow beings?'[11]

How we make decisions in that state of permanent doubt matters to everybody of course, and most situations in our lives feature 101 small decisions that we are barely conscious of making. Decisions are often framed in the context of strategy, and leadership as singular moments and matters of destiny, but they are more like repeated challenges and matters of character. Mostly we are not global leaders with a clear personal narrative featuring decisive moments and clear take-home messages. Mostly we are strangers to ourselves and each other, hungry for insight, meaning and refuge to get us through the day. I believe chess can and should speak to that more familiar experience of life.

The late English chess player, barrister and author Gerald Abrahams wrote that: 'In chess, one realises that all education is ultimately self education.' This idea is a timely consideration in our data-driven world. Chess lends itself to structured information and quantitative analysis in a range of ways – for instance the numerical value of the pieces, databases of millions of games, computerised evaluation functions and the international rating system. However, the value of the experience of playing the game is more qualitative than quantitative.

Like any competitive pursuit or sport, chess is an elaborate pretext for the production of stories. The benign conceit of rules and points and tournaments generates a narrative experience in which you are at once co-director, actor and spectator. Chess is education in the literal sense of 'bringing forth' and it is self-education because our stories about a game emerge as we play it, as we try to achieve our goals, just as they do in real life. Chess stories are of our own making, and they are often about challenges we overcame or failed to overcome. Every chess player knows the experience of encountering a vexed colleague who is desperate to share their tragic tale in which they were 'completely winning', until they screwed up and lost. And yet we also know tougher characters who recognise that taking resolute responsibility for your mistakes, no matter how painful, is the way to grow as a person and a player. As the child psychologist Bruno Bettelheim puts it: 'We grow, we find meaning in life, and security in ourselves by having understood and solved personal problems on our own, not by having them explained to us by others.'[12]

Chess can therefore give us valuable forms of meaning in ways that information, explanations and rational analysis cannot. A chess game is rarely meaningful as a given – it is not 'data'. The story only comes to life when we make meaning out of it, and then it becomes what some scholars call 'capta'. Chess has shown me that we need the unconventional language of 'capta' every bit as much as we need the present exponential expansion of 'data'. The philosopher of education Matthew Lipman puts it as follows in the context of children learning to think, but the point applies more broadly:

Meanings cannot be dispensed. They cannot be given or handed out [to children]. Meanings must be acquired; they are capta, not data. We have to learn how to establish the conditions and opportunities that will enable [children], with their natural curiosity and appetite for meaning, to seize upon the appropriate clues and make sense of things for themselves ... Something must be done to enable [children] to acquire meaning for themselves. They will not acquire such meaning merely by learning the contents of [adult] knowledge. They must be taught to think and, in particular, to think for themselves.[13]

The point of the capta/data distinction is that the power of chess lies not so much in the moves created by the games, but in our relationship to the stories we create through them. A chess game is rarely meaningful as a simple matter of fact – as 'data', the story only comes to life when we make meaning out of it, and then it becomes 'capta'. In the language of perhaps the greatest scholar of narrative thinking, Jerome Bruner, chess subjunctivises reality – it creates a world not only for what is but for what might be or might have been. That world is not a particularly comfortable place, but it is highly stimulating. It is a place, says Bruner, that 'keeps the familiar and the possible cheek by jowl'.[14]

In light of the power of metaphor, chess's role as a meta-metaphor, and the capacity of chess to illustrate that education is ultimately self-education, the question of what chess might teach us about life is worthy of some answers. The structure of this book mimics a chessboard's sixty-four squares, comprising eight files and eight ranks, alternating between dark and light. The collage that follows is broken down into eight chapters of eight vignettes featuring a sequence of key thematic contrasts, antinomies or juxtapositions: thinking and feeling, winning and losing, learning and unlearning, cultures and counter-cultures, cyborgs and civilians, power and love, truth and beauty, and life and death. What chess taught me about life is, among other things, that:

Concentration is freedom
It's the mattering that matters
Our autopilots need our tender loving care
Escapism is a trap
Algorithms are puppeteers
We need to make peace with our struggle
There is another world, and it is in this world
Happiness is not the most important thing

These distilled answers have emerged from a thirty-five-year relationship with chess that is still evolving. For about half of my childhood chess was central to my idea of who I was, and what the world was about. I loved the game with all the pain, need and longing that is wrapped up in love. I have loved chess as a child loves a guardian who keeps them safe, as a teenage boy loves a girl who represents love itself, as a young adult loves his newfound autonomy and his place in the community, as a student loves his teacher, as a friend loves his friend, and as a father loves a child. I am no longer sure exactly how I love chess, but it is in all these ways and more.

ONE

Thinking and Feeling

Concentration is freedom

When I search for my first experience of concentration, I find myself in the Beach Ballroom in my home town of Aberdeen. I am a young boy, I think eight, so not quite dangling my feet under the table, but still somehow placed there by the community, rather than choosing where to be of my own accord. I am competing in a primary school chess event against an older boy, and ours is the last game to finish before lunch.

I see the beach outside through large windows, some friends playing football on the nearby grass, and I sense a few grown-ups are still here to keep us on track. The opponent stood out for me because he came from a school – Mile End – that was somehow perceived to be bigger and better than my own school of Skene Square, about a mile away from it. Looking back I suspect 'more middle class' is close to the truth, but I was still shielded from such thoughts – youth, and chess, are great equalisers in that way.

I recall feeling depleted and hungry after several games already completed, but there was also this sensation of power, of knowing that I was already good enough to out-think and outlast him. He was at least two years older, so the prospect of beating him was doubly motivating. I recall feeling like I was in control, that I was competent and knew what I was doing. And I enjoyed the sensation that my opponent was floundering. My mind, body and soul were concentrated in bringing the full point home, and I loved the sensation of pending victory.

When I think of this scene now, over three decades later, I'm reminded of the Russian-American poet Joseph Brodsky. His life featured heart attacks, poverty and exile, but in an interview with the *New York Times* published on 10 December 1991 he said that he did not think he had really changed: 'I remember myself, age five, sitting on a porch overlooking a very muddy road,' he said. 'The day was rainy, I was wearing rubber boots, yellow, no, not yellow, green, and for all I know I'm still there.'

For all I know, I'm still there. That's how I feel about lots of my chess experiences – somehow so vivid and tender; as if those younger versions of me are still out there in unsuspecting nooks of the fabric of reality, playing. Those moments are touchstones for the memory. Mostly they are moments within scenes; snapshots rather than coherent narratives. Such snapshots can be pieced together across our lifetime. They are by no means solid proof of enduring personal identity, but they provide good circumstantial evidence.

What defines these moments is partly the experience of competence, but mostly it's the experience of concentration – the thing I miss most about no longer being an active chess player. The better you get at something, the richer and deeper the absorption becomes. The Hungarian-American psychologist Mihaly Csikszentmihalyi has built a large body of research around the state of consciousness called *flow*, characterised by intense absorption, loss of self-consciousness, meaningful feedback from the world and an altered sense of time. Flow experiences are deeply rewarding and they arise when our skill level and challenge level are optimally matched; too little challenge and we feel bored, too much and we feel anxious. In daily life we have moments of flow, but for enduring flow, little compares to a hard-fought chess game lasting several hours.[1]

Sitting down at the start of a chess game is like entering an eagerly anticipated party. All our old friends are there; not just the royal couples and their associates, and the reassuring straight lines of noble infantry, but also the convivial and elevating features of the place: the generative order, resonant harmony and latent beauty. Within this familiar pattern we know we have to navigate risk, but we feel fundamentally safe because the rules are sacred and inviolable. The contest might be confounding, but the outcome will make sense. While concentrating our experience of self is almost entirely projected into the caprice of the position on the board. And yet our need for identity maintenance lingers, because we are always a certain kind of person and a certain strength of player, and we literally *identify* with some moves more than others. But the sublimation of desire means that when we identify with *this* square, or justify *that* move, we merely experience intimations of the self, rather than a direct encounter.

The weapons we wield are civil and symbolic, but their function is brutality. All the emergent details of the battle feel ripe with meaning, and they need not be dramatic; a hunch, a trap, a transition – it all feels important when your figurative life is on the line, just as a cracking twig may tell us a predator is near. We search for good moves, but the process is as much tactile as visual – we are trying to feel our way through with intuition. The setting for a chess idea is always a confluence of the rules of the game, the strategic purposes of the moment and resistance from the opponent; while the plot of a chess idea will be a sequence of moves in which one state of affairs is transformed into another, leading to an evaluation of whether the change is desirable. There is no particular algorithm for finding good ideas, so mostly we amble among whatever seems interesting, trusting the important to reveal itself.

As tension rises, the responsibility to continually make decisions can feel unbearable. When we have stretched to maximum capacity but still can't fathom what will happen, the idea of luck starts to linger: a ghost of many names which no one really believes in, but everyone awaits. It feels as though stories of great consequence are unfolding and we are their author, yet every line we write will be edited by our co-author, who just happens to be our assassin. We are their assassin too, and our pulsating minds loom large within each other. Chess players experience unsovereign wills strenuously marshalling thought within stationary bodies – a profoundly unnatural state of affairs. That one sitting opposite, the other who reads my mind and shapes my actions; they want what I want, and we can't both have it. It is scandalous that they are allowed to figuratively kill me, and the only way to deal with the discomfort is to kill them first.

The game is not introspective in spirit. It may give rise to self-knowledge over time but that is never the explicit aim. Chess is also not quite like written exams, where we submit ourselves to being tested and lock ourselves into an intense encounter for a few hours, leaving the world outside behind. In chess the point is not just that we are tested, but that we are tested through hostile cohabitation. Every game is a place and time, and we share it with a figurative flatmate we have to live with for hours that can feel like years: someone who wants to damage your furniture, steal your precious objects and occupy your bedroom, before killing you. Chess is a test of the mind and will under social pressure. It reveals our response to a co-constructed reality, particularly our capacity to shape it in a competitive collaboration.

And it's wonderful! The tension of sublimated mortal combat is thrilling, and chess offers that kind of experience repeatedly and reliably. The game is like a drug and we play it to experience a change in consciousness: 'A swirl of deeply felt intensities' is how the anthropologist Robert Desjarlais aptly describes it. Rather than thinking of concentration as a narrowing of focus, like a laser beam, my chess experience tells me that concentration is more about summoning layers of oneself as sources of strength, while simultaneously purging psychic debris. Concentration is mostly a process of coherence-building, drawing forth different aspects of oneself. Some features of willpower, energy and attention are pulled into the self while others drop away.

The classic readings of Zen Buddhism include a story about concentration that I often read for inspiration while playing tournaments. It is called *Great Waves*:

In the early days of the Meiji era there lived a well-known wrestler called O-nami, Great Waves. O-nami was immensely strong and knew the art of wrestling. In his private bouts he defeated even his teacher, but in public he was so bashful that his own pupils threw him. O-nami felt he should go to a Zen master for help. Hakuju, a wandering teacher, was stopping in a little temple nearby, so O-nami went to see him and told him of his trouble. 'Great Waves is your name,' the teacher advised, 'so stay in this temple tonight. Imagine that you are those billows. You are no longer a wrestler who is afraid. You are those huge waves sweeping everything before them, swallowing all in their path. Do this and you will be the greatest wrestler in the land.' The teacher retired. O-nami sat in meditation trying to imagine himself as waves. He thought of many different things. Then gradually he turned more and more to the feelings of the waves. As the night advanced the waves became larger and larger. They swept away the flowers in their vases. Even the Buddha in the shrine was inundated. Before dawn the temple was nothing but the ebb and flow of an immense sea. In the morning the teacher found O-nami meditating, a faint smile on his face. He patted the wrestler's shoulder. 'Now nothing can disturb you,' he said. 'You are the waves. You will sweep everything before you.' The same day O-nami entered the wrestling contests and won. After that, no one in Japan was able to defeat him.[2]

We are all O-nami. When we succeed in concentrating, great power can flow through us and sometimes it manifests gloriously. Yet mostly we struggle to achieve the requisite state of heart and mind. People less wise than Hakuju simply tell us to concentrate, as if we should thereby know what to do, but concentration is not like a bulb that we can turn on and off with a switch, because we are not just the bulb; we are also the switcher and the switch. Humans are more like thermostats receiving and sending out signals, seeking the optimal 'mental temperature' as ambient conditions around us change.

Concentration is about building an alliance between parts of ourselves for whatever purposes we are caught up in. We succeed in concentrating when we manage to convene the dispositions that matter; for instance our awareness, attention, discernment and willpower, and then the assorted emotions that co-arise and come along for the ride, like fear, anger, determination, joy and hope. Concentration is a kind of cocktail of the soul. Only when our qualities are properly mixed and start to settle are we able to effectively zoom in or out of whatever we are caught up in. To concentrate is, literally, to coalesce.

We are not supposed to live at maximum concentration all the time. To do so would be strenuous, consume too much energy and run counter to the ebb and flow of life. And yet living well does depend on being able to concentrate when we need to – without that capacity to intensify experience, much that is rewarding in life passes us by. Not without reason does the ancient Indian philosophical text the *Upanishads* say: 'Those who achieve greatness on earth achieve it through concentration.'

Yet when normal experience is increasingly defined by overstimulation and our continual availability to others, to insist on concentration feels like an act of subversion. The challenge of concentrating is therefore only partly about the disposition of our mind and will; it is also about the context of our lives. Some phases of life allow for single-minded goal-oriented attention when concentration arises relatively easily – for instance if you are an athlete in training or a student with protected time to prepare for exams. However, many phases of life, including the one I am currently living through, call for multi-tasking, adaptability and flexibility. At the moment concentration is primarily about maintaining presence of mind and kindness as I try to submit with grace to my time being fractured.

Smartphone notifications tug at the muscle memory of my lower arms and work emails gatecrash my attention as unsolicited to-do lists. My mother calls to tell me about birthday cards I've forgotten to send and old friends find new ways of showing up; I'm pleased to see them, and dislike the part of me that feels diverted, and yet there are books to be written and time feels scarce. I am eager to build my new organisation too, but my youngest son wants me to build his train track. New bills come through the post that I have to query, but first there is lunch for at least four to conjure, while neighbours I have yet to meet build their kitchen extension one chiselled brick at a time.

These are First World problems, and I am grateful to have them. But at such times, without the refuge of concentration that chess afforded, it can feel as if life is living me, rather than the other way around. What is lost in focus on one form of life can be gained in a fuller experience of life as a whole, but not easily. As the political philosopher Matthew Crawford puts it: 'As our mental lives become more fragmented, what is at stake often seems to be nothing less than the question of whether one can maintain a coherent self. I mean a self that is able to act according to settled purposes and ongoing projects, rather than flitting about.'[3]

Concentration is an *achievement*. The etymological roots of concentration refer to bringing fissiparous materials together towards a centre, thereby distilling and purifying substances. We are those fissiparous materials and substances – we fly off in different directions all the time. Learning to concentrate is therefore an encounter with the nature of the self; a self that is embodied in flesh, embedded in culture and extended through technology.[4] Most other sports are defined by how well you use your limbs, and chess teaches us that, on closer inspection, concentration is also physiological; it's about how well you regulate your nervous system.

One of the things that impacts most on the quality of our lives is how much time we have to concentrate on things that we care about. Chess gave me this blessing: a glimpse of a life where it is permissible to have just one thing to think about most of the time, even if that one thing happens to be multitudinous in scope. Several years of my life were structured around the experience of concentration and I imbibed a great deal of silence in the process; you can't put a price on that. When Simon and Garfunkel refer to the sound of silence in their famous song I feel I know what they mean, as if I've heard it through chess. To see the chess pieces set up therefore looks to me like a gateway to a particular kind of freedom – the freedom to concentrate. In everyday consciousness we are compelled to make sense of uninvited stimuli and scramble through stories and memories to grapple with who we are. In chess, each position *invites* us to follow our thoughts; thinking becomes something that happens to us through us, with us, by us and for us. When we concentrate, we are the charmer and the charmed.

Yet the charm is an achievement that we risk taking for granted. We concentrate when we want to and when we must, rarely just because we can; and yet when we *try* to concentrate, we risk missing the point – our will becomes another element of consciousness to hold and tame, and we risk getting in our own way. Concentration therefore arises as a kind of paradox, when we simultaneously forget and find ourselves; when we know who we are without asking, and know what to do without getting in the way of doing it. In those moments of coalescence called concentration we are mostly fully ourselves, most fully alive, and free.

I. FREEDOM IN CAPTIVITY

If you were a hostage in the Colombian jungle and somebody gave you a broken machete you might try to escape, but with your hands tied under the eyes of armed captors, an attempt to *physically* escape would be foolhardy.

In the summer of 2008, Mark Gonsalves, an American military contractor held by the FARC rebel group for five years, opted for a mental escape instead, and used his broken machete patiently and determinedly to carve chess pieces, which were played on a painted piece of cardboard. This painstaking task took him over three months to complete, but the result was hundreds of hours of release shared among the fifteen hostages, including former Colombian presidential candidate Ingrid Betancourt.

Needless to say, this is no fairy story. The hostages painted a gruesome picture of their captivity, describing months of enforced silence and a campsite shared with a rats' nest. They slept on the floors of drug labs and marched for hours in chains. Ms Betancourt also remarked that there were some things that would stay in the jungle.

It seems fitting that the meticulous rescue mission was named 'Operation Jaque' ('Jaque' means check or sometimes checkmate in Spanish). Colombian security forces rescued the hostages first by observation over several months to track their movements, and then by taking acting classes and pretending to be FARC rebels, thereby tricking the captors into handing them over for transfer within the FARC group by helicopter. Betancourt later told a press conference she had no idea she was being rescued until she saw her captors naked and blindfolded on the floor of the aircraft. Only then was she told: 'We are the national army. You are free.'

Marc Gonsalves said that playing chess was 'a way for us to stop thinking about the cruel situation we were in', and his fellow hostage Keith Stansell added: 'We would sit chained and, thanks to this guy [who made the set] we were … just playing chess … When you are doing that you are free. Your mind is engaged, you are not a prisoner. That's the gain, that's the victory. And they [the captors] don't even know it.'

There are many stories of chess helping people to mentally escape from physical ordeals, but this is one of my favourites because the hostages gave testimony to something that every chess player knows. Chess is a source of escape, and an escape not merely away from suffering, but towards something beautiful. The Italian writer Umberto Eco captured this sentiment in a line from a fictional love letter that might have been addressed to chess: 'Only in your prison do I enjoy the most sublime of freedoms.'

The contention that concentration is freedom stems from a view that both concentration and freedom are forms of self-mastery over time. The freedom in question is not the lesser sense of freedom *from* constraint. That minimal freedom is sometimes called negative freedom because it is defined by having no positive content; the idea is that we should be free to do whatever we choose, and choose whatever we want, as long as we don't harm others. (The so-called harm principle is encapsulated in a widely quoted line with no authoritative source: 'Your right to throw a punch ends at the tip of my nose.')

The freedom that chess helps to cultivate through discipline and concentration is more like what philosophers call 'positive freedom'. The emphasis is not merely on what you are free *from* but also your freedom *to* do or be or become things of value; to pursue substantive visions of the good life, and clarify what they entail for flourishing as a person. The belief underlying positive freedom is that moral and spiritual freedom are not givens; they have to be cultivated. On this view, we do not always know what is best for us and sometimes have to spend a lifetime figuring it out. We can be rational and even wise, sometimes, but we are also unruly creatures of delusion and passion. Our freedom is therefore constrained not only by external chains but also by the nature of our own hearts and minds: our egocentric dispositions, our neurotic and selfish tendencies, our bondage to limited ideas of who we are and what life is for.

Learning how to concentrate is critical for appreciating positive freedom and for developing it, because positive freedom is ultimately about the transformation of consciousness over time, and we need qualities of concentration to attend to the quality of our consciousness. Positive freedom depends upon the capacity to concentrate because it involves preferring goal-directed attention to stimulus-directed attention; activities where we feel some agency, rather than those where we are merely entertained. Preferring positive freedom over negative freedom means, in practice, preferring to play chess rather than watch TV, even if one activity is more likely to inform you or make you laugh, while the other involves hours of strenuous concentration after which you might feel the bitter pain of defeat. Mihaly Csikszentmihalyi makes a related point explicitly in his research and writing. Since the experience of flow depends on the challenge level of an activity fitting one's skill level, and since we gradually get better at things through practice, our challenges have to become more complex for us to experience the rewards of flow. In this sense our love of concentration drives the growth of the complexity of consciousness, and thereby deepens our experience of freedom.[5]

Valuing positive freedom does not mean there is only one way of living well, but it does mean resisting the idea that what is of value is merely a matter of opinion. The claim is that a process of lifelong flourishing that involves, for instance, continual learning, absorption and growth through self-overcoming, ideally in service to some higher good, is ultimately a better life than one lived in pursuit of pleasurable experiences – for instance cheeky cocktails and delicious meals in scenic places with cheerful friends. Of course we can value both pleasure and flourishing, and exploring the tensions and compromises between them would lead us to deep philosophical waters, but this question of how to live often amounts to a question of what kinds of freedom matter to us most.

Freedom is not merely about contenting ourselves with being free from coercion, voting once in a while and buying whatever we can afford. Positive freedom is about believing there is scope for psychological and spiritual development within individuals and across society, and that we should all work towards that. Consider those prisoners of conscience who became moral exemplars, like Mahatma Gandhi, Martin Luther King or Nelson Mandela, all of whom lost their freedom for periods of time. While imprisoned, or living in unjust societies where that threat was never far away, their freedom from constraint was wrongly compromised, and nothing can properly compensate for that. However, in different ways their freedom to develop inwardly was apparently undiminished, and they remain moral exemplars as a result.

Positive freedom is therefore an inspiring idea, but also dangerous. For instance we might be told that our nation is sacred and that national civic service is both a duty and good for our character, or that classical music is better for our soul than pop music, or that chess is better for our mental health than computer games. In the language of Jean-Jacques Rousseau, the risk of promoting positive freedom is that people might be 'forced to be free', i.e. told what freedom *should* mean and then compelled to live in accordance with it.

But there is a risk in overstating this risk too. Positive freedom opens the door to the best and the worst of us, but it is grounded in a spiritual commitment to our better natures waiting to unfold, and a belief that with the right support they can and should prevail. If we rely on negative freedom, in theory it can lead to a flowering of individual agency, through creative inspiration and diverse manifestations of the good life; but in practice it often means we are at the mercy of advertisers seeking profit and politicians seeking election, who create fleeting preferences and needy mentalities that are reinforced by habit and convention.

When negative freedom is considered somehow more fundamental than positive freedom, rather than in some kind of balance or harmony with it, we risk becoming a meaningless, rudderless, anything-goes culture shaped only by prevailing desires, and not directed by any higher ideals. We might think we can ensure that our decisions are truly our own, and build our lives accordingly, but the balance of evidence suggests otherwise. At a societal level, the freedom that matters most might be the meta-freedom to choose which kind of freedom to aspire to, but the governance challenge is to make that a genuine choice. My own instinct is that cultural maturity leads us to understand that freedom is ultimately a kind of commitment. Freedom is about building a boat to sail on the open seas, but it is ultimately more like building than sailing.

My understanding of the relationship between chess, concentration and freedom is based on a view of human nature that evolved over two decades. It was while doing Philosophy, Politics and Economics as an undergraduate at Oxford University in 1997 that I first studied Isaiah Berlin's famous essay on *Two Concepts of Liberty*, where he warns the reader against positive liberty due to the danger of it leading to authoritarianism, and at the time I didn't have the intellectual resources to really understand the threat or to disagree. It was through a growing understanding of chess psychology that I began to think differently about freedom.

Writing *The Seven Deadly Chess Sins*, published in 2001, led me to look into the Christian idea of 'sin', which I was surprised to discover is less about immoral acts and more about a theory of human nature. What the idea of sin draws attention to is not our wickedness but our brokenness, vulnerability and fallibility; our relationship to ultimate reality is imperfect and we cannot help but make mistakes. Sin is therefore what the writer Francis Spufford convincingly calls 'The Human Propensity to Fuck Things Up'; any brief study of history will reveal that propensity in abundance.[6] The chess sins I selected were therefore about our latent tendencies to err based on our limited human apparatus, rather than mistakes as such, and the first of the seven was *Thinking*.[7]

Writing about sin in chess from this psychological angle shifted my intellectual centre of gravity away from politics and philosophy towards psychology. Soon afterwards I spent a year studying for a master's degree at Harvard on the relationship between 'Mind, Brain and Education', taught by distinguished scholars including Howard Gardner – famed for his research on Good Work and Multiple Intelligences – and one of my intellectual heroes, Robert Kegan. Kegan, I believe, understands as deeply as anybody what it means for a human being to grow and develop, and his work has informed my view of the world ever since.

My sympathy for positive freedom deepened through my Ph.D. at the University of Bristol, which was an interdisciplinary inquiry into what the process of growing wiser might mean in theory and practice. What drew me to the study of wisdom was a sense of being touched, moved and inspired by people and actions I considered wise, which were characterised by a compassionate disposition and a cultivated quality of discerning attention and deft communication.

My idea of what kinds of freedom mattered most was further refined during the six years I spent working at the Royal Society of Arts in London, from 2009 to 2016. I applied for a senior researcher job a few months after becoming a father for the first time, when

I realised I would have to travel much less than I had as a chess player, and when I was no longer sure what I was trying to achieve in the chess world. This job was in 'the third sector' of organisations that are neither public or private but liaise with both, and civil society is still my 'beat' – where I work. With the help of an understanding boss at the RSA, I adjusted to office life, developed a talent for fundraising and became director of the Social Brain Centre, which was an elaborate job title for a varied role at the nexus of journalism, academia and politics – ideally suited to my skills and interests. Compared with chess, where there is often a lethal opponent who wants to figuratively kill you, work also felt relatively easy.

The work covered a range of policy areas, and I developed a particular interest in climate change, but the intellectual premise of the job was that working assumptions about human nature in public policy have not caught up with our scientific and philosophical understanding. For many years government policies, particularly those informed by economic models, were designed on the assumption of self-interested rationality as a default for human beings; namely that we know what we want and will try to maximise whatever that is. I did not need much persuading that this is a deluded idea of who we are, because I already knew from chess that decisions of even the very best players – apparent paragons of rationality – are shaped by the influence of other players, memories of apparently unrelated games, and other emotional and pragmatic concerns.

Developments across academic disciplines in recent years have corroborated my chess experience. There have been significant shifts in our understanding of ourselves. Default human behaviour is much more automatic, more profoundly social and more embodied than the prior theoretical construct of the rational individual, *Homo economicus*, suggested. Rationality is a mode of enquiry, not a feature of being; rational is one of many things we can *do*, not something we *are*. We live and decide on the basis of conditioning, situational influences and 'social proof' – namely by looking around to see what others are doing. We are riddled with cognitive biases that shape thinking and we make different decisions depending on the momentary state of our bodies and how a given option is framed.[8]

A fuller appraisal of human nature therefore suggests that we are not merely complex, but actually fairly deluded most of the time. From that premise, freedom looks different. Even after formal education in childhood, there appears to be scope to continue developing in ways that go beyond mere skill acquisition or material prosperity. It seems to me that we are unfinished business. There is always scope to grow, not just intellectually but morally, epistemically and spiritually. The question is: how? It is no accident that most religious traditions have a path aspect to their teachings; whatever you think of their doctrine, many of the contemplative and social practices they promote are directed towards the cultivation of virtues, which might be thought of as embodied values.

I have no religious background, but these thoughts led me to design and lead a public engagement project about giving the apparently nebulous notion of 'spirituality' greater intellectual coherence. The process involved several hundred people including believers and atheists, and the silent majority who don't feel that belief is the key determinant of spiritual sensibility.

The spirituality project was popular and well received. I managed to build on it to find funds and network support to create my own organisation. Perspectiva supports research to better connect complex problems in the world with the inner lives of human beings; like what the connection might be between denial of our deaths and the denial of climate change, and how we might grow to meet the challenges of our time. Through writing and speaking and hosting events, we help a range of social change organisations make better sense of their attempts to improve the world. My career is not easy to define, but I love my work. I am in the world now, perhaps even too far in to ever get out again. Life has made its move, and has taken chess away, but everything I think about is permeated with my experience of the game, not least the experience of time.

2. TIME

The British comedian Stephen Fry tells a story of a student accosted by his headmaster while walking in the hallway. 'Late!'

says the headmaster. To which the student replies: 'Oh really, sir? So am I.'

Alas, I am pathologically late. I know that lateness is a kind of theft, stealing and spoiling the time of others, and part of me hates it, but psychologically it often feels like a matter of survival. Lateness functions like a cushion to protect the vulnerable parts of our psyche from their terror of unmediated social contact. Achieving punctuality stems from respect for others and basic organisation, but the unconscious sees things differently. *Failing to be late* means giving up on adrenaline, surrendering to the reality of time, submitting to existential capture, and potentially facing up to all the things we have skilfully suppressed for so long.

I am rarely late for impersonal things. I don't miss application deadlines or flights, though I sometimes cut it close, and if the occasion is particularly important, then I'll be sure to be on time. However, I confess I am late for most meetings with friends and family; usually by just a few minutes, but enough to feel safe. I do not plan to be late, and will convince myself that I have everything in hand, but I have observed the pattern of behaviour for long enough to notice it has its own coherence and emotional logic.

Once you have made your apology and received your forgiveness, explicitly or tacitly, you have been seen at a human level, however unfavourably, and it is much easier to connect deeply with the person you are with; otherwise it risks feeling too much like an appointment for a transaction. At work the issue is more complicated, because there is a risk of self-sabotage. For instance, in 2013, after labouring over a public policy report on climate change I was invited to meet with a high-ranking government official in Whitehall to discuss what it might mean for the government's communication of science policy, which is a significant indicator of impact in that line of work. But I was half an hour late for a one-hour meeting, and for no particular reason other than perhaps some impostor syndrome. I vividly remember being at home at my desk a few hours earlier, sensing the lateness coming on, but feeling unable to stop it. Part of the problem with being slightly late for psychological reasons is that when you are delayed for practical reasons like trains going slowly, then you are stupidly late.

And the whole drama probably is a little stupid. I am not proud of it, and in recent years, partly due to being a father with responsibility towards my children, I am late far less often. Still, I must confess that I am a little wary of those who are steadfastly punctual, as if they have nothing to retain them, nothing to hide or protect, nothing worthy to divert them from the false god of good timekeeping. I am more inclined to like and trust people who are a little late. I love listening to their stories of why they are late, and smiling as our eyes make contact and our souls say to each other: 'Ah yes, my friend, I see you.'

Curiously, my time management as a chess player was normally quite good, which is consistent with a broader pattern of sublimation. Chess allows you to do and be things you cannot be in the real world. Clock time is the feature of the experience of playing chess that is perhaps least well understood and appreciated by those who have some sense of chess culturally, but have never experienced it competitively. Clock time is to chess like sets are to tennis or overs are to cricket; they create the temporal form that sets the tempo of the contest. I think you have to have experienced taking a series of decisions under time pressure to even countenance the idea that chess might be a sport. The experience of the game is not contemplative or reflective in the way it can appear in cultural references; in practice it is a perpetual competitive injunction to resolve complexity as quickly as possible.

Time limits vary, and although the rules mostly remain the same, the rhythm, tension and meaning of the game alters along with the time limit. In general, the longer the game the more seriously it is taken, and most classical games typically give each player between two and three hours each per game. This time is punctuated by a certain number of moves when you are given part of your time (e.g. you have to make forty moves in 2 hours and then receive an additional hour to finish) or by having a set time for the whole game and receiving a small span of additional time every move (e.g. 30 seconds). The longer you have to take decisions, the less random the outcome feels. And yet randomness is sometimes thrust upon us towards the end of the game, and faster time controls are often used as tiebreaks to resolve deadlocked contests, and can even decide World Championship matches, so it pays to be good at all time controls as far as possible. Blitz chess for instance – three to five minutes each per game – is like the experience of being late; it's a guaranteed adrenaline rush, and a bit discombobulating, but it is often played for recreational reasons. It is strangely relaxing to feel the story of the position unfold so rapidly, as if you are white-water rafting on a river of meaning; you have a certain amount of steering control, but also know you are at the mercy of the river. In all time controls you can 'lose on time' by thinking for too long and running out of clock time. Such defeats can feel devastating, like an unreasonably sudden death.

Chess players measure clock time in hours, minutes and seconds, and board time in tempi. These two temporal streams are co-present in every moment of every game, but they do not fuse together. They are different dimensions of the same world. So you can also 'lose on time' in the sense that you squander precious tempi, fall behind in development, or lack the board time to put your ideas into practice before they are thwarted by the opponent's swifter schemes. These two aspects of time comprise two of what I consider to be the four main dimensions of chess and I call them 'ticking' – clock time – and 'time' – board tempi – respectively. The other two dimensions are material and quality.

Soon after we learn the basic rules of the game we learn that the pieces are 'material' and worth varying amounts of points (using pawns as the unit of currency, which are each worth one point). Queens are worth about nine points, rooks five, bishops and knights about three, while the king has infinite value. These values are not philosophically or mathematically grounded; they are just heuristics to guide thinking, and this is one of the challenges of playing chess well – those values permeate our thinking, but judgment is about much more than merely counting, because the value of pieces varies depending on the position.

Quality is much harder to measure, and includes things like the integrity of our pawn structures; through the process of capturing diagonally or being captured, pawns can become, for instance, isolated, or doubled, or doubled and isolated, or tripled. The placement of the weakest pieces determines the character of the game and the activity and scope of the more powerful pieces. Quality is also about subtle features of the position relating to king safety, piece coordination, control of important squares, and scope to improve our position. Chess at the highest level features a constant trading in the three dimensions on the board – material, quality and time – which produces situations of such complexity that you need a lot of clock ticking time to work them out.[9]

If you are not a little scared of time ticking away then you have not been paying attention to how utterly mysterious it is, and what it means for you. We are living and dying because of time, but we don't really know what time is. The tortured logic of resistance to time through lateness therefore goes something like this: if you submit to time by being on time, it will eventually kill you because your time is finite; but if you flirt with time by being late, it might admire your playfulness and let you live in perpetuity, knowing you have grasped that time is infinite. Of course this logic makes no sense, but it is not clear if time does either.

Days are all we really have. There is nowhere else to live. Most of us are blessed with around thirty thousand days, which should be enough to live well. But somehow those days go by, filled with meals, moments and meetings, and we rarely capture what exactly we did with them, or why. We judge the quality of our lives by our personal relationships, our social contribution or our achievements, but as the poet Annie Dillard reminds us, 'How we spend our days is how we spend our lives.'

Less poetically, how we spend our hours is how we spend our days. And our hours depend on minutes, which are built with mere seconds, and that reduction goes all the way down into the basements of reality, and God only knows where it goes after that. Thinking about time in this way makes me dizzy, and reminds me of one of my favourite literary quotations, by the Argentinian writer Jorge Luis Borges: 'Time is the substance from which I am made. Time is a river which carries me along, but I am the river; it is a tiger that devours me, but I am the tiger; it is a fire that consumes me, but I am the fire.'

The way chess alters our experience of time is a core feature of the game's cultural resonance and charm. And our relationship to time, and how we choose to nurture it, shapes our experience of freedom.[10]

If concentration is freedom, what exactly is set free? In chess the part of us that is set free most profoundly is the ego – the part of our psyche most invested in desire, attention and acquisition. Chess does not deny the need for such craving, but rather creates a safe playground for it, as parents do for tender young egos who seek praise and attention, and occasionally want to break things just because they can. However, every experienced chess player will tell you that their best results usually come from a wellspring of confidence that goes beyond ego. The moments chess players welcome but cannot really manufacture are those in which we sublimate our egotistical desires into successful operations on the chessboard, forgetting our neurotic concerns in the rapture of abstract achievement for several days in a row. In this sense, concentration is about getting out of one's own way, without surrendering agency.

That internal manoeuvre of being optimally present to the task and optimally distant from the self involves navigating the relationship between reality and abstraction. We tend to talk about abstraction as if it were a process of diluting or diminishing reality, but it can also be viewed as a way of deepening and distilling it. There are times we need to be abstract to make any sense at all – for instance when expressing a truth mathematically; and there are times when an abstract perspective helps to convey a particular kind of truth, for instance in conceptual art. It is precisely when concrete problems start to multiply in so-called real life that we need to move up a level of abstraction to make sense. An example would be when the family cannot function because the children are blaming each other for doing something unfair and the parents are blaming each other for not blaming the children in the right way, and every family member has a story of how every other family member needs to change, but nobody is zooming out to see the family operating as a whole. That *need* for abstraction is partly why chess seems so true to life. In the real world we often struggle to know what we are trying to do, and our energy is dissipated. In chess, due to the clarity of our purpose and the concentration of energy, the abstract world of pieces and squares often feels more real, not less, than the world outside it.

The quality of that abstraction depends on grounding ourselves in the logic of the game and the legitimacy of our opponent. Chess teaches you that there are constraints and limits on our desires, partly because of the game's own rule of law, but also because our opponent has the same rights as we do. Yet there is some dissonance at the heart of the game, because while we have to acknowledge that our opponent's competing desires are valid, we also have to snuff them out to survive. Those who know chess come to see that the opponent's competing reality is essential to our love for the game. Our intense encounters with other minds are fleeting, almost promiscuous, but they shape our relationship with our self, which shapes the character of our life.

3. YOUR CASE IS AN UNUSUAL ONE

In August 2008, a man named Stuart Conquest became British Chess Champion, finishing with eight points from eleven games (one point per win, half for a draw, zero for a defeat). Stuart Conquest is a great name, full of fortitude, worthy of a flag, a suit of armour and a deep sonorous voice. The repetition of the strong 't' suggests harmony, while the subtly embedded 'u' and 'qu' signal latent quixotic tendencies. The very name is enough to instil fear in an approaching army, and dazzle a thousand damsels. For several years he has been teaching chess in Gibraltar, where he is a local chess celebrity, but back then he lived in La Rioja, Spain, where he discerningly imbibed the local wine we see on our supermarket shelves at its source. Nonetheless, in 2008 he was the first English player to win the event in seven years.[11]

Stuart was a worthy champion. His form has always been wayward, but he is a seasoned professional with considerable flair, and his broad opening repertoire makes him nearly impossible to prepare for. At his peak in 2001 he was ranked 88 in the world, while career highlights include beating former world champion Mikhail Tal in 1988.

Stuart made history by becoming the first person from his school in Hastings to earn a place at Cambridge University, to study modern languages. However, he had recently become world Under-16 champion in Argentina, and was on a chess high, so he asked for a deferral. That year went well, so he asked for another, and another. The third time Cambridge said it's now or never, and Stuart decided to stick with chess.

Twenty years later he applied again to the same Trinity College in Cambridge, this time for Anglo-Saxon, Norse and Celtic studies. He wrote to the dean explaining his case, and received a reply with the memorable first line: 'Dear Mr Conquest, Your case is an unusual one.'

Stuart was interviewed, but did not get offered a place. I haven't checked in with him for a while, but I believe he sometimes regrets his original decision not to take up his offer. And yet who can say that the more conventionally attractive road would have led to a better life?

Stuart emailed me before the British Championship started in 2008, expressing disquiet with his recent form, celebrating a difficult puzzle he had solved easily, and asking for my mobile number in case he needed some help at the event. On reading this email, I said to my wife Siva: 'I think Stuart's going to win this year.'

It is difficult to put my finger on what it was about the email that gave me such conviction, but the tone was a mixture of tension, reflection, confidence and anticipation – perfect preconditions for concentration to emerge and deepen during the tournament. It was the tone of a man who knew his strengths and limitations, and was ready for a task that deeply mattered to him.

A steady performance throughout the event, with only a couple of scary moments, was enough for first equal (Grandmaster Keith Arkell made the same score). Stuart prepared for the play-off by studying his opponent's recent games on his laptop over a sausage and Egg McMuffin breakfast at McDonald's, where he correctly predicted the successful opening, and prepared an improvement, which led to an emphatic victory.[12]

Stuart's life decisions seem to have been about going his own way, rather than putting up with the prospective constraints of a more conventional path. That kind of decision is often framed as a form of 'opting out', but in many ways it is *opting in*. When you are in control of your own time you are free to have a more direct relationship with life, to choose where to put your attention and care, rather than be forced to conform to the patterns of prevailing cultural norms, typically manifest in the routines of work, home and family. We are different characters, and Stuart is a decade older, so we could not have lived each other's life, but Stuart has sometimes functioned in my psyche as a kind of chess alter ego, living the apparently free life I might have chosen had I stayed on the road playing chess.

And yet I know, and I think Stuart would agree, that our emotional connection to chess ebbs and flows, and on-the-road freedom can give rise to moments of disquiet and dislocation. Most professional players are time- and travel- and friend-rich, but typically semi-nomadic and financially poor. In some countries, serious chess players are financially supported by commercial sponsors, or by their governments, but most Grandmasters make only just enough money to live; usually from a combination of tutoring, writing and occasionally winning prize money at tournaments or being paid to play in professional leagues.

For several years I travelled from London to Birmingham to play in such a chess league. I was paid a few hundred pounds per weekend as a 'hired gun' for eleven games spread over five weekends, but I had to cover my own expenses, so it was a blessing that my teammate Grandmaster Daniel King used to drive to the event from close to where I lived. Dan is a grown-up in a chess world where many struggle to leave their youth behind. He is serious in intent, but funny, charismatic and a clear communicator; perhaps the best chess commentator in the world. His background includes a full family life and playing bass in a local band, and he was a role model growing up; his love of the game was infectious, and I found him to be good company. Yet truth be told, I was also motivated by the fact that those two-hour car journeys saved me about £40 per trip in train fares. This amount of money was not pivotal but it felt like an achievement – part of the game of life at the time – not to spend it when I didn't have to. After a few of these trips, in response to an email asking if the same arrangement would be OK again, Dan responded: 'I'll make my own way if you don't mind. I just want to keep a clear head before the game.' At the time I was hurt, and even a little dismayed, but now as an adult with children who rarely gets time alone, I admire the decision. Perhaps I took those rides for granted, perhaps I spoke too much in the car, or perhaps the decision was not personal at all. In any case I have learned to respect people who know how and when to draw their lines. Concentration depends on saying no, and so does any freedom worth having.

4. OPEN SECRETS

Towards the end of 2008, there was an open secret in the chess world. For almost a year it had been known that the thirteenth world champion, Gary Kasparov, was training America's number one, Hikaru Nakamura, one of the best players in the world. Kasparov was formally retired, but having been at the top of world chess for two decades he is a living legend and is still famed for his depth of opening preparation, which often gave him good positions near the start of the game. Playing Kasparov was often like waiting to be hit with a hidden weapon, or 'mugged in the street', as one Icelandic Grandmaster put it.

Kasparov and Nakamura chose to 'neither confirm nor deny' the rumours, and the collaboration was all the more powerful for being merely suspected rather than known. As the best horror films reveal, we are most scared of our own imagination. When you know you are facing Kasparov's preparation, you can steel yourself for the formidable challenge, but when you feel you just *might* be facing Kasparov's preparation, it is difficult to know what kind of psychological response to deploy. The open secret became public knowledge within a few months, and it was a relief for Nakamura's opponents to know what they previously merely suspected. Kasparov and Nakamura ceased working together soon after.

Open secrets are a profound phenomenon, revealing something fundamental about the social nature of human cognition and our capacity to hide things from ourselves and others. The cognitive scientist Marvin Minsky said that: 'You cannot think about thinking without thinking about thinking about *something*.' This statement helps to explain why chess is so often used in cognitive psychology experiments, where the relatively controlled and contained thinking environment helps to focus on the thinking process as such – not just thinking, but thinking *about* thinking, with chess playing the starring role as the *something* to be thought about.

But I think open secrets are a more profound entry point into the nature of thought. We tend to think with what we know about what we don't know. However, there are times when what matters is knowing what others know, and further, knowing what others know about what *other others* know. This experience of trying to hold multiple perspectives in mind and then think productively without dropping anything is an exquisite form of torture that, curiously, some people enjoy.

There is a notion of 'cognitive load' in psychology, which is about the number of items we can think about at one time, and 'seven plus or minus two' has been the conventional wisdom since the fifties, which is part of the reason why most phone numbers used to be six or seven digits long, before they were readily stored on our phones. The process of 'chunking' is how we grow in ability, in which larger groups of ideas are compressed into nuggets of meaning, which is why we struggle to remember even our own number without saying it in a particular way that reflects the chunks we know. Similarly, in chess, a standard castled king position at the side of the board contains five elements (king, rook, three pawns) but to an experienced chess player it is processed as one chunk. However, what we need to understand better from chess is not so much the perception of position, but the experience of how concentration ebbs and flows; how we replenish intellectual bandwidth so that we can keep examining the same set of things while also accommodating new things without the whole wave of thought collapsing in on itself. To concentrate well, we need that kind of resilience, because otherwise we keep on having to come back to the start of the process, and don't get anywhere at all.

This challenge is revealed by a logic puzzle that I love, which I learned from the philosopher of mind John Hawthorne. The puzzle concerns three men on an island who all have blue faces. It is wonderfully convoluted, so please suspend disbelief, forget common sense, and search for the Sherlock Holmes inside.

The situation on the island is a little delicate. The three blue-faced men see each other every day, but none of them can see his own face. They all know that their face is either red or blue, but if any of them discovers the colour of their own face they have to shoot themselves at the next stroke of midnight exactly. Those are the rules. A little twisted, I know, but clear enough to live by.

Careless talk costs lives, so they don't speak to each other, and never dare to see their own reflection. Yet despite the pressure and ambient tension, they live together in blissful ignorance for several years. Then one day a Scottish tourist called Jim arrives on the island, all the way from Glasgow. Jim chose this island because he was trying to shake off an incipient midlife crisis and couldn't face the tedium of another beach holiday in Spain.

However, Jim is an accountant, not an anthropologist. After a few perplexing days with the natives he could not handle the tension and felt an uncontrollable urge to make a West of Scotland wisecrack. To his credit, Jim was careful to tell them something he assumed they must already know, and after getting on his boat he said: 'At least one of you has a blue face, eh!' And off he went from the island, back to Glasgow.

Not that night, not the following night, but on the third midnight, all three men shot themselves. The first question is: Why? The second question is: What was the new information that Jim told them that they didn't already know? Many intuit the answer to the first question long before being able to articulate the answer to the second. Feel free to skip the next few paragraphs if you want to try to solve the puzzle.

The answer is epistemological in nature. It concerns the nature of knowing in general and the vital difference between private knowledge and public knowledge. To solve the blue-face problem we need to grasp the layered and social nature of knowing – who knows what about whom and how does that knowledge perpetuate itself, or change through the sharing? We also need to concentrate and think productively, proactively eliciting insight rather than waiting for it to volunteer itself. In this sense the puzzle reminded me of chess thinking, where we inch our way towards a decision one micro-judgment at a time.

A useful step towards solving the puzzle is to query the purpose of each of its elements, for instance asking whether it would make any difference if the new information was heard by each person separately; and it would have. In that case nothing would have changed – there is something about hearing the line together that is pivotal. That point is in itself fascinating because it reminds us that even the meaning of basic factual information is not independent of context.

It also helps to think hypothetically about Jim's comment on the same island if it were inhabited by just two people. In the two-person scenario, if they know that at least one of *them* has a blue face, and they look at a blue face, and nothing happens that night, they know the other person cannot have seen a red face or they would have shot themselves. Exactly the same logic applies to the other person, which means that if they both see blue faces they kill themselves on the second night, but live all day on the second, knowing their fate. The challenge is much harder with three people, mostly because of our limited mental capacity, but the same kind of logic applies.

The new information that arose from Jim's comment takes the logical form: 'A knows that B knows that C knows that at least one person has a blue face (where the three perspectives are interchangeable).' Before the tourist came, 'A' only knew that 'B' knew – he knew nothing of 'B's' knowledge of 'C'. At first blush it is not clear why that matters, but something mortally significant does change – the counterfactual question 'If I had a red face, what would happen?' yields a different answer. In order for something to 'happen' at midnight, or for a non-event at midnight to be substantive information, it must be possible for someone to think that someone else might think that *someone else* sees two red faces, because that is the only way that any of them might ever imagine that someone could kill themselves.

This disparity between the brute fact that there are three blue faces, and the necessary hypothetical that one of them, seeing two blue faces, could nonetheless imagine that another might think there are two red faces, is what makes this problem so hard. What happens is that it is possible for A to think that he has a red face, imagine that B might think that he has a red face, and then think that B, knowing that C knows that at least one has a blue face, might then conclude that his face was blue and kill himself. A simpler way to look at it is that if I had a red face I would be removed from their consideration over the new question of who has the blue face, and the two-person scenario takes over. In this case all three men are waiting for the resolution of the two-person scenario by the second night and when it doesn't come they all conclude that they can't have a red face, and that they must therefore have a blue face.

This puzzle provides a useful reference point for contrasting thinking styles and inclinations. Some people immediately latch on to rules and the underlying analytical and logical structure of the problem, while others cannot get away from the bizarre and macabre context and what they assume must be a subtle trick or some kind of psychological allegory. But why are their faces blue? Why are they on the island in the first place? Surely they would talk to each other? Others feel the logic burn through the problem and can quickly screen out extraneous details; they become obsessed with the underlying rationales, finding it hard to think of anything else. Those who find the setting and plot absurd and implausible may see the logic as gratuitous and tedious and are only too happy to forget it about it. Neither reaction is wrong.

The puzzle is both utterly fascinating and vivifying, and an absurd waste of time. Some say the same about chess; in fact three distinguished writers have pithily dismissed the value of the endeavour as such. Sir Walter Scott called chess 'A sad waste of brains', George Bernard Shaw said chess is 'a foolish expedient for making idle people think they are doing something very clever', and Raymond Chandler went further: 'Chess is as elaborate a waste of human intelligence as you can find outside an advertising agency.'

I don't agree with these statements, but they sting because there is some truth to them. I do not regret a second I spent playing chess. If anything I regret not playing more when I was good enough to get even better. Most moments at the board were impassioned and life-giving, and those that were not were necessary to create the meaning: major needs minor to be properly heard, joy deepens through sorrow, light invites shadows. The experience of concentration is so intense and the battle so meaningful that you feel scintillatingly alive. So, no, Messrs Scott, Shaw and Chandler – frankly, what do you know? It is not about pretending to be intelligent, as you appear to be pretending with your pseudo-assessments. How much board time did you put in? Come back after a few thousand hours of competitive thinking and I very much doubt you will think that time was wasted.

Chess is not a waste of time, but time is scarce and there is more to life than chess. In the context of concentration being not just an experience of positive freedom but also a way of developing it, there is an open question of just how much time we should spend on pursuits like chess. Chess simulates life as well as being part of life, but it falls short of the sensuality and plenitude of the world beyond it. Potential world champions aside, the game can and should be a spur for a full life, a kind of parallel training ground of self-discovery and development, honing oneself not so much for the next chess game but for the life outside it. In that life beyond the game, we are also tested, valued and needed, perhaps more than we currently know.

5. ASKING PERTINENT QUESTIONS

Once upon a time, when my first son Kailash was three, he wanted to hear about Jack and the Beanstalk, again. He was story-hungry and sleep-resistant so I briskly detailed the implausibly magic beans, the unexpected sprouting and the youthful Everyman climbing up the fabled legume to find an unlikely castle, before climbing down with pilfered treasure, as the Anglophobic blood-loving giant breathlessly gave chase: 'Fee, fi, fo, fum, I smell the blood of an English-mun.'

While doing my best not to condone violence, or foster prejudice against tall people, I relayed how Jack swiftly took a handily placed axe to chop down the beneficent beanstalk. When I conveyed how the hapless giant hit the ground and 'fell asleep for a hundred years', I was glad Kailash did not ask what that really meant, but was stunned by a different query: 'When the beanstalk is chopped down, Daddy, what happens to the castle at the top?'

I congratulated him on a wonderful question, and told him I would think about it and tell him in the morning, by which time I was glad he had forgotten.

I still don't know the answer. Perhaps the castle is an emergent property of the beanstalk that dies with it and disappears. Perhaps the castle is independent of the beanstalk, which is merely a new path to get there. Perhaps it's just a story, and we should not take the question too seriously. But I love that spirit of enquiry. Of course, children's questions can be incessant and aggravating, but those disarming moments where the familiar is recast as perplexing are among the most precious gifts of being a parent.

There are many different ways to frame the educational value of chess, but if I had to sum it up in one word, it would probably be: 'questions'. If I had three words it would be 'questions about relationships'. As the writer Marina Benjamin puts it, to ask a question is to invest in attentiveness, to declare a stake in the answer, and that is one of the many gifts of chess; you cease to be a passive recipient of information, and become an active learner – an intrinsically rewarding experience.

Playing chess is about posing questions to the opponent, and answering the questions they pose you; the little questions are always nested inside bigger ones. As you get better at the game you zoom in to the most important questions quickly, and you can sense they are the most important questions because they speak to the conceptual ambiguity that holds your attention. Your overall question is: 'How can I checkmate the opponent's king?' But the recurring questions that help you answer that include: 'What am I trying to achieve here?', 'What happens if I go there?', 'What do I do now?', 'How will he respond to that?', 'What does that knight *want*?'

The anti-philosopher Friedrich Nietzsche saw more deeply into questions than most: 'We hear only those questions for which we are in a position to find answers.' The educational value of chess is that it makes asking questions a reflex, and the experience of getting better at chess is finding that your questions get richer and more pertinent. A great deal of chess improvement is about cultivating the inclination to look one move deeper than you typically would, but that effort depends on being concentrated enough to care. The chess lesson for life is often framed as the importance of being one step ahead of your opponent, but I think that aim is to challenge ourselves to push beyond our cognitive comfort zone, to enquire of the place where we naturally want to stop thinking: Is this it? Is there not perhaps more to be discovered here?

Most of the studies on chess thinking are related to expertise, and really they are about perception; they deal with our visual 'take' on positions, rather than with thinking as a productive process. Chess ability stems from noticing patterns over time and recognising them in related contexts. Patterns are the raw material of the chunking process; they are constellations of pieces that we gradually come to understand as competitively meaningful. Sometimes that's a pawn structure, sometimes a square, sometimes a relationship between pieces, and sometimes all of these things and more combined; the better you become, the more the whole position is experienced as one single pattern.

Recognising patterns characterises expertise more generally. For instance, when a personal bodyguard makes a dynamic risk assessment about how to protect a VIP from harm, they will consider patterns – factors like visibility, mobility, density of people and weather conditions. If the emergent overall pattern from these micro-patterns combined feels 'risky', for reasons they can't always articulate, they will form a judgment – for instance, to take a different entrance, or a longer but safer route home.

However, chess in particular may have something to teach us about the *know-how* of concentration: exactly how we direct attention towards the right things in the right way with the right intensity over several hours. In practice, regardless of our ability, concentration comes and goes, forms and collapses, builds and then crumbles because there is an upper limit to what we can hold in our heads at any one time, as the blue-face puzzle indicated. As players, we move towards our upper limit and away from it again and again, rhythmically, like waves. Stronger players see more patterns, and more ideas with fewer items of thought, because through thousands of hours of learning we have become efficient at knowing what to connect and what to separate.

In difficult positions, against worthy opponents, thought is sometimes strenuous and we can't always hold each thought stream fully. As we peer into the unfolding position, it is as if we are driving more or less automatically, as if it's second nature, until new possibilities flash before us like bikes emerging from side-streets, and then we are brought back to the challenge of steering consciousness; and at such moments the edifice of thought we had built is likely to collapse. If we are not careful, we can spend far too many minutes in this state of perpetual irresolution, in which we seek but don't find an answer to what is happening, because there is just too much meaning in the position for our minds to process it. One thought wave comes towards the shore of attention, and carries more or less water, and then collapses, and that process goes on. Sometimes we know what we have seen, and can move towards a decision, but sometimes the water overwhelms us, and we turn away from the shore.

The naïve view of thinking is representational: namely that we are building pictures of what is happening in the position in our heads – a bit like taking photographs as we go and looking at them one by one – but that's not how it works. If somebody mentions there is a cat stuck up a tree you already know what they mean without having to see in your mind whether the cat is, for instance, Siamese or Persian, or whether the tree is deciduous or evergreen, and the lack of those details won't stop you from automatically generating ideas about how the cat got up there or how it might get down.

Similarly, if you ask a Grandmaster about the chessboard in their head, you will find it doesn't have a size or a shape or a colour. What we have is an implicit sense of the rules of the game, the relationships between the pieces and the prevailing strategic purposes. We know these things in the way that we know how to walk and talk; these features of thought are second nature and they swirl around more or less consciously as we await the felt sense *in our bodies* that we are ready to take a decision. Moreover, the stronger the player, the more abstract their visual image will be. Just as fluency in a language arises when we become less self-conscious about speaking, expertise in chess is about not having to strain to hold the imagery of the position in mind. The eyes of our mind are not blind; we do see something – mental imagery known as eidetic imagery – but what we see in our minds is qualitatively different to what we see on the board.

Vladimir Nabokov seemed to understand this point, and described it evocatively in *The Luzhin Defense* from the perspective of his Grandmaster protagonist, Luzhin:

He found therein deep enjoyment: one did not have to deal with visible, audible, palpable pieces whose quaint shape and wooden materiality always disturbed him and always seemed to him but the crude, mortal shell of the exquisite, invisible chess forces. When playing blind, he was able to sense these diverse forces in their original purity. He saw then neither the Knight's carved mane nor the glossy heads of the Pawns – but he felt quite clearly that this or that imaginary square was occupied by a definite, concentrated force, so that he envisioned the movement of a piece as a discharge, a shock, a stroke of lightning – and the whole chess field quivered with tension, and over this tension he was sovereign, here gathering in and there releasing electric power.

Why does understanding thinking in this way matter? In my work as director of a social change charity and as a philosopher of public policy, I have come to believe that the world's most challenging problems are ultimately problems of thought. Many complex problems in our lives and in the world cannot be properly understood or experienced unless we can consider several ideas and ways of thinking together at one time. However, if all we can do is hold them, we won't be able to actually think with them or about them; we will be those thoughts, but we won't really *have* them. The physicist and philosopher David Bohm puts the challenge like this:

> The general tacit assumption in thought is that it's just telling you the way things are and that it is not doing anything – that 'you' are inside there, deciding what to do with the information. But I want to say that you don't decide what to do with the information. The information takes over. It runs you. Thought runs you. Thought, however, gives the false information that you are running it, that you are the one who controls thought, whereas actually thought is the one that controls each one of us.[13]

What Bohm is alluding to is our need to get better at thinking about thought without being run by thought; to find a vantage point outside whatever system of facts, associations and language forms are shaping our idea of what is happening. The essence of our thinking challenge today is that the world's problems are profoundly interconnected but our ways of knowing and acting on them are fragmented. And our ways of knowing are fragmented partly because we are not trained to think of how things connect from a young age. If anything, the inclination is trained out of us. Academic progression, alas, is a function of specialisation, not integration.

To make a good move on the chessboard you need to know what is happening on the kingside, the queenside, in the centre; you need to keep track of each and every piece, key strategic battles and tactical pitfalls and so forth; and you have to somehow bring those features of the position together and make your own judgment. Likewise with, for instance, biology, chemistry, physics, economics, psychology, politics, sociology, philosophy, theology: they are ways of thinking about what is ultimately the same position – life – and we need to bring them together as a matter of priority.

Chess taught me that you need to see the whole position in all its reverberating dynamism to make good moves, but also that it is impossible to think about everything at once. In the early twenty-first century the position we face as a species includes questions of what to do about, for instance, preventing mass unemployment in an age of artificial intelligence and robotics; protecting the truth when lies are easier, more exciting and travel faster; strengthening democracy in a time of political alienation; and how to collectively confront our ecological crisis when material-intensive economic growth is still the world's prevailing policy objective. These vexing issues, and more, are all connected; they manifest as patterns in the position conceived as a whole, but how we are able to act on them stems from ways of knowing and perceiving and thinking. We will struggle to address them without a more concerted effort to see how they co-arise and co-constitute each other. And we will never do that if we start from a vantage point that sees each problem as a discrete issue, ciphered off to be analysed by a distinct discipline. Einstein was right when he said we cannot solve our problems with the same thinking that caused them.[14]

6. MAKING PLANS

It has been said that we don't plan to fail, we just fail to plan, but this seems facile. Planning has its place. Sometimes we fail in spite of planning, or because of it, and sometimes we succeed thanks to our plans, but not in the way we intended.

The 1958 film *Inn of the Sixth Happiness* is based on the true story of the British housemaid Gladys Aylward, who sets off alone for China in the 1930s to become a missionary. In the climax of the film, as the Japanese invade, she heroically leads a hundred children over the mountains to safety. Colonel Lin Nan is a Chinese officer who falls in love with Gladys, but his love conflicts with his sense of duty. When an elderly local mandarin asks Colonel Lin Nan why he chose in favour of duty, the colonel ruefully says that his life is planned. The mandarin responds that a life that is planned is closed, and while it may be endured, it cannot be *lived*.

There is a Jewish saying that captures this sense that life's quality lies in its inherent unpredictability: 'Man plans, and God laughs.' This statement can be understood philosophically or religiously, and I am not sure which way I prefer. When I was eleven years old, I did not plan for chess to be a large part of my future, but I can trace my chess development and my current understanding of planning to the moment that £200 worth of Batsford chess books arrived at my home in Aberdeen; they were my reward for solving a chess puzzle correctly, and for my name being the one picked out of several from a prize-draw hat in London. On the one hand this was a simple stroke of luck, but it doesn't feel like that to me now. Three decades later that pivotal moment looks and feels more like providence than chance, as if it was *supposed* to happen, though I can't explain exactly what that means.

When I opened the boxes in my bedroom, one stood out from the others. It was a huge scarlet softback, with the photograph of an imposing moustached man staring at me on the cover, and lots of thick black lettering signifying strength and importance: *Alekhine's Greatest Games of Chess*. Alexander Alekhine was the fourth world champion, who lived a tumultuous life and held the title for most

of the second quarter of the twentieth century (1927–35; 1937–46).
Here was the kind of tome that silently commands you to open it,
but I feared for its creasing and arching spine every time I did, as if
Alekhine might suddenly admonish me for harming it.

Alekhine endured two wars, had three wives, found himself
living in countries invaded by Nazis (France) and Bolsheviks
(Russia), wrote a doctoral thesis on the Chinese prison system,
and died in Portugal under suspicious circumstances involving a
3-inch-long morsel of undigested meat. He allegedly choked to
death, but many historians believe the food was planted inside
his windpipe after the fact by Soviet assassins who felt he had
betrayed the motherland, or by French agents who sought revenge
for Alekhine's alleged collaboration with the Nazis. Portugal was
neutral during the Second World War and its tense aftermath, and
it is possible that the Portuguese authorities preferred not to ignite
controversy.

A fuller description of Alekhine's life and death story is beyond
our scope, but in July 1944 he wrote to the journalist and chess
player Juan Fernandez Rua with the following rueful reflection:

> The best part of my life has passed away between two world
> wars that have laid Europe waste. Both wars ruined me, with
> this difference: at the end of the first war I was 26 years of age,
> with an unbounded enthusiasm I no longer have. If, sometime,
> I write my memoirs – which is very possible – people will
> realise that chess has been a minor factor in my life. It gave me
> the opportunity to further an ambition and at the same time
> convince me of the futility of the ambition. Today, I continue
> to play chess because it occupies my mind and keeps me from
> brooding and remembering.

In 1946, while still world champion, and just before learning
that money had been raised for him to defend his title in England,
he died (or perhaps was killed) impoverished and alone, with his
chess set on the table in front of him; one of millions of tragedies
directly or indirectly caused by war.

I learned from the big red book that Alekhine's games were deep – he saw many moves into the position – and substantial – they were conceptually rich, and classical; he had absorbed existing chess knowledge and had moved beyond it. He was a rounded player with no obvious preferences or weaknesses. Alekhine is quoted as saying that a chess Grandmaster needs to be 'A combination of a beast of prey and a monk.' We need aggression, but our fire has to be under control. We need to reflect and focus, but with a view to winning.

I came to feel this idea viscerally around 1990, in a suburban house in Glasgow, where I sat with a couple of other proto-adolescent boys, along with our chess guru for the evening, Iain Swan. Iain is a teacher by profession, and one of Scotland's most dangerous attacking players, but that night he was trying to get us excited about what looked like an utterly lifeless endgame position – a position where there was material equality, few pieces left on the board and no contact between the opposing forces. At such moments there is no intellectual or competitive tension for chess players to get excited about.

Each side had just a single dark-squared bishop and two rooks, and three pawns on each wing that were only ever so slightly asymmetrical. When Iain asked us to formulate a winning plan for Black, we looked at each other in disbelief, and none of us could muster any significant sense of purpose. As is often the case in life, our imaginations were trapped by the conviction that we were bored. We were neither beasts of prey, nor monks.

The game was Eugene A. Znosko-Borovsky – Alexander Alekhine, Paris 1933, and I will never forget how that dull drawish position sprang to life through the orchestration of Alekhine's willpower. Seemingly out of thin air, the monk conjured an elaborate scheme that we were supposed to have guessed, while the beast of prey executed it with precision.

This kind of 'will-in-motion' involved mysterious ideas like 'exchanging one pair of rooks', 'centralising the king behind our main asset', advancing and trading off the isolated rook's pawn to create a weakness in the opponent's position, gaining space on the queenside, and then winning based on 'the principle of two weaknesses'; which was news to us at the time but is basically about overstretching the opponent's defences and then pouncing with your superior mobility; the side that is defending is generally tied up with defending certain pieces or squares, which makes the defensive forces less nimble than the attacking forces.

Alekhine's ideas were not in any sense sufficient to win the game at an objective level. The position was equal and there were plenty of defensive resources for the other side. That's not the point, however. For the first time in my life I felt the power of planning in chess, and sensed that willpower grows in proportion to our sense of purpose. I am grateful to Iain, because that night I remembered the big red book at home that was packed with Alekhine's games, and I set about studying them diligently.

Many assume that chess is all about such planning, but mostly it's about coping and adapting, which often means guessing and tricking. Chess taught me that the real purpose of planning in life is not so much to get to where you want to be, but to strengthen the willpower that you will need to get to a good place of any kind. Clarifying purpose through plans is about knowing how you want relationships to change. When you begin to feel the relationships moving in the right way because of how you set your intent in motion, purpose grows at compound interest, just like the grains of rice on the chessboard squares.

At those moments where we succeed in clarifying our purpose and acting on it with vigour, it is as if our will looks up and sees itself through us, smiling as it goes. Not without reason did St Francis of Assisi say: 'Start by doing what is necessary, and then do what is possible. Soon you find you are achieving the impossible.'

7. THE RIGHT KIND OF DIFFICULTY

I sometimes wonder whether chess is a prisoner of its own image. The game is perceived to be difficult, and therefore associated with strategy and depth. These positive qualities lead to chess imagery being used for marketing purposes, or to subtly signal to an audience that a character is cunning or sophisticated, as often happens in films just before somebody puts arsenic in the claret.

It's always good to see chess in the public domain, but the semiotics of chess often perpetuate the idea that the game is highbrow or elitist, and only accessible to really brainy people who love maths and button their shirts all the way up, or wannabe aristocrats with illusions of grandeur, who use the game to project a cultivated image.

As anybody who has played a chess tournament will tell you, the reality is very different, and chess is probably the most inclusive and meritocratic game on the planet. Learning the rules of chess is much easier than learning the alphabet. Eager five-year-olds can compete with their great-grandmothers, and nobody can safely predict the result.

And the exquisite but challenging fact is that insofar as chess is difficult, it's difficult in a good way. It's not difficult to learn or to play or to enjoy, because anybody who can think a thought can do that. The difficulty with chess is the difficulty of mastering it, which is a rewarding lifelong project.

The marketing challenge for chess is a subtle one, because most forms of marketing involve making difficult things look easy. Convenience sells, while effort does not, and yet the real rewards of the game come from the difficulty; from the pleasure of trying to make *fewer mistakes* than your opponent.

The bind is that if chess is difficult then it's exclusive, but if it's not difficult, what's all the fuss about? This is what I mean when I say that chess might be a prisoner of its own image. The only way to 'break free', I suspect, is to overcome widespread unfamiliarity with the experience of playing the game. Difficult things become less exclusive when everyone is expected to do them.

8. DISCONCERTING MOODS OF UNCERTAIN ORIGIN

In early December 2008, in a generic hotel room in Palma de Mallorca, Spain, I was submerged in a disconcerting mood of uncertain origin. I did not know quite what I was feeling or why, but there was a sense of being displaced from myself. I did not recognise my mood and could not identify with it in a way that would allow me to properly experience or encounter it. To be estranged from one's surroundings is not unusual, but to feel estranged from your own mood is even more vexing.

The experience was not emotional as such, but more like an atmosphere, a whole cocktail of feelings that were not so much within me, as between me and the world, mediating that relationship. It was the middle of a week-long international tournament and I was the highest-rated player and top seed. I remember thinking I ought to be a serious predatory Grandmaster, full of energy, willpower and competitive zeal, but in fact I was indecently mellow. I was not unhappy as such, but somewhat bewildered, because I found it increasingly hard to convince myself that winning chess games ought to be my main purpose in life.

That malaise might partly have been a function of timing. While the hotel was very pleasant, the organisers decided, in the interests of the few players who would also be tourists, that the games should begin at 8.30 p.m., long after morning optimism and afternoon alacrity have shuffled off to another time zone. So I spent my days waiting, reading, buying postcards I was never likely to send, and overeating at the bountiful buffet downstairs, before struggling to find form at the board, and typically finishing after midnight.

I remember it was late afternoon, and the sun, especially shy in recent days, was retiring once more. As a seasoned professional, I should have been deep in preparation, firing up the engines for the battle ahead, but I found that my appetite for opening theory was completely gone, and it was disaffecting to keep looking at chess positions on the screen as a kind of menu, when I was not even looking for a meal. I was more focused at the board, and although I underperformed, the tournament was not a disaster. When playing we are mostly released from self-consciousness, and I was still professional enough to solve whatever problems arose in my games; in fact it was a kind of relief to do so. But for several days I was not myself, or at least I was not my idea of myself.

We become so familiar with our moods – elated, bored, anxious, tranquil, restless – that we forget how important and mysterious they are. Moods are important because they are signals that life matters to us, that it is in our natures not just to function in the world but to *care* about it. Moods are mysterious because unlike mere emotions, we find ourselves *in* a good mood or a bad mood; we don't *have* a good mood or a bad mood, and this is not just a quirk of language. Moods do not seem to come to us 'from the outside' or 'from the inside', but from the relationship between them, what existentialist philosophers call our 'being-in-the-world', or from what we might think of as a moodscape. One reason that 'Concentrate!' feels like a naïve injunction then, is that it does not take account of mood. Before we can concentrate we first have to be in the mood to do so, and that challenge is not just about the task at hand but our existential predicament as a whole.

Moods are rarely clear; they are often inchoate, diffuse or misty, and tend to be inherently ambiguous. Moods linger, and sometimes we try to shake them off and fail. They determine our sense of what matters at any moment, often subverting our prior sense of what should matter. And moods are not always active in their orientation: just as often they are suffused with inertia. The statement 'I'm not in the mood' may sound lethargic and negative, but it is also a revelation. Our mood is essential data about how well attuned we are to the task at hand.[15]

The philosopher Martin Heidegger is notoriously hard to understand, but he places mood at the heart of his theory of human existence. For Heidegger, moods (*Stimmungen*) are the means by which we *find ourselves* in the world, and how we orient our sense of belonging to it. Our moods are fundamental to perception and thinking, which is always *thrown* in some way by them, and our emotions are partly about how we get to grips with that. Moods are the setting that allows any kind of sense of plot to arise because they shape our capacity to care and direct our attention. In Heidegger's language, the fact that things are able to matter in a given way is 'grounded in one's attunement'.[16] The commentator Charles Guignon puts it like this:

Our moods modulate and shape the totality of our Being-in-the-world, and they determine how things can count for us in our everyday concerns. Heidegger's point is that only when we have been 'tuned in' to the world in a certain way can we be 'turned on' to the things and people around us. Moods enable us to focus our attention and orient ourselves. Without this orientation, a human would be a bundle of raw capacities so diffuse and undifferentiated that it could never discover anything.[17]

Perhaps a love of chess is love for the *mood* of the game. If you enter a chess tournament hall and sit and watch what is happening, there is not usually much to report, but there is definitely a mood to be sensed and appreciated. I experience the mood as ambient incipience; the palpable intrigue that arises when, on every board, something is under way *and* about to happen. I have come to love this state of expectation, in which there is a sense of being held tightly in perpetual motion. When I say the meaning of chess is implicit, I am referring to that experience of unfolding significance.

Implicit comes from the Latin root 'entwined'. The point is not that life's meaning is interwoven in chess positions, like pesto in pasta or honey in porridge. The implicit meaning in chess is – if you'll permit me – more like the meaning that arises when two bodies become entwined in love-making. Meaning arises not because two things are together but because the experience of intercourse is like becoming a different form of life, and sometimes so intense that we feel altered, transformed and, all being well, transcendent. Although sex is considered explicit, the meaning of the act is implicit – entwined in the process itself. The act subsumes most of the meaning of talking about it, and f-ing the ineffable is rarely wise. I hesitate to say that chess is better than sex, but it is perhaps more reliable. Chess suspends us in a heightened state of luscious cogitation for hours at a time, like a diffuse, prolonged and strictly silent orgasm.

TWO

Winning and Losing

It's the mattering that matters

'Wash your necks,' said our team captain Mr Russell. I remember his friendly countenance, dark-framed glasses, multiple moles and abundant nasal hair; he was the pre-eminent grown-up among the grown-ups, the doyen of Scottish junior chess at the time.

'Wash your necks,' he said. 'Keep yourself fresh and alert. And dig in! Try your best!'

All the neck-washing in the world was not going to save us. In chess, as in many competitive endeavours, Scotland–England matches are often a form of ritual humiliation. Sometimes we – the Scots – are better and simply win, but more often there is a triumph of hope over experience in the buildup, and palliative consolations afterwards. How hard we fought, how proud we should feel. No matter how badly we lost. Almost every Scottish competitor knows this trope of being the courageous warrior who becomes the noble loser, and most of us are tired of it. Two decades later, becoming British champion in 2004, the first Scot to do so since 1946, helped. Holding the title for three years was all the sweeter for putting those formative feelings to rest.

Back in childhood, 'Away Home Game' was the title of a short local newspaper article about me, a Scot living in England (Whitton, Middlesex) who had returned to Scotland (Bearsden, Glasgow) to compete against England in 1988. The article was published before the annual Scotland–England under-12 match where teams of twenty players played two games in one day against their opposite numbers. I was number ten in a team of twenty, one of forty young children facing off in pairs on rectangular tables in a large sports hall. It was a familiar chess scene, apart from the uniform sweatshirts, Scotland's royal blue against England's vermilion red. I lost my first game, but have no memory of how it happened.

In the next game I outplayed my opponent, chess-speak for demonstrating superior understanding. I won 'the exchange', giving me an advantage of rook against knight, which would usually be decisive because the rook controls far more squares and has greater capacity to infiltrate the opposing territory. More generally, Scotland had played better than usual, and you could sense the excitement in the room; not that we would win of course, but that we might *lose better than ever before*.

My game was the last to finish and I could sense a small swarm hovering around my table: teammates, adult supervisors and interested parents. On a brief walk away from the board while my opponent was thinking I was advised by an onlooker that if I won or drew, it would be the highest score we had ever made against England. Whoever said that did not understand either chess psychology or child psychology, and I could not handle the pressure. I knew only that I should win, but that thought often acts like an antidote to winning. The key is to *allow yourself* to win, but that is precisely what is precluded under pressure to do so. I started to drift, and squandered some pawns. I remember feeling resentment towards my rook, somehow so unresponsive to my plight, so helpless against the coordinated force of his knight and pawns that were about to become queens. I had to resign, which adults typically do by stopping the clocks, but children often do it as seen in the movies. I knocked over my king.

Then I cried, on and off, for hours. At first I cried at the board, hiding anguished eyes with my team sweatshirt, in full sight of everybody. I eventually managed to move and sat nearby, but there was more protracted sobbing, soon comforted by my mother, who had come to collect me, and then there were some more tears in the car on the way home. It felt like everybody had told me it did not matter, but that only heightened the sense of trauma, because clearly it did. The failure was seen by too many people I had wanted to impress, too many people for whom chess mattered, which profoundly mattered to me at the time.

The sense of being watched is part of the chess experience, even when it is hard to say who exactly is watching and how much they care. Sometimes there are spectators in the same room watching our horizontal position vertically on analogue or digital demonstration boards hanging near our tables, sometimes there are other players sitting next to us or loitering nearby who glance at our position, and sometimes there is an online audience. Even without a live audience we record our games in algebraic notation. The vertical ranks are numbered one to eight, the files are lettered A–H and the piece names are abbreviated to single letters, e.g. 1.Nf3 means knight to the square 'f3' on the first move. Whoever is watching, there is a sensation that posterity has a stake in our moves, as if we are carving into reality, and leaving a trace for ever.

This responsibility of making irrevocable decisions in a public forum is part of the reason chess feels like it matters. The more personal and important and public the game, the more personal and important and public the result. The centrality of this point is highlighted by Simon Barnes in *The Meaning of Sport*: 'It is the mattering that matters ... All sports represent the collision of wills: people or teams who want the same thing and have to cause somebody pain to get it. The more it matters to the athletes, the more vivid the experience for the spectator.'[1]

Competition is the social construction of mattering. Things that matter can hurt you, and when you are hurt it is natural to say the thing hurting you, the competitive context, does not matter after all. But we build the competitive context together; the rules, the scores and the rankings are precisely what create an experience worth having for participants and spectators. To know and relish the narrative adventure, the peril and the plight – that is what matters, and not the competition as such. Punching the air in delight at victory or holding our heads in our hands in defeat may look different from, say, blowing out birthday candles, welling up while saying our wedding vows or anguished sobbing at funerals, but they tap into the same pattern of how we make meaning together.

In Confucian thought there are 'as-if rituals', which are things we do as if they were true, for instance lighting incense so that our ancestors smell the sweet smoke. Such actions have real effects because in the process of pretending they are true for us, we evoke feelings of humility and respect, and momentarily gain a fuller perspective on our lives. The Western version of the same idea is 'fake it until you make it', but the Confucian idea is deeper, because it's not about any old performance, but about rituals that we undertake in the process of developing our character, which are usually exacting in some way, forcing us to reach beyond our grasp. Chess can be seen as an as-if ritual. At some level we know the results of the game do not ultimately matter, and yet we play as if they do, and thereby evoke qualities of mind and character that might otherwise lie dormant. Chess does not matter until we make it matter and it matters all the more for that.[2]

What is important is not the result of the game, that's true. But it's not the whole truth. Taking part is 'the important thing', but that's not the whole truth either, because we cannot *really* take part, we cannot feel fully what there is to be felt, unless we act as if the result counts. What matters above all therefore is that we *care*. Whether we win or not is important for our personal quest and narrative, but not for our shared civilisation. Our gentle but firm acceptance of competitive significance is a sacred duty of sorts, because it is this shared commitment to making things matter that gives meaning to life.

Our record of competitive success is reflected in our chess rating, which is also a key feature of the social order of the chess world. Just as our competitive results do not really matter, and yet feel like they really do, so it is with our rating. Chess ratings reflect relative strength in a self-contained system of measurement devised by Professor Arpad Elo around 1960. Our rating changes according to a formula based on how our performance deviates from expected scores. The World Chess Federation, FIDE (*Fédération Internationale des Echecs*), issues ratings that start around 1000, and a player is likely to be making lots of mistakes up to about 1500, when they'll become an average club player with some basic chess sensibility. Many players plateau around that level, but improving club players stay on steep learning curves up to 2000, when they are likely to have mastered a wide range of ideas and be one of the better players in their area. By 2200 a player can put up a fight with professional players, though they will typically lose, and as skill becomes further refined, it gets even harder to improve.

At 2400 you become an International Master if you can also achieve three qualifying norms in international events, where you have to play above that level under certain conditions relating to the abilities of your opponents. At 2500 a similar process applies for becoming a Grandmaster, when you have to combine the achievement of that rating with three international tournament performances of 2600 or above where at least three Grandmasters are playing. Both IM and GM are titles conferred for life, but there is a big gap in playing strength between the two titles, reflecting greater breadth, depth and acuity of understanding. It can take many years to go from IM to GM and many never manage it. At the time of writing in 2018 there are well over 3,000 International Masters and about 1,500 Grandmasters in the world. Chess players know that our ratings, like our IQ, are a very limited way to reflect our diverse and varying capabilities. For instance just as IQ says little about our kindness or creativity, a chess rating says nothing of our style of play, how acute our understanding of particular positions can be, nor quite how dangerous we can be on any given day. Even so, we are typically self-conscious about ratings, because they are such a clear marker of our relative status in a world that we care about.

My highest published rating was 2599, just a point shy of my personal target of 2600, which was the unofficial level for the unofficial title of *Super Grandmaster* when I was growing up. There is a certain amount of rating inflation over time, so 2600 today merely places you in the top 10 per cent or so of GMs, many of whom peak during the exacting process of attaining the title and then dip well below even 2500. The level for the unofficial title of 'Super GM' has unofficially increased to 2700, and there are about fifty players of that standard. You need to be around 2800 or above to be a World Championship contender, and there are only a handful of such players. As a child I never dared to dream beyond 2600. That was the number that mattered to me when I realised I might be good enough to get there, but for some reason – perhaps because Scotland's chess culture was not particularly developed, perhaps because being diabetic is a physiological constraint at the very highest levels, or perhaps simply because I had other interests – I set my target there. And looking back, I wonder if I perversely enjoyed the absurdity of narrowly missing out. Having a published rating of 2599 three times, which briefly fluctuated beyond my goal between lists before falling back down, gave me the impish satisfaction of both achieving my goal *and* not achieving it.

We set ourselves more or less achievable aims for all sorts of reasons. In *Cigarettes are Sublime* Richard Klein argues that the persistent attempt to give up smoking is often a precondition for continuing the habit, because there is something about the process of giving up that is compelling and therefore addictive. Similarly, diets are notoriously self-defeating, and lots of people earnestly put on their running gear only to go out into the park, sit on a bench and look at the river. We are full of contradictory desires. I now wonder if 2600 was not so much a goal, but more like a safety valve; a numerical limit beyond which I might have been captured by chess for ever.

My highest-ever world ranking was 139 in 2005, when I was twenty-eight, just a couple of good tournaments away from being in the world top one hundred players. Doubtless I could have kept climbing, and it still hurts to think that, but there were also limits. My encounters in competition and analysis with world champions including Magnus Carlsen, Viswanathan Anand, Vladimir Kramnik, Rustam Kasimzhanov, games against elite Grandmasters like Lev Aronian, Alexander Morozevich, Alexander Grischuk and Peter Svidler, and regular encounters with England's world-class Grandmasters Michael Adams, Nigel Short, Jon Speelman and Luke McShane, revealed my limits to me. I was good enough to think and tussle with the very best players, but not to prevail or even survive against them consistently. Mostly they beat me, and not always with significant effort. Amidst thousands of international competitors I was among the cream, but not the cream of the cream. Magnus Carlsen, on the other hand, could hardly get any creamier.

9. HOW THE STRONG WEAKEN THE WEAKER

Towards the end of 2013 Norway's Magnus Carlsen became the new World Chess champion at the age of twenty-two. A year later he became the highest-rated player of all time, with an international rating of 2882 – a dizzyingly high figure for chess players.

I played Magnus at the Dresden Chess Olympiad in 2008, when he was only seventeen, but already a world-class Grandmaster who looked certain to reach the summit. We played a strategically rich game, and I may even have had some advantage at one point, but I was irresolute in the late middlegame and became short of time. I remember vividly how Magnus set up a tactical opportunity for himself several moves before I saw it coming. When the natural sequence of moves followed and he executed his idea I felt this overwhelming surge of energy and strength coming in my direction. It was as if I had been sparring in the ring for a few hours and more or less holding my own, then lost focus for just a millisecond, only to be hit with a ferocious right hook that knocked me to the floor.[3]

Magnus's life has been completely dedicated to chess, and he has been supported from a young age by his mother, father and two sisters, who often travel with him to events, partly to keep him happy and grounded, but also to deal with administrative matters so that he can focus on the chess. Magnus was a fully worthy winner in 2013, and it was helpful for the chess community that we could now be completely unequivocal when people ask us: 'Who's the best?' In addition to supreme excellence in all aspects of the game, Magnus brings glamour and global star quality, for instance modelling G-star RAW clothes with actress Liv Tyler and beating the billionaire Bill Gates in nine moves, executed with just 12 seconds of thinking time, on a Nordic talk-show clip that went viral online.

If Magnus has a flaw as a world champion, it's that his life story does not speak to a geopolitical zeitgeist as Bobby Fischer did during the Cold War, and Kasparov and Karpov did as the Soviet Union imploded. But that is hardly his fault. He compensates for his zeitgeist deficit with, at least in the public eye, his apparent normality, which is a huge asset for the chess brand. Yet I was a little sad when Magnus became world champion. My sadness was not just because I know and like Viswanathan Anand – 'Vishy' – whom he had supplanted (more on him later). Nor was it about my tendency to resist popular narratives like 'Magnus is unstoppable'. The disappointment and feeling of emptiness that followed were more about the way it happened.

Each of the reigning champion's three losses had an avoidable quality in which the mistakes felt unforced and uncharacteristic. You can say that once, but three times? At some point you have to accept the brutality of competition. The strength of really strong players lies precisely in their ability to make other strong players play below their strength. The first two losses came from fairly simple positions, where clear thinking indicated few objective problems, but Magnus's will and relentless accuracy wore Vishy down, and the psychological pressure made it hard for him to calculate. Game nine was different. Vishy built up a promising position, then could not make the most of his resources, and blundered to his third defeat. The match was almost alive and kicking, but again came these uncharacteristic mistakes: the brilliant attacker misplays his attack, the amazing calculator miscalculates.

Did Magnus do that to him? I think he did. Vishy may feel that he only had himself to blame, but these lapses were not about lack of effort, they were about nerves and concentration, things he did his best to control, for instance by being physically fitter than he had been for years. But it is not always in our power to influence the full spectrum of competitive qualities that we need to win. I think the sense in which Magnus weakened Vishy is more primal, like the way one boxer dominates another through eye contact before a punch has been thrown, or the way a lion will compel another to lie on their back in submission to forgo any test of dominance.

The strong weaken the weaker because strength is ultimately a function of the will, and in a context where there is no escape, one side's will ultimately yields to the other. Any weak-willed thought that the opponent may be fundamentally stronger is therefore fatal, not least because of the curious – almost geometrical – qualities of willpower. Competitive willpower is distinct from mere effort, because it is not about honing our own performance, but rather what we muster to impose on the opponent. Willpower is zero-sum in that context; as one side's willpower grows, the other's weakens. Moreover, willpower seems to rise or fall with compound interest, building on itself with momentum, almost like a law of nature. There is evidence for this phenomenon in tennis, in which the side who won the previous point is disproportionately more likely to win the next point, and also in football penalty shootouts, where the side that shoots and typically scores first has a big advantage because the other side always feels like they are trailing and therefore submissive.[4]

These curious features of willpower help us understand why, in a contest that should be close, the players often look far apart. When only one can ultimately survive, the weaker player often submits in spirit to spare themselves the humiliation of effortful hoping in what they know in their hearts to be a hopeless case. In a single game the role of willpower is not quite as significant, because there are so many variables and chance plays a role, but in a match of several games there is no avoiding the fundamental question: Who is stronger? Which one of us has to die? Sometimes the competitors do not know, which is why the match happens, but when they already know, even if only in their own hearts and minds, the result is a foregone conclusion.

* * *

Ernest Hemingway once remarked that: 'As we get older, it is harder to have heroes, but it is sort of necessary.' I feel that way about world chess champions.

In most cases, success means sacrifice. The closer you look at the level of dedication required from a tender age to become the best and stay there, and the single-mindedness and vertigo that entails, the less sure you are that you would ever want to be that person. In Gary Kasparov's early autobiography, *Child of Change*, he remarked that a normal childhood was the price he paid for becoming world champion. Kasparov gave a talk at Oxford University while I was a student there. I asked him if this price was worth paying and my question was sincere. He said yes, as you might expect, but sounded rueful, referring to lost opportunities to, 'you know, just go out and play with the other children'.

The difficulty in having heroes is also that as we get to know the best players as people, we find that they seem to suffer as we do. The stars achieve more, and perhaps feel more fulfilled, but they are still awash with desire, frustration and envy. They also get hungry, tired and irritated, and fear losing what they have. When maturity allows us to see our heroes as human, their heroism feels like part of the human story we share with them, rather than a single superhuman story that is theirs alone.

I have met and played with several world champions, but the one I know best is Viswanathan Anand, who was champion from 2000 to 2002 and 2007 to 2013. Vishy is a living legend in the chess world, particularly renowned for his speed of thought and play as a youngster, often winning games using only a few minutes of his clock time. He became world class as his natural speed interacted with technical skill and eager use of computer technology to prepare openings. Vishy knew me from my chess writing, and we first met when we were both playing on the stage at the Calvia Olympiad in Spain in 2004. I had recently featured in a profile interview for a magazine that included questions about food, so his opening gambit was not 'Hi,' but rather: 'Anybody who likes south Indian curries with coconut milk can't be that bad.' I am fond of south Indian food because my wife Siva comes from that part of the world. Soon afterwards we had lunch in Chennai with Vishy and his wife Aruna, where said curries were duly enjoyed, and we have been friends since then.

Hemingway's recognition that heroes are necessary applies in my case to Vishy. Partly because I have come to know and love India through marriage, and partly because I liked Vishy personally, I wanted him to be world champion; that meant watching at times as he retained the title, and at other times as he strove to reclaim it. Just as we often end up supporting a football team by accident, and then follow them for decades, chess players don't do a cost–benefit analysis of the players we like. Our heroes appear through the questions we ask of life, and we live some of the answers vicariously through them.

10. BEING WOUNDED

It has been said that when you find yourself at the gates of heaven, God will ask you: 'Where are your wounds?' And if you say: 'I have no wounds,' he will say: 'Was there nothing worth fighting for?'

For some, coming to terms with the idea that God may not exist is the biggest wound of all, but whatever your view of ultimate reality, our wounds may be the best part of ourselves. The nature of the wound is always unique to our personal story, and yet the uniqueness of our wounds is something we share. The Christian philosopher Richard Rohr even calls Christianity, the world's largest and most influential religion, 'the way of the wound', which is consistent with the idea that the individual significance of one life and death can be, paradoxically, universally relevant.

There is a joke that nails this point. A professor was lecturing about uniqueness not really being so special, because, after all, everyone is unique. A troubled student at the back of the room put his hand up and proclaimed: 'Excuse me, Professor, but I disagree. I happen to be the only person in the universe who is *not* unique.'

Wounds are unique in that paradoxical sense of being completely universal. If we decide something matters to us, we are always vulnerable to wounding: within chess games and tournaments, and life in general. As long as we resolve to care about something, we remain vulnerable, a fact that social researcher and bestselling author Brené Brown develops beautifully in her work on human emotions, calling vulnerability 'the magic sauce' that holds relationships together. It might even be the shared experience of vulnerability that bonds chess players together as a global community – we know how easy it is to go wrong, and how much it hurts when it does.

Caring enough about something to be vulnerable may be an essential part of maturation, and it is noteworthy that many initiation rites in traditional cultures feature intense suffering or deprivation that we have to deal with before fully 'growing up'. Physical wounds can damage your life beyond recognition, but the psychic wounds incurred from abuse or grief or injustice can be every bit as serious. Less existential, but still deeply visceral, are the wounds incurred from sporting defeats, which can knock careers back several years as the vanquished, rather than merely defeated, lose their will to compete. Yet there are ways to turn towards our wounds and allow them to heal us.

In 2014, I was struck by the young Dutch Grandmaster Anish Giri's remark that Vishy Anand was 'too wounded' to have a real chance of winning the Candidates tournament, which was then under way in Khanty-Mansiysk in Russia. The winner of this event was to challenge Magnus Carlsen for the title, and Vishy, surely, had no wish to relive the experience of his crushing defeat the previous year?

It is indeed hard to fight an enemy like Carlsen, who is not only respected but *feared* by many of his rivals. On the other hand, the Russian Grandmaster Alexander Grischuk made the astute point that the winner among the candidates would be a completely different person as a result of the process, such that even this 'new Anand' emerging victorious would be a difficult opponent for Carlsen.

An inspiring thought, and a reminder of the wellspring of power we tap into at the moment we feel that our wounds are either healing, or bearable as they are. Just when people thought his career might be over after losing his world title, Vishy completely outplayed the tournament favourite and then world number two, Levon Aronian, in the first of fourteen rounds, and went on to challenge Carlsen for a second match in Sochi, Russia. He lost again, but gave a much better account of himself.

I suspect the psychological basis for Vishy's return to form was an acceptance of Carlsen's superiority. Just as Vishy had for several years been close in strength to Kasparov, but not quite as good, I think he reconciled himself to the same relationship to Carlsen – he was a worthy opponent certainly, but just not quite as strong. Only by letting go of the frustration of not being world champion could he allow himself to be at ease with merely being world class. He has lost to Carlsen periodically in the interim, but at the time of writing he still appears to love the game, occasionally plays brilliantly and remains in the world top ten players. The idea that there are no limits to our ability is not always true, kind or helpful. Sometimes accepting that we cannot be the best of the best is precisely what allows us to be the best we can be.[5]

11. THE DIFFERENCE BETWEEN EXCELLENT AND EXCEPTIONAL

It is helpful to deconstruct the skill set of the very best player in the world, for whom chess has mattered since he was a young boy. Carlsen's capacity to outlast his opponents is partly a function of will, which means he plays not just as if winning mattered, but in a way that constantly challenges the opponent to maintain the same level of commitment on every move – a task that few can manage.

Even before he became world champion, the defining feature of Carlsen's play was, well, that he beat everybody. Despite having virtually no match experience, he managed to become the undisputed world number one by winning, winning and winning some more. He had the invincible sheen of Roger Federer before Rafael Nadal, Tiger Woods before the infidelities, or Barack Obama before he was elected.

The gap in strength between Magnus and myself is approximately 300 rating points. In lay terms, based on the statistics that underpin these numbers, that means if I played Magnus today I would have a very slim chance of drawing, virtually no chance of winning, and very high chances of losing. It is small consolation that even elite Grandmasters who live and breathe chess in a way I never have are often rated a hundred points below him, which begs the question of what makes him not merely good, but singularly strong.

I believe the core of Magnus's strength is his capacity to outlast his opponents, and that this quality depends upon several other skills and dispositions coalescing in a way that is hard to match.

First, and perhaps most important, he very rarely blunders. He cannot avoid inaccuracies – small imprecisions in the move-order sequence of his ideas, for instance – but he very rarely makes significant mistakes based on missing major tactical opportunities for himself or the opponent.

Second, he is completely *at home* while playing. He revels in the competitive tension of being at the board and is in absolutely no rush to get away.

Third, he manages to be deeply self-confident while retaining both objectivity and a good feeling for the fallibility and vulnerability of the opponent.

Fourth, he is extremely versatile, and there are no positions that he does not like. He once remarked: 'Having preferences means having weaknesses,' and this readiness to go wherever the logic of the position may take him makes life difficult for most of his opponents who do have preferences.

Fifth, he has an excellent sense of timing, of knowing when to change the nature of the position to pose practical problems. This is a particularly subtle competitive skill that manifests as a sharp killer instinct: a sense of when to chase and how to pounce.

Sixth, he has the energy of youth, and makes the most of it by carefully managing his diet and lifestyle. This energy allows him to stay alert in the final moments of the game while others begin to fade.

When I look at the above six qualities, I find that I have only a good share of the third, fourth and fifth when I am playing well, but that I can't compete overall, which means that the longer the game lasts, the more likely I am to screw up. Stronger Grandmasters may have more of these qualities, and some even have all six from time to time, but I think there is only one player who has all of these qualities, almost all of the time, and that is Magnus.

On one memorable occasion, the Wijk aan Zee 2013 tournament, I watched online as Magnus ground down another former prodigy, Russia's Sergey Karjakin, who would later challenge him for the world title. Magnus steadily applied pressure over almost a hundred moves, even though his advantage was slight for most of that time. Everybody has their limits, though, and Sergey eventually cracked through a succession of small mistakes and then a blunder.[6]

Of all the non-fiction writers who have tried to make sense of chess as an outside observer, Julian Barnes is perhaps the most perceptive, particularly when he notes a profound binary quality in the language chess players use to talk about the game:

> When you eavesdrop on the chatter of chess, you discover that it reproduces and confirms the game's compelling mixture of violence and intellectuality ... half the language has a street-fighting quality to it. You don't just attack a piece, *you hit it* ... Getting your opponent into time trouble, you try to flag him; playing a sacrifice, you sack a piece, as you might sack a city. And since violent verbs require victims, your opponent's bits of wood are personified into living matter: 'I want to hit *this guy* and *this guy*.' Interwoven with all this is a more polysyllabic language of theory and aspiration. A move may be *natural or artificial, positional* or *anti-positional, intuitive or anti-intuitive, thematic or dysfunctional* ... And what are the two players seeking? The *truth of the position* ... They are struggling to *prove* something; though an outside observer might not *believe in* it ... Thus high ambition combines with low brutality; there seems to be no middle vocabulary developed by the players.[7]

These words ring true. The neutral language used to denote what is happening is algebraic notation, which details what the moves are – e.g. 1.d4 Nf6 – but when narrating we struggle to conceal our dual natures, and speak either in the tenor of an action film or as a kind of scripture, never in the language of, for instance, the BBC Shipping Forecast, which is celebrated for its lullaby-like quality of neutral nautical description – say 'Low Skagerrak 1008 expected Baltic 1003 by midnight tonight. Lows Plymouth and Rockall, both 1011 … Rain later. Good, occasionally poor.' I love listening to the shipping forecast, not because it says anything really, but because its indecipherability represents the benign mystery of life more generally.

I know chess too well to see it that way. The game has many flavours and not all of them are sweet. Chess is a study in truth and beauty, but it is also a violent contact sport; a geometric cage fight. What makes *contact* are two psyches obliged to try to destroy each other, and in that confrontation there is nowhere to hide. All the violence is sublimated, but a sense of latent terror is always present. At moments, in the heat of the battle, *Clockwork Orange*-style sadism can emerge. A dark excitement can arise from figuratively crushing our opponent, as if we were nonchalantly kicking them in the head while laughing. These are dark thoughts, I know, but they are not gratuitous. Grandmaster Boris Gulko makes a mild and peaceful impression in person, but he famously advised one his students: 'Understand, chess is a game for hooligans.'

I was already a Grandmaster when I heard Gulko's counsel for the first time, and I found myself wincing in recognition of something I had sensed for a long time. I wondered whether not being a thug at heart was the reason I have struggled to feel fully at home in the chess world, but that would be too easy a consolation. There is a brutality in the world of winning and losing, which makes sense for an intimation of war, and there is also a depth of experience that you will never know until you have put yourself on the line, and I am grateful for that. To know that sense of something mattering deeply from the inside and fighting with every ounce of our being – as if for our lives – gives rise to a feeling of *honour*, an old-fashioned value perhaps, but one we should not forsake.

12. THE REALITY OF TALENT

In the summer of 2002, I received a week of training in the home of World Championship candidate Artur Yusupov in southern Germany. The training was exacting and I came to realise how poorly I calculated variations compared with most other Grandmasters. Calculation is required for advanced tactical ability, in which you have to consider lines of play known as variations with care and precision and you need sustained concentration in order to make accurate decisions, often for several moves at a time.

Calculation is the part of the game that is most concrete and mathematical and where humans have to be relatively machine-like – for some it comes naturally, but I knew I had to work hard on it to rise within the Grandmaster ranks. This skill is paramount for converting positional advantages which often require us to momentarily lose control in a tactical sequence while we transform one form of dominance for another; when we fail to do that our advantages can dissipate, which often happened to me – I was much better at getting good positions than at converting them to victory. I had other virtues relating to knowledge of the opening phase of the game, positional understanding and psychological strength, but I tended to eschew calculation because I found it painful and difficult.

At Yusupov's house, for a whole week I was forced to calculate six hours a day, but it transformed my play and soon afterwards I shared first in the World Open and began to approach the world top hundred on the rating list. I felt palpably strong, the board began to look clearer, and I was hungry to compete with the best. Even so, a complicated variation that I might calculate correctly because of weeks of training and twenty minutes of strenuous effort at the board would be seen in the blink of an eye by a player like Magnus Carlsen, even as a young teenager.

After one particular hard day's analysis, I was left alone to watch the film *Amadeus*, originally a play by Peter Shaffer, concerning a rival composer's murderous envy of Wolfgang Amadeus Mozart. Just before leaving Artur remarked that the theme of the movie, the inequality of talent, was a very important one for chess players. It was the only English-language film in the house, but to this day I'm not sure whether he was trying to give me a hint. The plot concerns the competent and esteemed composer Antonio Salieri, who is consumed by resentment at the unmistakable chasm between Mozart's blossoming musical genius, which he craves, and his own mere ability, which looks mediocre by comparison. The story is told retrospectively by Salieri, from an insane asylum. It is a brilliant film.

I have never felt envy with Salieri's intensity, but I do know the discomfort of encountering somebody who does what I pride myself on doing well, only several orders of magnitude better. Talent is not one thing but several; a mixture of genes, early relationships, learning environments, growth opportunities and practice habits that fashion ability and the disposition to learn, but inequality of talent can still feel quite palpable. While analysing positions with world champions like Anand, Kramnik and Carlsen, for instance, their superiority in moving between accurate variations, sophisticated judgments and effective decisions has an effortless quality, like a language spoken fluently, without any trace of a foreign accent. I take some consolation from having been close enough in strength to elite players to recognise just how far away I was.

Max Ehrmann's classic prose poem *Desiderata* was on my bedroom wall as a child. I took comfort from the line: 'If you compare yourself with others you may become vain or bitter, for always there will be persons greater or lesser than yourself.' Chess constantly forces you to confront this idea. In most cases you can imagine closing the gap, or winning next time, but every so often you feel the brute fact of your inferiority, and if you are not careful it can feel like a kind of shame. When your identity is wrapped up in being the best you can be at one particular thing, it can be crushing to encounter others who are unambiguously better.

Our sense of shame in inferiority can be subsumed by qualities of character – for instance the grace of humility and the deeper self-belief it engenders – but not easily. Talent often evokes envy, and envy corrodes character.

Magnus Carlsen has been called 'The Mozart of Chess', because his play can look so effortlessly profound and beautiful, but he combines this elegance with formidable martial qualities and a steely will to win. I thought again of Salieri in the context of Carlsen's relationship to one of the USA's finest-ever players, Hikaru Nakamura, whom I managed to defeat in 2004 when he was not yet world class. Nakamura has been a mainstay of the world top ten and regularly within the top five of the rating list. He is a class act with steely determination and creative flair, and he continues to improve, so when he described himself as the main threat to Carlsen in the long term in 2014, it was not a groundless assertion.

And yet, he is not as good as Carlsen, and it is hard to imagine that he ever would be. You can sense this chasm in the fact that Nakamura called Carlsen 'Sauron', the ultimate and virtually omnipotent evil force in *The Lord of the Rings*. Perhaps intimidation is built upon this kind of internalised envy – we are not just scared but also attached to our inferiority in some sense, and the feelings that engenders. As the writer Sally Kempton once put it: 'It's hard to fight an enemy who has outposts in your head.'

Being inferior to someone at something you love despite your very best effort can be painful. You can try to explain such pain away, but it will linger as long as our identity is invested in competitive success and the status that comes with it. With some distance from chess I now think this predicament, which arises in every walk of life, is ultimately a spiritual problem we have to transcend. When confronted with our inferiority, the answer is not to console ourselves by targeting people below our level, to work a bit harder for the next opportunity, or run off the frustration in the park. Those shifts will not resolve the sense of dissonance that arises when you give everything you have and find it is not enough. The only ultimate escape, in the language of Robert Kegan, is not to solve the problem but to allow the problem to solve you.[8]

When we have done all we can to satisfy the ego's craving for validation, we have to turn the pain of inferiority into a justified insurgency against the sovereignty of the ego. The way out of the pain is to see who we are from more profound vantage points. Depending on your religious or spiritual perspective, allowing the problem to solve us might mean recognising the ultimate absurdity of the game we are involved in: a glimpse into the absurdity of life as a whole gives us a taste of reality from a perspective other than our ego's desire to win.

Another way to allow the problem of ego pain to solve us is to see, along with perennial philosophy, that we and our rivals are in some deeper sense co-constituted; we are fundamentally the same *interbeing* and share a reality that is bigger than both of us.

Allowing thwarted competitive desire to help solve us could also mean allowing our competitive identity to dissolve. We can come to realise that there is nobody there, really, no essential self for whom this pain needs to be felt. In the evocative words of Buddhist teacher Mark Epstein, we sometimes need to 'go to pieces without falling apart'; to break down the constructed identity we have been invested in so that we begin to see that the boundaries between ourselves and the rest of the world are porous. Rather than our reality being subsumed by the egoic desire to compete and win, on reflection it is not clear where we end and the rest of the world begins. From that perspective, winning looks very different.

For some, the only answer to the sovereignty of our ego is a more straightforward theism, in which we develop a relationship to something that is truly 'other', a relationship to something for which and through which we are not an ego seeking achievement, but a soul seeking home.

I do not think any of these approaches is the uniquely correct one, and there is still a time and a place for the raging ego that wants to win at all costs. Still, living well means having some capacity to temper our natural desire and envy. It helps to hold the significance of chess, competition and ego in a larger and ultimately truer perspective.

13. SPONTANEOUS COMBUSTION

In the summer of 2005 a middle-aged neighbour who lived alone approached our home looking unusually distressed. With bemused indignation, and the excited relief of a survivor, she told my wife Siva and me that the previous night, while she slept, her glass table had exploded. There was no external cause, and it did not just crack or even shatter, because when she emerged to see what had happened, there were thousands of smithereens scattered all over her living room.

It does happen apparently, though extremely rarely. Glass is an unusual substance, suspended somewhere between liquid and solid. I am no chemist, but my mother-in-law Dr Vatsala Srinivasan is. She tells me that glass does not have what is known as a 'first-order phase transition', which separates liquids from solids, influencing properties like density. Glass can be thought of as a highly viscous liquid or an amorphous solid, while some chemists say it is a different kind of substance altogether.

Whatever glass is, it is not completely stable. Glass explosions happen with a certain kind of tempered glass that is fairly thick and covers a large surface area. The material expands in the heat and then cools unevenly, with thick rubbing up against thin in a confined space, leading to a build-up of tension that sometimes has to break out.

We had a glass table at the time too, and although the chances of it exploding were minuscule, the very thought was too much for our imaginations to bear. On the same evening we heard of our neighbour's story, my wife Siva instructed me to dismantle the table and put it in the shed, where it lay for several months before we gave it to a friend, all the time looking pretty solid.

We are more like glass tables than we typically imagine. Mostly we are solid, but we can and do crack up. Sometimes we are broken by accident or force, and sometimes we explode for no apparent reason. The idea of spontaneous human combustion is bizarre and disputed, and appears to be a highly rarefied phenomenon if it happens at all. In so far as it can happen, it is probably not 'spontaneous', but caused by other factors, for instance a mixture of extremely high alcohol content in the blood and a smouldering cigarette being in the wrong place at the wrong time.

But even if the chances of literally exploding are extremely low, we do figuratively explode all the time, and not just with anger. Sobbing is a gentler form of explosion; convulsions of the body shaken by the soul's will to health. And whenever we laugh we explode conceptually, intuiting the contingency of the patterns that constrain us, and glimpsing forms of vitality on the other side of the structures we think and act with every day.

During a chess game it is not straightforward to channel anger, feel sorrow or laugh heartily. Our hearts, minds and wills are often full of emotions, not just fear and hope but also anxiety, exhilaration, desire and longing; but our bodies are stationary for hours at a time – a far from natural predicament. This combination of volitional and emotional drama and physical inertia means that our nervous system is often close to falling apart. And since we cannot channel our feelings physically, they manifest on the board. The most painful way this happens is when we blunder. Blunders are not just inaccuracies but major and often decisive errors, for instance leading to a loss from a winning position. Mostly we blunder when we are placed under pressure, but sometimes the slip is bizarrely unforced.

The phenomenon of blundering has something of Freud's death wish in it. Psychoanalytic theory is full of references to destructive and self-destructive tendencies that run contrary to our desire for pleasurable experiences, but the most elegant expression of the idea came from Freud in his book *The Pleasure Principle*: 'an urge in organic life to restore an earlier state of things'. In a chess context, that sounds like the understandable urge, in an overwhelmingly complex game, to relieve the tension by setting the pieces up and starting again, which is effectively what happens whether we win, lose or draw. Trying to win when the opponent will not cooperate increases the tension, which can be unbearable; the tension sometimes becomes so great that we self-destruct. Psychologically we might pretend to ourselves that we are doing all we can to compete, but for an important and neglected part of us it can feel like dying is the only way to survive.

The death wish runs deep. Freud believed human history could be seen as war between the two 'heavenly powers' Eros and Thanatos: between the urge to love, to preserve, and the urge to destroy. Eros and Thanatos are intertwined at all times, like Yin and Yang, but today Thanatos has new resonance in the latent ubiquity of suicide bombing, and in the sense that the life force of Eros may have become corrupted; pervasive ecological degradation suggests that, tragically, we may be unable to stop ourselves from destroying our only home.

In chess the death wish manifests as blundering, and blunders rarely 'just happen'. There is always a psychological build-up either within the game or in its broader life context that makes self-destruction more probable, and perhaps even attractive. Sometimes we appear to want to harm ourselves to protect ourselves, but our reasons for doing so often remain unclear, even to ourselves. In this sense, blundering is vulnerability made manifest, but sometimes vulnerability is elicited as the intensity of willpower in one player erodes the will to resist in the other. I have been on both sides of this equation; as one side plays better and grows in determination, the other is inclined to make mistakes and start to wilt. Sometimes you are up against such strength of will that you would do anything to get away from it, which can make losing a welcome relief. As indicated above, Magnus Carlsen seems to thrive on making this phenomenon manifest in his elite but awestruck opponents.

Professional players will rarely simply collapse, but they will sometimes leak their sense of unconscious inferiority through forms of substandard play that allow them to disavow their responsibility to wholeheartedly compete. We still willingly put ourselves in an existential arena for hours on end, because the intensity is delicious and we rarely feel more alive, but then bathos enters into the world of would-be heroes; the beauty, the logic, the story waiting to be told – we squander it all with trivial errors that are beneath us.

The anguish is maddening. For instance when, in 1991, Grandmaster Vassily Ivanchuk from Ukraine lost a high-stakes game in Brussels that would have given him a chance to challenge for the world title, the *British Chess Magazine* described the moment as follows: 'Immediately after the play-off was over, he walked out into the street, and, to the shock of passers-by, emptied his lungs with a blood-curdling scream.'

Watching a player you like and admire lose a painful game is not as bad as losing one yourself, but our own memories of loss cut deep, pain stays vivid, and even vicarious experience is palpable. Thinking back to watching Vishy's loss in the final game of his World Championship Match with Magnus Carlsen in 2013, he made an avoidable blunder in a complex position where he had winning chances and I felt like I was in physical pain for some time afterwards. Much of that pain was the projective identification any fan might feel when their favoured competitor loses, but it was also about identifying with a particular kind of regret.[9]

I don't know exactly how Vishy felt, but I tweeted at the time: 'An unpublished draft of Dante's Inferno includes a circle of hell where you learn how it feels to lose an important chess game.' After blundering you sometimes wonder if your self will ever feel whole again, if you will ever recalibrate all the broken pieces of your psyche. Chess players feel a close bond for many reasons, but the experience of post-traumatic survival is one of them.

14. CEASING HOSTILITIES

Brian Wall, an American amateur, is not known for great games, but I will remember him for a great quote: 'Chess is basically a fight between the pain of losing and the pain of thinking.' On reading this, I suddenly appreciated the role of the draw offer in our game, which affords a release from both kinds of pain. In life, there is nothing quite like the draw offer, though perhaps there should be.

A game can be drawn for a range of reasons, including stalemate (no legal move can be made, but the king is not in check), fifty moves are completed without a pawn move or a capture (this rule prevents a game going on indefinitely without anything changing), a threefold repetition of the same position (often in the form of perpetual check, when the king cannot escape, but nor can it be checkmated), or a player running out of time when his opponent no longer has 'mating material', i.e. sufficient forces to deliver checkmate in any plausible way.

In all time controls, acute time pressure can arise, and it is not unusual for a player with a decisive advantage on the board to agree to a draw because he risks losing on time before being able to give checkmate; giving rise to a paradoxical feeling of pained relief. In addition to all these technical possibilities, at any stage of the game either player is entitled to play his move and just before pressing the clock propose that the point be split, usually with the dangling words: 'I offer a draw.'

This provision can be abused or overused, but it is always psychologically revealing. The offer is technically only valid after you have made your move, and only stands for that particular moment in the game. You are not supposed to offer a draw more than once before your opponent has offered in return, but this rule is often broken. At the World Cup in Reykjavik 1988, former world champion Boris Spassky, long since past his prime but still dangerous, offered reigning world champion Gary Kasparov a draw on move eleven. The position was balanced and Kasparov declined, but soon made an unforced error. After a few deft manoeuvres, by move nineteen Spassky had achieved a position that looked merely slightly advantageous, but it was the kind of advantage that was likely to steadily grow, and Kasparov had nothing in particular to look forward to. Having been world champion, and no longer feeling hunger to prove anything, Spassky purportedly said Russian words to the effect: 'I am giving you a last chance. If you refuse the draw now I will wipe you off the board.' Kasparov wisely accepted.[10]

We learn about the draw offer soon after learning how the pieces move, and rarely question it, but on reflection it is without parallel in other games. Imagine a tense football match – let's say an old firm Celtic–Rangers game in Scotland, with no goals after 35 minutes. There is still plenty of competitive tension, scarves are flying, fans are singing, and then the managers meet on the touchline and tell the referee to blow the whistle because they have agreed a draw. Such an outcome would seem scandalous in a spectator sport, which is important given that this is what some would like chess to be.

That said, in life there are some parallels to the draw offer. Negotiators use the technique of 'bracketing' to allow them to proceed with other aspects of a potential agreement while leaving the most contentious language choices until later; that's a kind of draw offer because it's about choosing when to make temporary peace and postponing the need to fight. Moreover, in the context of divorces we often call upon mediators to help provide a safe way to *conclude* a process without necessarily fully *resolving* it. That said, the draw offer is not merely a pragmatic way to reduce conflict, but also a form of fraternisation, a proposed gift exchange that turns a putative enemy into a kind of friend, but which can also be viewed as a form of treason.

In this respect the closest historical parallel to the draw offer may be the poignant story of the Christmas truce between British (and French and Belgian) and German soldiers who came together in the no-man's-land between trenches in 1914. There are numerous primary sources detailing this historical moment, which included soldiers singing songs, swapping sweets and cigarettes and maybe even playing football, but perhaps the most moving account is among the most bleak, from Alfred Anderson of Scotland's Black Watch, who recounted his experience almost ninety years later as follows:

> I remember the silence, the eerie sound of silence. Only the guards were on duty. We all … just stood listening. And, of course, thinking of people back home. All I'd heard for two months in the trenches was the hissing, cracking and whining of bullets in flight, machinegun fire and distant German voices. But there was a dead silence that morning, right across the land as far as you could see. We shouted 'Merry Christmas', even though nobody felt merry. The silence ended early in the afternoon and the killing started again. It was a short peace in a terrible war.[11]

When warfare is so brutal, who can blame the peacemakers for wanting a break from it? 'Let's be friends' invariably sounds like a good suggestion, especially in wars that are as senseless and stupid as the Great War. And yet, in principle there must be rare moments where war is necessary and justified. The dignity of chess is that it respects the perennial place of warfare in our psyches but sublimates the violence so that nobody gets physically hurt. In that context, the draw offer is a way of saying: In light of the position on the board, I don't think this game is worth getting hurt for, do you? Sometimes the opponent agrees, but often they decline our offer and tacitly say: actually, yes, I do.

I was a live commentator for game seven of the Kasparov–Kramnik World Championship match in London in 2000, which featured an agreed draw after only eleven moves. The final position was equal, perhaps even 'drawish' to discerning eyes, but there was no need to cease hostilities immediately. Only a few hundred spectators paid for seats, but hundreds of thousands were watching online and the main sponsors of the event, Braingames, had chosen this day to come to the venue to see what they were getting for their money. I don't think they came back.

Kasparov lost the match mostly because in this game and several others he could not break down Kramnik's 'Berlin Wall' defence, an opening variation that quickly leads the game into an endgame where Kasparov's position may have been slightly superior, but where his extensive preparation and attacking prowess was almost irrelevant. After the completion of game seven, one of the main match organisers, Ray Keene, accosted Kasparov about the unfortunate timing of this short draw. Kasparov apparently responded: 'You have your problems with the match, Ray, and I have mine.'

Some dislike draws in principle, seeing them as unmanly truces for timorous creatures who can't stomach the demands of competition. Clearly some games are drawn due to little more than mutual fear of losing, but a draw can also be a reasonable outcome of a hard-fought contest, and we know that chess almost certainly should be a draw if both sides play well. It is rare to play a full game without making a mistake, but to the best of our knowledge there is no way to force victory if your opponent does not go wrong. Moreover the drawing margin – the range within which the result with best play should be a draw – often feels very wide. The closest parallel to the wide drawing margin in chess might be how doctors reassure a parent expressing concern that their child is not yet speaking or eating or sleeping as they know that other children of the same age are. Anxious parents are often told that there is 'a wide range of normal'. Similarly, draws happen for a wide range of normal reasons.

Trying to solve the draw problem is like trying to rescue war from peace, but the forces of Eros and Thanatos cannot be severed like that. War and peace, like death and life, are co-constituted. No wonder attempted solutions to chess's perceived draw problem seem unnatural; for instance banning the draw offer entirely, restricting the offer to beyond a certain stage of the game, disincentivising draws by awarding three points for a win and one for a draw. All these approaches have major flaws relating to the fact that draws can and indeed *should* be the outcome of a well-played game. The philosopher and, arguably, great mystic Ludwig Wittgenstein famously wrote that 'the solution to the problem of life is seen in the vanishing of the problem'. I think something similar applies to 'the draw problem' in chess. The spontaneous cessation of hostilities is part of the beautiful game, part of its exacting agony; it can disappoint spectators, but perhaps without the knowledge of a possible escape the tension would simply be too much to bear.

For the vast majority of chess games, I see no need to change the rules of engagement. There is nothing inherently wrong with draws as such, and the players should not be punished for following the logic of the moment as they experience it. Yet when spectators watch professional players there is something *right* about the competitive logic that one side ultimately has to prevail. At the highest levels, the audience is an integral part of the mattering that matters, and premature draws violate that understanding.

I therefore have sympathy with an approach to draws that I first heard from Rustam Kasimdzhanov, who became world champion after winning a series of brutal knockout competitions in Libya in 2004. The way I interpret the proposal is that even in tournaments that are not knockouts, each contest between players should end with a decisive outcome. While as players we can agree to a draw from any position, as *performers* we are obliged to keep playing each other at progressively faster time controls until someone wins. If the game is drawn after the normal time control, we play a faster rapid game. If that game is drawn, we play an even faster blitz game. As the games grow faster and blunders more likely, a conclusive result will eventually occur. Chess is civilised, yes, but it is only worth watching when it is a game for civilised gladiators rather than mere civilians. There is no place for physical violence, but for the game to be a worthy spectacle there needs to be a ritual sacrifice. The crowd has to feel that blood will be spilt. Someone has to kill to live, which means someone has to die.[12]

15. ONE STEP AT A TIME

Chess can be brutal, but it can also be blissful. In May 2008 I spent a memorable week in Porto Mannu in Sardinia, where a friendly and scenic international tournament was taking place. I took time out from my Ph.D.-writing to be a chess player again, part of me that I missed at the time. In this particular event a deep sense of togetherness was palpable; a shared social and humanistic experience that is often generated by the pretext of competition. After experiencing competition in such contexts, it is no surprise to discover that, etymologically, competition means 'to seek together'.

I am not sure what people who do not play chess see when they witness a chess tournament – perhaps mostly tables and chairs. Personally I see a microcosm of civilisation. There is a benign meritocratic microclimate, where mistakes are normal and forgiven. I see a diverse subculture that values beauty and truth while upholding the rule of law. And I see a form of life with its own special language for telling stories about games, long after they have happened.

It helps when you are playing in a paradise, with a great atmosphere – a notion that is hard to pin down, but we know it when we feel it. Porto Mannu is blessed with a lush green landscape surrounded by rugged mountains, where white sand greets deep turquoise water stretching towards a clear blue sky. There is also the gentle whisper of the sea, freshly squeezed orange juice, and you are only ever a few hours away from your next encounter with a sumptuous Italian meal.

The nature and combination of people tends to be pivotal to the curation of atmosphere, and the organisers were discerning about the overall demographics and personality of the event. There were about 100 players, with a judicious balance of Italians, foreign participants, professionals and amateurs, young and old. The tournament was also very inclusive – for instance two wheelchair users seemed entirely at home, and one participant with Parkinson's disease was accompanied by his supportive wife, ensuring that he could execute his ideas with his own hands.

Porto Mannu 2008 was also a family event. Many who were not playing were nonetheless glad to be part of the tournament community, which added to the festal feeling – this place, this experience, this activity, these people – it all matters. There was a strong sense of kinship, with everybody seemingly glad to share this precious week together. And when the clocks started, friendship became the context for our shared need to express and assert ourselves in competition. That year was especially rewarding for me because I won the event outright.

Before travelling to Sardinia, I did everything I could to leave the world behind – all my work and phone calls and emails were made in advance so that I had the luxury of living and playing one day at a time, with nothing but my games to divert me. We often play our best when we feel free to enjoy whatever is arising. In this sense *finding form* is about caring deeply about the exacting process of getting oneself ready, but *being on form* is often simply about being ready, and there is a complex relationship between the two;

approximately the relationship between mood and concentration we have already considered.

In Porto Mannu 2008 I was very much 'in the mood' to play chess. While the tournament is remembered as one thing that happened, one moment of time, the games themselves had their own moments, and a particular tempo – they each lasted for several hours, but their meaning is etched in my mind in a micro-narrative form. Our episodic memory is like that more generally; our lives are stories within stories within stories.

In round one, the German master Norbert Friedrich was solid, as experienced German players typically are, but he was too solid for his own good, so I just had to wait until he drifted into a passive position and imploded.

The Argentine Grandmaster Garcia Palermo was clearly playing for a draw, but I managed to keep enough tension in the position to deter him from his regular cigarette breaks and perhaps he collapsed under the physiological strain.

Chess was by then a hobby for the Dutch Grandmaster Dennis De Vreugt, and I sensed he would rather be on the beach, so I quickly fixed the pawn structure and began some heavy manoeuvring. He grew impatient, and a flurry of activity led to a hopeless endgame.

The Italian amateur Pozzini has a modest rating, but his hairstyle and designer glasses made him look like a blues brother, so I was not taking any chances. He ventured his favourite wing gambit, which involves an early sacrifice, but I gladly grabbed the errant pawn and weathered the speculative attack.

The Peruvian Grandmaster Julio Granda Zuñiga is fully worthy of his impressive name and had defeated me before, so I was definitely a bit scared, but I just made the moves that seemed necessary before he allowed a winning sacrifice. It felt remarkably easy to beat such a formidable player.

The Romanian Grandmaster Mihail Marin is a renowned chess writer and analyst and insists, for complex reasons, that we should call him 'Bob'. On move 21, after a tense opening, I played a very strong anti-positional move – a move that defied principles (in this case about blocking one's own pieces) and yet worked because of a more discerning appraisal of the position – that was a highlight of my tournament. I had Bob on the ropes, but I could not find a decisive blow.

Italy's young Sabino Brunello was already almost a Grandmaster, but his openings were predictable, so I could almost guarantee the favourable technical position I achieved and then nursed to victory.

Playing Black against the Russian Grandmaster Oleg Korneev was the tournament decider. Korneev looks and plays like Vladimir Putin on steroids, and I was under sustained pressure for seven hours. He grew visibly frustrated and almost lost by trying too hard to win, but I was glad to draw and thereby enter the last round a point clear.

On entering the tournament hall I was intercepted by my opponent, the intrepid Igor Naumkin, another Russian Grandmaster, but less fearsome than most. He offered me a draw while we were still standing, which would give me outright victory of the event, but I shook my head and initially declined because I was hungry for another good game. But the opening did not go well, I started to worry about pushing my luck and acquiesced to sharing the point. Only then, when the work was done, did I put on my cut denim shorts and allow myself to be on the beach. Only then did I surrender my thoughts to the shimmering Mediterranean sea. Only then, when the sun was finally upon me, it started to rain.

16. SYNCHRONICITY

When our ego wants immediate gratification and we long for attention through achievement, it is easy to lose track of what it actually takes to perform well. So much ability is squandered by those who fetishise the final results of a competitive encounter and forget to enjoy the incremental competitive process. It took me twenty years to understand that to win tournaments I needed to concentrate on playing one game at a time, one move at a time, while also respecting how difficult it is to achieve that blessed state of mind.

Once I needed to score four out of four to qualify for the Grandmaster title, and a fellow competitor, English Grandmaster Neil McDonald, advised me playfully that this was an impossible task. However, he saw no reason why I could not win the next game and score one out of one, and do this four times in a row. The subtlety was lost on me at the time, but at the British Championship in Swansea 2006 I was faced with the same 'impossible task', and managed to heed the advice.

On the eve of the final round I was returning by bus to my hotel, having fought my way back into contention with three straight wins. We were playing in what is known as a Swiss tournament format, where we play opponents on a similar score, accrued from wins and draws, and prizes are determined by our aggregate score after the last round. I was paired with English Grandmaster Jonathan Parker, whom I was due to play the following day, and we both had seven and a half points from ten games. At stake were the title of British champion and the cash prizes.

If the game was drawn, we were guaranteed a good financial outcome of at least £5,000 – a big pay day for most professional players – and we could compete for the title in a play-off, where the games are faster and more capricious. In that case the pain of losing is somehow diluted by the shared understanding that the outcome has been slightly randomised. Since only one player from the chasing pack could make eight points, but several could make seven and a half, agreeing to a draw would have been a pragmatic thing to do.

The last round in a chess event is like the decisive moment in any sphere of life. When what happens next determines an outcome we have been working towards for quite some time, the significance of whatever we are caught up in catches up with us, and suddenly becomes palpable. For some, that embodied sense of occasion focuses the mind, while for others it overwhelms it. Some excel at job interviews while others flounder; some relish their chance to score in the penalty shoot-out and some are crippled by the fear of missing. I do not have any pat advice about how to handle such moments well, but I think the key is to find your own path, your own version of the middle way. You have to take the moment seriously but not too seriously, to forgive yourself for your inevitable mistakes, and yet not forsake your responsibility to perform at your best. We need to learn, somehow, to relax into the tension.

Each critical occasion seems to me to be a different kind of encounter in disguise; perhaps with memory, with luck, with hope, or some other invitation to the challenge of self-overcoming. In this case, my encounter was with fear, particularly my fear of losing in the last round. Losing when it really matters leaves a lasting taste and often defines our event, but this year I was more aware that the need to 'end well' is a craving for comfort for its own sake. Comfort has its place, but it does not chime well with the sublime beauty of the game, which arises from an existential encounter with risk and death.

There is a case to be made for pragmatism of course, not least to pay the bills, but I think we know when the desire not to push ourselves is sponsored by neurotic fear rather than good judgment. Such was the case here. I had to find the strength and composure to 'feel the fear and do it anyway', as the T-shirts say. This feeling grew stronger while I was sitting on a bus to get back to my accommodation and a young man sat down on the seat in front of me. He was wearing an orange promotional T-shirt for a famous brand of pens. The words on his back read 'Parker: Aim High!'

Jonathan Parker, my opponent, was very much on my mind, and so was my prospective game strategy. I have a healthy degree of scepticism towards such coincidences, but sometimes the scepticism feels indulgent because the experiences are self-evidently valid. This particular coalescence of implicit question and symbolic answer, for instance, could certainly have arisen by chance, but it was so apt and so timely that it removed all doubts about playing for a win the following day. The game that followed was probably the best that I have ever played, and it allowed me to retain my British title for the third year in a row.[13]

Looking back now, over a decade later, part of me regrets that I did not manage to arrange my life in such a way that I could play more, and build on this momentum. I was not yet thirty. A few more tournaments and a bit more work on the game might well have catapulted me to a higher level of play, but instead this proved to be a peak moment, after which I went back to my Ph.D., explored a range of other career options, and life moved on. In 2006 the game still mattered to me, but other things began to matter more, and I do not regret life expanding beyond chess. In particular, my hunger to learn was no longer satisfied by the game, and nor was my desire to grow. As the tennis legend Martina Navratilova once put it: the moment of victory is much too short to live for that and nothing else.

THREE

Learning and Unlearning

Our autopilots need our tender loving care

In the autumn of 2002 I was enjoying some melting ice cream after dinner in student accommodation at Harvard University. A friend remarked that he particularly enjoyed ice cream in the semi-liquid, post-snowball, pre-milkshake state. I share the same preference, and offer this memory now because I think my reaction may have been influenced by my experience of being a chess player. I immediately thought of myself as an eight-year-old, looking curiously at my mother's eighties-style perm, while emerging from a family visit to the swimming pool.

Not so typical perhaps, but what immediately entered my mind when I saw the melting ice cream was the idea of transitional states, and I offered a comparable example. Permed hair in the process of drying is neither completely straight nor completely curly, and I remember liking it that way. The content of the two instances is very different, but the form of the relationship is similar. For me, the pattern matched, and I expected my dessert companions to see my point. Instead they looked at me like I was an alien life form, and swiftly polished off their ice cream.

My thinking was perhaps eccentric, but by no means crazy, because melting ice cream and drying hair both change their form, and are comparable *processes*, even if they are very different *things*.

In *The Stuff of Thought*, Steven Pinker writes: 'The power of analogy does not come from noticing a mere similarity of parts ... It comes from noticing relations among parts, even if the parts themselves are very different.'[1] One of the ways chess thinking might transfer to other domains is in the disposition to see dynamic patterns of relationship as the constituent elements in any situation, and the fundamental features of life more generally.

Chess is not about relationships in the interpersonal or emotional sense, but the game is much more *ecological* than it might initially appear. I don't mean that chess fosters environmental concern, a common conflation, but it generates a form of ecological perception; the reality you experience is an emergent relational process rather than a collection of objects.[2] Thinking ecologically is not about trees and otters and streams as such, it's about a view of the world in which the relationships between things are primary and the nature of things is defined by the nature of those relationships, and the relationship between *them*.

For instance, the knight has a beguiling character in chess; it is eccentric compared with the other more linear pieces because it hops over enemy forces, frequently attacks pieces of higher value and always controls colours of squares different from the square it occupies. Many if not most opening sacrifices feature the knight galloping into the opponent's position at an early stage of the game and sacrificing itself to destroy the opponent's composition and composure, like cavalry in warfare, charging towards enemy lines. Kasparov's infamous defeat to the computer program Deep Blue in game six of a match in 1997 is a good case in point, with the machine's knight sacrifice for a mere pawn on move eight creating havoc and causing Kasparov to resign on move nineteen. However, in any given position the characteristic features of the knight are much less important than its relationship with other pieces and the prevailing purposes of the position, which might for instance call for the noble steed to be a defensive piece, keeping the king warm for the whole game.[3]

Nature is a symphony of systems, and humans are an increasingly loud part of that symphony, but we need help to hear the music.

The late Gregory Bateson communicated the value of this kind of perception with great acuity: 'The major problems in the world stem from the difference in the way nature works and the way people think.' He also said, in a line that speaks directly to the experience of chess competition: 'It takes two to know one.'[4]

Chess can perhaps play a part in closing the gap between the way nature works and the way we think because at any given moment a chess position is suspended in a form of dramatic tension, and the sense of 'What will happen next?' is fundamentally about 'How are the relationships going to change?' The question of what you should do in chess, as in life, is a function of how you can tweak and rebalance existing relationships so that they begin to feel more aligned with the purpose at hand. Chess can therefore help you think of the world in relational and systemic terms, and perhaps even cultivate some ecological sensibility, which the world badly needs more of. As the philosopher William Ophuls puts it in his book *Plato's Revenge*: 'The wisdom and the ethic [of ecology] follows directly from the ecological facts of life: natural limits, balance, and interrelationship necessarily entail humility, moderation, and connection ... For all these reasons, ecology will have to be the master science and guiding metaphor for any future civilisation.'

It would be asking too much of chess to think of it as the key to creating a new civilisation, but the game can help us improve the relationship between mind and world in ways that are not trivial. The game serves to highlight perspectives that can transform our understanding of how we might think more clearly and wisely, for instance through ecological perception, but also related notions like systems thinking, learning to love mistakes, noticing our patterns of attention, our automaticity, and appreciating the importance of unlearning. These ideas are presented in a linear narrative here, but they are more like a hermeneutic circle; they define each other to a certain extent. It is natural to chase after what we don't know with what we think we know. Sometimes, however, it helps to stop chasing for a while, so that a new way of seeing the world can emerge. Only then can we chase away what we never really knew in the first place.

A chess position can be thought of as a *system*, and probably should be to fully appreciate the game's educational value. Systems thinking is a form of perception above all, imbued with understanding that wholes have properties that do not exist in the sum of their parts, and that everything is connected to a greater or lesser extent. Defining 'system' too tightly risks reifying it into one thing of many, which obscures the premise of systems thinking, namely that the fundamental features of life are not things at all, but more like relational processes.

The subtle issue with systems thinking is that while in one sense systems are ubiquitous, it is also true that the idea of 'a system' is a human construct. It helps to recognise that our own systems of thought create the idea of systems, which means the boundaries we draw to separate systems in the world may be very useful, but are always somewhat arbitrary. If forced to define 'a system', I would say it is any process involving multiple interrelated elements that lies within a conceptual boundary that is drawn by humans to highlight a perceived function or goal.

Systems thinking can sound niche and exacting, but systems are not exotic, they are within and between everything. The solar system includes Earth's atmospheric system. We organise our lives on this planet through a political system which tries to govern an economic system, which relies on material resources provided by natural systems, and also on the perpetual creation of consumer demand through a semiotic system of persuasion called marketing. Marketing works on our nervous systems to increase our desire for all sorts of things we don't need but might like, for instance doughnuts enhanced with pearl sugar, strawberry jam, pink icing and Madagascar vanilla cream. These unreasonably tasty doughnuts subvert our appetite control systems that evolved with a weakness for densely calorific food to aid short-term survival, particularly under stress. A shift in demand for such doughnuts at scale impacts upon related supply chains and ecosystems in ways we never suspect while licking tasty remnants from our lower lips. Over time, systemic influences reinforce cravings for doughnut-like products in obesogenic cultures which eventually destroy our immune systems, our health systems and the ecosystems on which life as such depends. The breakdown of systems that aid our quality of life caused by a confluence of other systems is partly why activists speak of 'the system' as a whole, and don't necessarily refrain from eating doughnuts. Instead they say: 'We have to change the system!'

In chess the system is deceptively simple and the key question is where its boundaries lie. The elements are the pieces, the squares and the rules, which together create a myriad of relationships, and the overall purpose of the game is to checkmate the opponent's king. While any given chess position is best thought of as a complicated system, the game in motion is a complex system, partly because human systems are influencing and influenced by what is happening, and partly because the position keeps changing, and those changes have emergent properties that change *how* the position is changing. Our manoeuvres and exchanges lead to positional transformations, for instance changes in pawn structure alter strategic purposes, the nominal material balance shifts when pawns get closer to reaching the other side, where they can become queens, build-ups near our king become 'attacks' that have to be defended against, and sequences of moves that change the material balance operate as combinations of ideas, rather than mere move sequences.

Perhaps the challenge of thinking systemically explains why chess is so difficult. Indeed, the comedian Stephen Fry aptly described chess as 'ludicrously difficult'. If a person doesn't like things that are difficult, they won't like chess, which is fundamentally about loving the struggle of reaching beyond our grasp. The love of difficulty naturally leads to a curiosity about mistakes. If we are too precious about getting the right answer on a regular basis, chess will infuriate and depress us. These challenging features of difficulty and error are the heart and soul of the game, and a neglected part of the story of why we come back for more. The late Viktor Korchnoi, possibly the strongest player never to have become world champion, seems to agree: 'As a rule, the more mistakes there are in a game, the more memorable it remains, because you have suffered and worried over each mistake at the board.'[5]

Since ludicrous difficulty and inevitable mistakes are two of chess's main assets, it is no wonder that chess is a stiff marketing challenge. In effect, the unvarnished selling pitch would be something like: 'Play chess! It is extremely difficult and absolutely maddening. You will definitely screw up and possibly feel like an idiot, but you will love it. Hurry while stocks last. Two players for the price of one!' Of course, in reality, chess promoters sell the sizzle and not the sausage, by foregrounding themes of depth, strategy, play and intelligence. I wonder, however, if something might be gained by making more of the game's role in helping us experience difficulty and mistakes, which is the character-forming terrain where educational value is deepest.

17. THE LOVE OF MISTAKES

In the year 2000, in the bleak splendour of Torshavn in the Faroe Islands, I lost a game to a young Russian Grandmaster called Alexander Grischuk. 'Sasha' was in the process of a swift ascent to the world elite at the time and already outrated me by a hundred points, but there was something about the way I played that suggested I was far too relaxed about losing.

Later that day I was approached by two experienced and friendly Grandmasters: Alexander 'Seamus' Baburin is a tall and forthright man who had emigrated from Russia to Ireland, and former Soviet champion Lev Psakhis is a naturalised Israeli who is wise and mischievous in spirit. Together they asked me what happened in my game that day, as chess players do. 'I learned,' I said, and I thought this answer was clever, but I will never forget the response.

'You know this has to stop!' said Baburin, with unexpected force. 'This is not university now. Every time you mess up you say you have learned. You are not here to learn, you are here to win. You always talk about your lessons ...' He had no formal investment in my chess development but he looked genuinely pissed off, as if I was wasting my ability and somehow betraying the spirit of the game. I had squandered winning positions in my games against Baburin himself more than once, without appearing too perturbed, and it felt like he had been waiting a while to share his advice. No doubt I was visibly taken aback, because in a gentler and more contemplative tone, Psakhis added: 'Maybe you should teach your opponents a lesson?'

As indicated, deep learning requires us to play the game 'as if' the result really mattered. Without that commitment we risk remaining trapped in a self-fulfilling narrative of being a learner, which I think Baburin and Psakhis were keen to release me from. If we really want to learn we have to care, and sometimes we learn more when we care about winning rather than learning.

The etymological meaning of 'expertise' is about having tried and having been tested. One way to think about what defines an expert is that they have been tested so much that they have exhausted most if not all the errors one can make within a given domain. An expert is someone who makes so many mistakes over the years that they start running out of unfamiliar mistakes to make. However, one of the subtle mistakes that I was still making was to play as if learning from mistakes was the point of competing. I am grateful to Baburin and Psakhis for that short conversation, because as a competitor I toughened up considerably over the next few years.

And yet I could never fully shake off the notion that chess was an arena for learning first and foremost. As a young player I remember being almost mesmerised by my mistakes – 'Did I do that?' – and I am still intrigued by the thought processes that lead people astray. I do not know exactly why I feel drawn to looking at what went wrong, but I find it comforting somehow, as if understanding my mistakes makes me real and keeps me real. There is something about looking steadily at how your mind goes awry that is profoundly intimate, like looking in the mirror and feeling compassion gazing back. The closest analogy I know comes from the children's story *The Velveteen Rabbit* by Margery Williams Bianco, which my mother used to read me as a young child. The story includes a beautiful exchange between two stuffed toys:

Real isn't how you are made … It's a thing that happens to you. When a child loves you for a long, long time, not just to

play with, but REALLY loves you, then you become Real ... It
doesn't happen all at once ... You become. It takes a long time
... Generally, by the time you are Real, most of your hair has
been loved off, and your eyes drop out and you get loose in
the joints and very shabby. But these things don't matter at all,
because once you are Real you can't be ugly, except to people
who don't understand ... once you are Real you can't become
unreal again. It lasts for always.

Our flaws make us real and in many ways our mistakes are the best
part of us, the part of us that is most human and most worthy of
love. I have always sensed this, so it was a delight to discover an
intellectual tradition that places mistakes at the heart of an ongoing
conversation between ourselves and the world.

Most readers will know of Albert Einstein, with his big eyes,
mystical statements and famous equations. And most know
Sigmund Freud, with his patrician beard, his various complexes
and his interpretation of dreams. But I imagine relatively few
readers will have heard of Jean Piaget, with his owlish glasses, his
stages of cognitive development and his fascination with children's
mistakes. In my view Piaget's intellectual contribution was every
bit as profound as Freud's or Einstein's. Einstein himself said of
Piaget that his main idea was 'so simple, only a genius could have
thought of it'. It takes one to know one.

Piaget is often thought of as a naturalist and a scientist, and
he presented himself as such to the world, but recent intellectual
biographies reveal that he had several mystical experiences
in his life and that his ultimate interest was philosophical, to
reach an integrated understanding of science and religion. In
his autobiographical writing Piaget reflected on reading the
French process philosopher Henri Bergson when he was still a
teenager: 'The identification of God with life itself was an idea that
stirred me almost to ecstasy.'[6]

Piaget described himself as a genetic epistemologist, a forbidding
expression that probably did not help with name recognition, but

grasping this self-description is an important part of understanding the unique value of his contribution. Genetic epistemologist means something like 'one who studies the origins of knowledge'. The origins of knowledge are experiential and psychological but also philosophical, biological, social and spiritual. Piaget's insight was that people vary enormously not just in what they know, but in *how* they know the world; the manner in which their minds structure and interpret what there is to be known. Moreover, this 'how' is something that evolves as a life process that appears to inhere in the *relationship* between mind and world rather than being any feature of the mind as such.

Piaget's entire world view can be gleaned through his fascination with mistakes. Through a variety of revealing tests, Piaget showed that younger children systematically make errors that older children do not. Piaget's most famous experiments were about the conservation of properties like number, liquid, mass, area, volume, length and weight; properties that stay constant (conserve) when their container or context is changed, even if they look very different. In perhaps his best-known task, a child, typically between three and ten, is shown two identical beakers, containing the same amount of coloured liquid. Then liquid from one of them is poured into two taller, thinner glasses. The child is then asked whether there is still the same amount of liquid in the two tall thin glasses as there is in the one of the two original glasses that still has liquid. The water quantity has not changed, but some children answer 'No, there is more in the tall thin glasses,' while others say 'Yes, there is still the same amount.'

Mistakes in assessing the conservation of liquid are not the same as basic arithmetic errors or errors with language, because they reveal a broader truth; in many cases a child cannot override what they perceive with what appears to be easy to understand. Piaget's work has received a range of methodological critiques, but this central idea has stood the test of time and remains profoundly relevant.[7] The reason children's errors matter is that they illustrate what it looks like to be trapped inside a form of perception; not to lack knowledge as such, but to be too embedded in one way of seeing the world to imagine there are other ways to see it.

At the heart of Piaget's work is the distinction between *being* one's thoughts and feelings and *having* them. That perceptual shift from, for instance, being your anger and acting it out to having your anger under your control makes a huge difference in our general capability. This subtle but profound mechanism of moving from being subject to things (ideas, feelings, perceptions) to having them appears to be inherent to the life process rather than merely unique to childhood.

A related example from Robert Kegan's analysis of Piaget makes the point vividly. Imagine two brothers are on the top of the Empire State Building. The three-year-old looks down and says: 'Look at the people, they *are* tiny ants.' The eight-year-old replies: 'Yes, the people *look like* tiny ants.' One of them thinks what he sees, while the other can think *about* what he sees. Were the eight-year-old to try to correct the three-year-old, it is unlikely that he would be understood – that capacity to theorise about perception is precisely what his younger brother can't yet do. As Kegan puts it: 'He is not individuated from them; he is embedded in them. They define the very structure of his attention.'[8]

This inquiry into 'the very structure of attention' is one of many defining issues of our time, not least because the demands of advertising and social media on our attention are considerable. In a distracted world that is inundated with information but increasingly hard to understand, we need to reclaim our capacity to make sense of our experience. That means unlearning many of our maps of the world and our habits of mind. The collective challenge is not so much what we know, but how we know, which means thinking differently about how we learn, and therefore reimagining what good education would look like.

18. THE NEED FOR EVIDENCE

On a frosty day in February 2013 I was one of nine people gently checking each other out across a round table in a high-rise office building on the south side of the River Thames. The meeting was full of words like 'power', 'confidence' and 'fidelity'. I felt like I had skin in the game because there was a lot of money at stake; but this was not a legal office and these were not divorce proceedings. The agenda was how to devise and complete a rigorous quantitative study of chess in education. 'Power' is a statistical term conveying the likelihood that the study would detect an effect of chess on education if there was an effect there to be found. 'Confidence' was about the robustness of any such a finding, and 'fidelity' was about the process of the chess intervention being consistent and true to its purpose in each place it was tested.

The four academics from the Institute of Education at the University of London knew they would potentially be doing the research, and they seemed dispassionate, as if the meeting was an extension of their day jobs. Two senior staff from the Educational Endowment Foundation looked under thirty, but they would be the ones to establish whether the project was viable and fundable. They seemed excited, as if they had already been given a green light from elsewhere and knew the right answer was yes, but they had to be seen to be doing their due diligence. And then there was a friend of mine, the director of the chess and education charity Chess in Schools and Communities (CSC), Malcolm Pein, who had developed a comprehensive chess teaching programme over several years and had access to the schools where the research would happen. The potential prize was evidence not only that chess in schools made sense, but that it might make particularly good sense for the poorest children; a dream result for those like Malcolm who love chess as much as they dislike inequality of opportunity. And then there were Malcolm's wingmen conferring moral and intellectual support: Sandy Ruxton, an experienced policy researcher and chess aficionado, and me, deeply grateful to have grown up playing chess in a regular state school, and hoping others would have similar opportunities.

The conversation did not go quite as I hoped it might. Often despite their better judgment, educational professionals are institutionally bound to care more about test results than the social and emotional contexts and thinking dispositions that arguably give rise to them. A policymaker spending public money is acutely aware of being accountable to the taxpayer, so they need to know that educational gains are caused by the active ingredients in chess as such, and not by the mere fact that pupils are, for instance, sitting down and taking a breather from normal lessons, or because the time allocated to chess reduces or eliminates something else that is having a negative impact.

The agenda of the meeting is therefore best understood in juxtaposition with suggestions about all the things that should be taught in schools. Those who have sound reasons for suggesting the inclusion of one thing rarely have good reasons for justifying the exclusion of another. Educational recommendations often seem compelling until we remember that there are a certain number of teachers, pupils and hours in the day. And yet it goes on: 'There should be more …' they say, and there is no natural stopping point here: 'Drama, art, music, citizenship education, martial arts, poetry, sport, cookery, computing, financial literacy, foreign languages, thinking skills, meditation, design and technology, mediation skills, grammar, yoga, science, history, chess!'

Chess? Prior to any formal research, few would doubt that chess might make a valuable contribution to educational outcomes. On the face of it, the game should teach us how to think under pressure, to plan, to concentrate, to improve our reasoning by considering competing ideas, and so forth; and the fact the game has wide cultural and historical resonance and is so cheap and inclusive adds to its viability. In many countries, for instance Armenia, where the game is on the national curriculum, this case has already been considered and accepted. However, at the time of the meeting, and without broader cultural support for the game that reduces the need for validating research, there was little compelling evidence that chess in particular should be part of a national curriculum or a major feature of school life.

In one sense, the meeting went extremely well and the research proceeded as planned, but I remember feeling quiet desperation at the time, as if what the room seemed to be agreeing to do risked missing the point entirely. The three chess players in the room *knew* that chess informed education in a profound way and we were eager to share stories that might begin to explain why. However, there was nothing about the discussion or the proposed research process that made our experience seem relevant. We were welcome to be there, and we chipped in now and again, but in terms of what the funders were hunting for, and the tools their academic hunters were planning to use, we were bystanders with no relevant insight or formal standing to influence events.

The money eventually rewarded for the project was £689,150, which is significantly better than a slap in the face with a wet fish, and gives some idea of the ambitious scale of the research. The aim was to measure the effectiveness of CSC's thirty-week programme on 4,009 Year 5 (age nine to ten) pupils across one hundred schools with varying socio-economic intakes in terms of their standard attainment test (SATs) results in mathematics at the end of that Year 5, compared to control groups, with some secondary outcomes relating to English and science also considered. The evaluation of this landmark study into chess and education was published towards the end of 2016. The conclusion was effectively as follows: no evidence of effect.[9]

This outcome felt like a minor disaster for those who believed in the cause of chess in education at the time, partly because we felt sure the result would be resoundingly positive, but also because we sensed the research was not quite right in ways that were less to do with methodology than the philosophical assumptions that were baked into the research design.

The Educational Endowment Foundation's mission is to change policy to help disadvantaged children, so they wanted to show that if you do X (chess curriculum), there will be evidence of Y (better SATs results compared to control groups) within a specified time frame, in this case one year. That is precisely the kind of effect that policymakers are looking for because it allows them to justify investing funds in the intervention, so I understand their approach. The value of a scientific method, and the reason it confers authority when it is on our side, is that results don't always go as we want or expect them to. However, our fear was that this result would be seen as the final and negative word on chess and education in general, rather than one result from a rigorous but narrowly conceived study.

'No evidence of effect' does not mean 'evidence of no effect' and that distinction makes all the difference. To make fuller sense of the relationship between chess and education, we need to think more broadly and deeply than a single quantitative study, no matter how rigorous it seems to be. The first problem is that the underlying research philosophy is old-fashioned and unenlightened. The randomised-control trial approach is typically grounded in a perspective known as positivism, where social and psychological phenomena are modelled as if they were amenable to the techniques of natural science. However, it is much easier to separate constants and variables in the natural world than in open-ended ecosystems like a child, in a class, in a school, in a community, in the world. It may be harder, for instance, to understand what 'works' in education than it is to find cures for cancer.

Second, the target is questionable. What the research sought to measure was slight short-term improvements in certain scores, but that indicator is surely not the strongest evidence of chess having educational benefits more broadly. Third, even if we accept these two big strategic commitments, it's not clear that any effect on ability will become clear as quickly as within a year. Chess seeps into your thinking in all sorts of subtle ways, and educational benefits might not occur until years or even decades later. Fourth, what if the conditions that randomised the trial actually distorted the results? What if there is some kind of placebo effect within chess teaching that means you have to believe it is good for you for it to work properly?

The fifth and most fundamental limitation of the research is that for many positive outcomes, *how* chess is taught might matter more than the fact that it is being taught. Perhaps the 'active ingredient' being transmitted is something about a manner of thinking and being in the teacher that is particularly well imparted through chess; some of us have been lucky enough to experience that, but it may not be easy to replicate.

Albert Einstein said that education is what remains when what has been learned has been forgotten, and the ineffable thing that remains might be the key outcome. I can think of several chess players I learned from, but if asked what exactly I learned, I can only point to something about their manner of being and exposition and a few turns of phrase that encapsulated it. For instance, I remember Richard James, author of the celebrated book *The Complete Chess Addict,* using the expression 'as it happens' to describe several different variations in chess opening theory. I also recall him explaining that Anatoly Karpov's rook lift to the third rank to attack Artur Yusupov's kingside in a decisive encounter in their World Championship Candidates matches in 1989 was only successful because Yusupov's pawn was on h6 rather than h7. I was twelve years old and I did not fully understand the difference at the time, but I did absorb the underlying lesson, namely that attention to minute detail decided a game at the highest levels, and that notion motivated me for years.[10]

The chess and education research question is far from exhausted. I believe the game *potentially* fosters a variety of learning and thinking dispositions like sustained concentration, inclination to find evidence that challenges one's own ideas, the will to use knowledge, emotional comfort with mistakes, visceral awareness that several great ideas can be ruined by one bad one, 'grit' – the capacity to recover and persevere, and so forth. If the focus is on mathematics, for instance, chess probably helps to foster improved spatial memory, some kind of geometric intuition, a taste for purposive calculation, some kind of cognitive appetite for pattern recognition, rapid application of basic arithmetic for swift decisions, discerning evaluation of complex outcomes, and so on. Matthew Lipman, an esteemed proponent of teaching thinking skills, captures the value of such dispositions more generally: 'The child who has gained proficiency in thinking skills is not merely a child who has grown, but a child whose very capacity for growth has increased.' When considering the educational value of chess, this point is a profoundly important.

The problem is that none of these subtler effects is straightforward to demonstrate in our current educational paradigm, nested as it is within a society that struggles to see the world clearly, to value what matters and measure it accordingly. The research design we seek would test whether chess helps foster thinking and learning dispositions in ways that have yet to be conceived, and I think that aim is connected with the more profound challenge of how we perceive reality as a whole. While I believe chess has an important role to play in education, the intellectual resources for making that case lie outside of the current construction of the question. The most fundamental issue is clarifying your rationale for the education outcomes you are trying to achieve. Do you want better exam results, or would you be content with something more significant but relatively nebulous like 'more refined perception' or 'happier children'?

The question of what we are trying to learn and why is the domain of the philosophy of education, which is regrettably and tragically niche today. It is a sign of wayward civilisation that we don't take the living questions – what and how should we learn, and why – more seriously, because the answers create and recreate the world. Moreover, how we answer shapes the culture, institutions and power relationships that permeate society, which means that asking the questions more often and answering them better is a source of political hope. As philosopher of education Zachary Stein puts it:

> Education must no longer be something that is kept behind closed doors and that requires special privileges and capital to get. In a world pushed to the brink of crisis, education, like energy, must be made abundant, free, and healthy, if our species is to survive. Everyone everywhere must have access to educational resources that are good, true, and beautiful, even if only so that solutions can be found in time for the billions of community-level problems that are reverberating across our planet ...[11]

19. HOW TO GIVE PRAISE

Soon after my first son Kailash was born I competed in an international open that included the Scottish Championship, held inside the City Chambers in Edinburgh. It was a homecoming tournament of sorts, partly because I was travelling up from London, but also because Paul Motwani, Scotland's first Grandmaster, originally from Dundee, was flying in from Belgium.

I became aware of Paul when I played him in a simultaneous display at Bon Accord Chess Club in Aberdeen when I was eleven years old. A simultaneous display typically involves a professional player taking on several opponents and moving from board to board, awaiting a move and then quickly making one of their own before moving to the next. I recall dangling nervously on a wooden chair in Harlaw School's dining hall, asking some adjacent junior players what our prospective opponent looked like. They joked that he was seven foot tall with thick and expansive ginger hair and that his eyes were so piercing that he had to wear sunglasses.

In fact, Paul's peaceful countenance is threatening only as a disguise for the controlled aggression of his play, and that night I was squeezed, clamped and crushed. I heard him say 'well played' to others who resigned before me, so it troubled me slightly that although I received a smile and a nod, I did not receive the same compliment. Impressionable youngsters notice everything.

However, the following day Paul coached a group of juniors, and I came to understand why he is considered a great teacher. I tried hard to earn the praise I felt I deserved, and thereby came to deserve it. For attention-seeking youngsters, the praise of an admired adult is a powerful tonic.

Paul's teaching made a big impression on me growing up. I have always been inquisitive, sometimes to a fault, but whenever I made a comment about a position, no matter how obtuse or misguided, Paul had a way of highlighting the positive and sounding sincere, without hesitating to show the shortcoming of my ideas with authority. His respect for people precedes but does not obscure his respect for the truth of the position, and he has gained numerous friends and fans as a result.

Paul's other achievements include winning the World Cadet Championship and numerous heavyweight scalps, but I will always think of him principally as a teacher who knows how to give energy to others rather than taking it away.

In weekend congress events in Scotland, there was always a wide range of events across ages and abilities, and after the last games had finished it would take the arbiters a while to process the results, figure out who the prize winners were and stuff the cheques in the envelopes. In these moments Paul would often give a short public talk on a demonstration board, with a formula that the crowd knew and loved. He would show a game step by step, ask a question of the audience on almost every move, select somebody with their hand up, patiently await their full answer, ask their name, congratulate them on some aspect of their answer that was important, whether or not it was actually right, and then he would dip in to a carrier bag and find a chocolate bar of some kind which he would throw across the hall, adding a little game of 'catch' to proceedings. Everybody wanted one of those chocolate bars, and not because of the chocolate.

Several years later, I find myself doing something similar. I have many years of experience teaching young children, including an informal class at my son's primary school for about fifty minutes early on a Friday morning. At the end of every term I take my own bag of confectionery into school, and model the same procedure, the heart of which is discerning praise, proportionate reward and the modelling of serious fun.

I have found that if you pay close attention, children's desire for praise is palpable, almost like it is water for flowers, and the attentiveness to what exactly is said is striking. Chess has taught me to be generous in praise, but also as precise as possible. People need to feel seen, and they do when you convey your appreciation for exactly how they have tried. We may forget how a flying chocolate bar tasted, but the right kind of praise forges a connection that lasts for ever.

As indicated, chess players are intuitive systems thinkers because we learn that if we do not see the relationships and interactions that define the whole position, we are likely to misunderstand the parts – the pieces – and put them on the wrong squares. Chess can therefore be a source of tacit *learning* about systems. The game cultivates a form of perception that can help us reimagine the world and our place in it, but we have to keep paying attention.[12]

In the middle of September in 2005, I woke up and looked in the mirror, and saw a natural disaster. There was a red spot on the front of my nose, clearly visible and gradually swelling. On most days that wouldn't matter, but this was my wedding day. There would be so many people and so many photographs, and I felt embarrassed, frustrated and in one sense lonely – nobody else would take my problem seriously. We had spent so much time and money getting a new suit, a quality haircut, and I even had socks that matched my tie, but when I looked in the mirror all I could see was the spot. For a short while my sense of self collapsed; I was that spot, and I saw the pending wedding, almost literally, through it. I had lost perspective.

After getting ready for the day and looking in the mirror again I suddenly realised that the slight protrusion there on my nose was not really me. Not me at all. I am this occasion, all the years and people that have shaped me, all the beloved family and friends who had travelled from far and wide to be with us. I am a lifelong husband making a solemn commitment to my wife-to-be after all that we have been through together. I am old school friends, old chess friends, old teachers, my family, and now my family-in-law too. I can see their faces, and they are smiling and wishing us well. These people formed me and need me, as I will need them. In the Zulu language there is a word for this kind of realisation – *Ubuntu*: 'I am because we are.' I am grateful to that spot for acting as my unsuspecting messenger; by heightening neurotic self-concern it made me expand and transform my perspective to transcend it.

When we think in systemic terms some humility should arise, because it becomes clear just how conditional and interdependent everything seems to be, including ourselves. We are not at the centre of the universe, but some confidence may also arise from that thought, as we notice that we are also much more than we previously thought we were. Noticing that we can begin to see

ourselves and the world differently helps us realise that we are
responsible for what we choose to see. We can be map makers as
well as map readers, and the relationship between map reading and
map making has a dignity and a reality of its own. Teachers are those
who know their terrain well enough to help us read maps, while
great teachers also help us find ourselves in maps of our creation.

Consider how we joke about the caprice of the weather.
Meteorologists get a hard time for not always being accurate in
their forecasts, and they have to contend with a dynamic non-
linear system, which means one thing does not necessarily lead to
another. Multiple causes (changing data observed in land, sea and
air) create multiple effects (as observed in land, sea and air), but
those effects quickly become causes of their own; yet not all of them
do, and not to the same extent, so the predictive picture quickly
becomes hazy. Today's three-day forecasts are better than one-day
forecasts a few decades ago, but the weather is notoriously hard
to predict accurately beyond a few days, regardless of the power
of predictive technologies. Then consider that human beings are
much more complex than the weather.

Jean Piaget's inspiration for understanding human beings was
not psychology but open-systems biology: the study of life as such.
Chess is teeming with life. A chess position might appear to be a
closed system that is predictable in principle, even in the context of
its exponential possibilities. However, chess games typically include
at least two conscious human organisms who come to the board
with all their idiosyncrasies, myriad life contexts and openness to
the elements. The philosophical jury is still out on what it means to
say that humans have free will, but we definitely have *agency*. We are
open to influences outside of the position, including distractions
out of the window, unbidden moods, surprising memories and
cups of piping-hot tea. More importantly, our response to the
interaction of those things is inherently unpredictable.[13]

To put the point technically, humans are complex adaptive
systems. We are *complex* rather than merely complicated. We are
not just hard to understand but impossible to predict, due to our
emergent properties. For instance when a chess player realises they

missed a key resource on a previous move an emotional reaction of anguished regret might follow, affecting our capacity to miss a good move in future. A memory of the past shapes the present and influences the future in joyously random ways.

We are also *adaptive* in the sense that what we do is not deterministic. We don't merely react to what happens to us, as a reliable constant in a chain of variables. Sometimes we *respond* instead, by reimagining and redirecting whatever causal process we are caught up in, which makes us a key variable. The wonder of being human is that even if, somehow, absolutely everything could be known about us, nobody could be quite sure what we would do next.

20. THE JOY OF TEACHING

'If you want to build a ship, don't drum up people together to collect wood and don't assign them tasks and work, but rather teach them to long for the endless immensity of the sea.'

This beautiful suggestion from the French writer Antoine de Saint-Exupéry is often used to make sense of leadership, but it makes me think of teaching. At its heart, teaching is not so much about conveying knowledge as modelling a state of being, a sensibility; a feeling and disposition that is visceral as much as cognitive. Teaching allows us to spend time in a state of sympathetic friendliness with other people, something that arises when you share a larger context of enquiry akin to 'the endless immensity of the sea'.[14]

Sympathetic friendliness is a good way to characterise what we need when we are trying to work things out. Chess teaching usually takes the form of private tuition, so it starts with the student, about knowing who they are, what chess means to them and why they think you might be able to help. Personal rapport is important, because thinking is a revealing activity, and you need to feel free to express your thoughts, even when they seem fanciful or embarrassing.

As a chess teacher I try to establish mutual understanding that the point of the exercise is not an abstract pursuit of truth or ego aggrandisement, but a deeper and more enduring enjoyment of a game that is rewarding because it is exacting. Chess is pleasurable not in spite of its difficulty, but because of it.

All chess players structure their thoughts with patterns of some kind, and in most lessons I simulate typical challenges and compare notes with students on our respective thinking processes. I also do what I can to encourage certain positive competitive habits of mind, including confidence, patience and tenacity.

However, while teaching students how to know, how to think and how to compete are important, the real challenge is teaching them how to *look*, because it all begins there. The art critic John Berger wrote that: 'A drawing of a tree shows not a tree but a tree being looked at,' and the same might be said for a chess position.[15] The most important task for the chess teacher is helping students to direct their attention, because chess skill is marked, above all, by looking at the right things in the right way for the right amount of time.

There are no short cuts to this sort of perception; it is not a curlicue added to expertise, it is the expertise as such. Such perception cannot be directly taught, but it can be encouraged and partly modelled. You can give the student a glimpse of better perception in their own minds by carefully directing their attention until you feel like you are beginning to see the same things in a similar way. You then hope that this experience of looking better and seeing more is sufficiently inspiring that they keep playing and practising enough until such vision becomes their own.[16]

More technically, there are some theoretical ideas and recurring patterns that good players really ought to know, so part of the job is conveying knowledge. The ease with which we absorb such patterns depends a great deal on our age, with younger players picking them up unconsciously and connecting them seamlessly, while adults typically strain to digest them, because they often feel obliged consciously to compare and contrast them with things they have seen before. Adults can try to be more childlike in their learning, but it is not easy. Asking someone who has been playing more or less the same way for decades to see a position with a beginner's mind is like asking someone to remember to forget what they think they already know; it's a form of epistemic torture.

Moreover, since our understanding of what is happening is grounded in perception, asking someone to understand a position completely differently is like asking them to first see their own eyes, and only then look outwards; like having your vision checked by Satan. Adult players can and do improve, but it requires a more reflexive approach to learning. As the complexity theorist Edgar Morin put it in a celebrated UNESCO report about the future of education: 'Learning about learning, which includes integrating the learner into his knowledge, should be recognised by educators as a basic principle and permanent necessity.'[17]

Above all as a chess teacher I try to share my love of difficulty, and my joy in confusion. A student learns nothing if they are simply confused, but once they start to get interested in what exactly they are confused about, we are getting somewhere. Wrestling with difficulty together generates intimacy – a word not often used in the context of chess. The intimacy of shared attention is one of the game's many secrets. Any parent will know the intimacy of shared attention from looking around the world with a young baby or child and identifying things together, knowing that they are sharing the same reference points. Shared attention is a prismatic revelation: I, you, that: therefore we! I suspect most chess players do not realise that this intimacy, the intimacy of shared attention, is a large part of what keeps them coming back to the game.

We are accustomed to learning being directed at the part of us that is conscious and deliberative. It is widely thought that chess must teach you to 'plan', 'think ahead', 'be strategic' and so forth, and there is some truth there, but these notions often arise from a misguided folk psychology. A useful counterpoint from popular culture are the training scenes in the classic film *The Karate Kid*, where Daniel-san is excited to learn karate from the master Mr Myagi, but finds himself sanding floors, shining cars and painting fences, with periodic and very subtle instruction from the teacher about the requisite body movements. Only after two days of hard labour, when he is about to quit in fury at not being taught karate, does Mr Myagi show him that he has been 'learning' by cultivating the necessary reflexes in his automatic system. He blocks the punches by 'painting the fence', he fends off kicks by 'sanding the floor', and he defends instinctively and perfectly precisely because he is not thinking about it.

It is hard to accept that we are mostly automatic systems.[18] Research from social psychology suggests that between 95 and 99 per cent of psychological and bodily processes are automatic in the sense that we can do them without discernibly conscious thought. Once a situation is repeated and previous expectations and patterns are activated, conscious thought becomes unnecessary, which is why people driving on familiar routes often arrive at their destination without remembering any details of their journey. We do need conscious reflection in novel or socially complex situations, when we wake up out of our automaticity just enough to imagine that we are thinking creatures,[19] but the idea of 'automaticity' refers not just to a trait, but a way of living. We are not merely creatures of habit, but habit-forming creatures; our modus operandi is to familiarise ourselves with our places and our tasks so that we don't have to think about them. The result is that we are not consciously aware of most of what we do.

A blow to self-esteem through a failure or an insult, for example, mobilises previously rehearsed patterns of thought and behaviour like explaining it away, scapegoating, projecting our faults on to others, all of which serve to restore our sense of self-worth. In a famous article on 'The Unbearable Automaticity of Being', J. A. Bargh and T. L. Chartrand comically refer to these self-serving automatic processes as 'mental butlers' who know our tendencies and preferences so well that they anticipate and take care of them for us, without even having to be asked.

I don't think of my autopilot as a butler, and I don't think of it as a pilot in the sense that it flies a plane either. Mostly I experience my autopilot as a kind of artificially intelligent being that is dispersed within me, at once everywhere and nowhere, and tantalisingly close to being human but almost completely unrelatable. My relationship with the autopilot is characterised by a painful absence of connection and by gratitude, because I can feel that there is something miraculous I want to attend to and appreciate, but when I search for reciprocity it is not there – I am not there in the automatic system, and yet without whatever is there, I would not be at all. This strange loop of self-reference is wondrous and almost mystical, but it can be experienced as a kind of frustration. The part of me that is conscious seeks an I–Thou relationship with the part of me that is unconscious, a relationship between two beings, but all I can experience is I–It, a relationship between *my* soul and *that* system.

I therefore imagine the autopilot as lonely, as if it is reaching out to us to relate but cannot find a way to connect. The autopilot is the part of us that is always present, vigilant and looking out for our interests, but psychologically it is forsaken and completely cut off from social experience. That perspective on the autopilot is a little weird, I know, and full of projection, but just as we can love plants and look after motorcycles as if they needed our attention and affection, we can love our autopilots, and personally I choose to live 'as if' the autopilot needed our tender loving care.

With this view of ourselves in mind, learning is about giving the automatic system *what* it needs to make sense of the world, and unlearning is about using our conscious awareness to examine and improve *how* we perceive and know. Most of chess literature is unhelpful in the sense that it perpetuates the idea that what you need to improve is knowledge rather than skill, or 'know-that' rather than 'know-how'. Yet in almost any sphere of life, we get better mostly by thinking in practice or in training that simulates practice as closely as possible. Many school and university students, for instance, let themselves down by stocking up on what they are supposed to know, without setting aside sufficient time to practise what they are supposed to *do*, namely convey what they know in response to unpredictable questions under exam conditions. Many think the exam context is a neutral delivery platform for a mental download, but it is a completely different ecological condition, calling for a different set of thinking dispositions and bodily responses.

Sometimes we improve at chess by a kind of conceptual osmosis whereby our pattern-recognising and priority-setting abilities enrich and upgrade themselves simply through exposure to the game, but this is rare after childhood because our conceptual frameworks become more rigid and it is harder for new forms of perception to develop because the old concepts get in the way. Once our playing ability has stabilised, the challenge is therefore to be forensically discerning about where our thinking went awry – what did we assume, what did we miss, what did we want too much, or fear too little? This form of enquiry, which chess made available to me, was my main vehicle of identity formation and development, and something that has shaped my personal and professional life ever since.

It is hard to say how exactly this process works, but it is broadly about the conscious part of the system tacitly recognising the unconscious part, honouring its power for good and bad, and taking better care of it in the knowledge that it is a precious part of oneself. That is where the unlearning process begins, as you realise that most of your mistakes are based on things you thought you understood, but did not.

In the second decade of my life, by regularly analysing my games, I spent thousands of hours forensically examining how thoughts and emotions arose automatically and how they shaped decisions and results. Being good at chess is about being an intuitive choice architect, rapidly framing complex problems for opponents in a way that maximises the probability of mistakes.

In the celebrated behavioural economist Daniel Kahneman's terms, much of chess improvement is characterised by putting 'System 2' (the effortful, conscious system) to work on 'System 1' (the fast, automatic system). Over time, I attended to the other part of me often enough to know that the relatively conscious part of me was the most important, even if the relatively unconscious part was more powerful; just as in chess the queen is much more powerful than the king, but the king ultimately matters more.

This precious space of investigation and correction, where the part of us that is conscious and deliberate tenderly cares for the part of us that is automatic and habituated – that mode of being is the front line of freedom and vitality; it is the place we need to keep returning to in order to remain awake to ourselves. I believe the quality of this relationship between our pilot and our autopilot, between our conscious and our unconscious, is one of the most important relationships in our lives. We experience the relationship mostly through activities we love and identify with, whether that means craft, art, music, cooking, martial art, sport; anything requiring attention and discipline and self-awareness that includes some kind of feedback from the world. Living with an awareness that we are this relationship between conscious and unconscious processes is a desirable middle way; neither surrendering to the automatic system nor ignoring its defining role in our lives.

21. FINDING THE TESTING ROOM

They say if you're the smartest person in the room, then you're in the wrong room. When we reflect on how the people we most admire became so admirable, the saying sounds only slightly exaggerated.

To admire somebody is to recognise the challenges they have overcome, appreciate the efforts involved in doing so, and value the experience and expertise acquired in the process. The most admirable people tend to be in the habit of testing themselves against people 'smarter' than themselves. Gary Kasparov is one such person. He was at the pinnacle of world chess from 1985 to 2005. When he turned fifty in 2013 his long-time personal aide Mig Greengard wrote a short essay to celebrate, including the following line: 'After nearly fifteen years of observation, my guess is that the constant Kasparov "upgrade" process is a consequence of his relentless pursuit of really smart people to argue with. There is little he likes more than to challenge an expert with a contrarian theory ... he always learns something, always takes something away to ponder, even when he's insisting his friend/victim is completely wrong.'

After dominating world chess for two decades, Kasparov retired from competitive play while still top of the rating list. He is still a professional chess dabbler, constructively sticking his oar in now and again, but his focus is on campaigning against the Putin regime, promoting chess in education and generally being the Russian public intellectual of choice.

I admire Kasparov's decision to retire every bit as much as I admire his chess achievements. It takes courage to close the door, and Mig again hits the mark about Kasparov's motivation. Retiring was: 'Another challenge for this most competitive of individuals, a competition with himself to make Kasparov the human rights activist, author, and lecturer as relevant and fulfilled as Kasparov the chess champion.'

Seeking out those other figurative rooms where you are tested may be admirable, but it's not pleasant or easy. In this respect I'm reminded of talking with my friend Grandmaster Luke McShane about the need to develop a societal measure of happiness to rival or complement gross domestic product (GDP) as a touchstone of societal progress. Luke was characteristically sceptical, and he used Kasparov to question what we should most value.

Kasparov can be charming, but he also seems pugnacious, relentlessly driven and domineering. I don't think of him either as particularly friendly or as particularly happy. But perhaps that's the point. His restless discomfort is what propelled him to be so inspirational. While he may or may not be conventionally 'happy', his full, varied and successful life appears to have been very well lived.

In the early eighties Gary Kasparov persistently sought out the room where Anatoly Karpov sat, the reigning champion, and a person then 'smarter' than him. After prevailing in a series of tough qualifying matches, Kasparov earned the right to challenge for the world title in Moscow in 1984. The rules stated that the first player to score six wins would win the match, regardless of how many draws there were. Karpov was in great form and took the early lead with four victories after nine games, but then something changed. It is said that Kasparov stopped trying to win and simply resolved not to lose, and matured from boy to man in the process. He soaked up the pressure, bending but not breaking, and finding the composure to learn from Karpov rather than just trying to defeat him, while still staying in the match.

The strategy almost did not work. After sixteen straight draws, Karpov won a fifth game. From game twenty-eight onwards Karpov needed just one more victory to remain world champion, and it looked like a foregone conclusion that Kasparov would psychologically see the writing on the wall, and bow to his inevitable defeat. But somehow he held on. This particular display of tenacity, maturity and bloody-mindedness is what makes Kasparov not merely great but perhaps the greatest player of all time; the roots of his later dominance of the game stem from this epic match and his heroic determination not to give up. After four more draws Kasparov won on game thirty-two, his first victory ever against the world champion. It is hard to imagine the sustained competitive tension at even this stage of the match, and the disbelief Karpov must have felt about not being able to win one more game. But there were twenty-three more draws. And then, a sudden shift in the balance of power. Kasparov won games forty-seven and forty-eight. Both games were of a reasonably high quality; from looking at them, my judgment is that Karpov was wilting a little bit, but he had not collapsed psychologically. He was still leading 5–3, and needed only one more victory. On the other hand he had not won since game twenty-seven, while Kasparov had won thrice and was now in the ascendant.

What happened next is controversial. The match was terminated. The contest had lasted for five months, from 10 September 1984 to 8 February 1985. It was winter in Moscow and the match organisers' lease on the venue, the Hall of Commons, had long since lapsed. The Hall of Commons was apparently needed for other things, including funerals, and while that detail was not pivotal, it is the kind of friction that disturbs the status quo just enough to question the entire endeavour. Nobody could be sure how long the match would continue. Karpov might suddenly win or Kasparov might build on his momentum and win the next three games. Just as likely there would be another series of draws.

The FIDE president of the time was the Filipino political scientist Florencio Campomanes, and it remains unclear to this day exactly what led him to end the match at this juncture. He claimed that he was doing it for the good of the game and the health of the players, but it felt odd after two straight victories by Kasparov, and both players claimed they wanted to continue. There might have been political motivations relating to a judgment that Karpov was completely exhausted and a preference within the Soviet leadership to keep Karpov as champion; he was more instinctively loyal to the existing communist regime, while Kasparov was an agitator by nature, and more aligned with emerging political winds. Still, the evidence for high-level political interference of that nature is not particularly compelling, not least because Karpov was still objectively the favourite to win the match.

Mikhail Gorbachev became General Secretary of the Soviet Union a month after the match ended, and his policies of economic restructuring, Perestroika, and political openness, Glasnost, emerged a year later. It is hard to say if and how the political changes influenced the psychologies of the players, but the match was rescheduled for September 1985, and this time there was an upper limit of twenty-four games. The match was again very close, with Karpov having to win the final game to retain his title, but Kasparov won after a virtuoso defensive and counter-attacking display.

There were three subsequent Karpov–Kasparov World Championship matches, all of which were extremely close, but each time, often in the last game, Kasparov retained his title. Karpov remained a great player, but he never really engaged with the necessity for computer preparation and he gradually slipped down the world rankings and retired. Meanwhile, Anand sought out Kasparov, as Carlsen sought out Anand and everybody now seeks out Carlsen. And so it goes on. Each David becomes his own Goliath.

22. BOREDOM

Sitting still and thinking looks boring, and sometimes it is, but as the mindfulness meditation teacher Jon Kabat-Zinn puts it: 'When you pay attention to boredom it gets unbelievably interesting.'

To take one example from the chess world, Magnus Carlsen sometimes uncharacteristically loses his way, but most of the time he recovers with an extraordinary display of strength. For instance, in the Gashimov memorial event in April 2014 he lost two games, but ended with four wins, including an impressive victory against one of his main rivals Fabiano Caruana. Around this time, some started to wonder if Magnus had some kind of boredom strategy as a deliberate attempt to self-motivate. The Chessbase website editor Frederic Friedel put it as follows: 'Magnus is so strong that he is simply bored. I know from personal experience that he bores easily. So he has come up with a new strategy to make things more interesting for himself: play like an idiot in the first few games, move to the bottom of the table, and then try to win the tournament anyway.'

It is true that Magnus often looks bored, but the idea that he loses on purpose seems ridiculous, unless it is an entirely unconscious process, in which case it becomes fascinating.

In this context I remembered the line of Friedrich Nietzsche: 'Is life not a thousand times too short to bore ourselves?' I wondered at first if somebody with an intellect as powerful and active as Magnus's could really be bored, and if so, whether I really understood what boredom is. Leo Tolstoy defines boredom as 'the desire for desires', which chimes with the fact that at twenty-three Magnus had already achieved everything a chess player could want.

A deeper reflection from the poet Dylan Thomas claims: 'He who seeks rest finds boredom. He who seeks work finds rest.' This idea would make the losing-to-win strategy plausible, since to really create work for himself a player needs to manufacture obstacles on an otherwise under-stimulating path to victory.

If this seems elaborate, our need to escape boredom is no small thing. The philosopher Blaise Pascal famously remarked that all of our miseries stem from not being able to sit quietly in a room alone. Understanding boredom, and how to conquer it, is the key to understanding craving, which Buddhists will tell you is the most important thing to understand about your mind, and your life.

Deeper still, the writer Richard Bach says: 'In order to live free and happily you must sacrifice boredom. It is not always an easy sacrifice.' If boredom is about not knowing what to aim for, *sacrificing* boredom is about transcending the idea that the purpose of life is to satisfy desires. That transformation of perspective is a spiritual breakthrough, however, not an everyday achievement, so it may be that we need the experience of boredom and, therefore, ways to allay it.

I consider chess an antidote to boredom. The game simultaneously obliges us to attend and yet escape the familiar contours of our minds; it is not that chess frees us from the autopilot, but it lets the autopilot play in one of his favourite playgrounds.

And our autopilots always have work to do, navigating all the systems they control within us, to guide us through all the systems we are part of, based on our sense of purpose as they understand it. In the process we are often pulled by the autopilot towards whatever is novel and intriguing – maybe this? Maybe that? Our job is to decide whether to follow its lead, or take ourselves somewhere else. We have to be particularly careful not to be led astray by ideas that are charming or solutions that seem exciting, just because they free us from boredom. What we are attracted to or impressed by is often not what matters most in a given moment. In chess, as in life, we must always strive to distinguish between what is interesting and what is important.

23. WHY DOES THE DEVIL HAVE ALL
THE BEST TUNES?

There is a beautiful Irish blessing: May you be in heaven a half-hour before the devil knows you are dead. I find it beautiful because it is double-edged. At first blush it is just about wishing someone to be safe, but the deeper point is that our relationships deepen through observing each other make mistakes, or making them together, including moral indiscretions, letting people down, and the redemptive acts of apologising and forgiving. We are often loved not merely in spite of our mistakes but because of them, aptly captured in the greeting-card phrase: 'You will always be my best friend – you know too much!'

But can we learn from our idea of the devil, and might something be lost if we are always on the run from him? Paul Morphy was one of America's finest-ever chess players, considered the unofficial world champion around 1859. In the autumn of 1861, when the American Civil War was already under way, Morphy indirectly competed with 'the devil' and defeated him, during a visit to the home of Reverend R. R. Harrison in Richmond, Virginia. During a walk around the house Morphy was drawn to a painting, *The Chess Players*, by Morits Retzsch. In the painting, a young man is playing chess with the devil, the stake of his game nothing less than his soul. The artist depicts the stage in the contest where it is apparently the young man's move, and he seems to be realising his position is hopeless. Despair is visible in his features, while the devil has an air of nonchalant cruelty.

The story goes that Morphy looked closely at the position in the painting, as I would have, or indeed as any serious chess player would have. It is not clear where every piece is placed, but the contours are visible and some intelligent guesses can be made. Before long, Morphy hurried over to his friend like a paramedic ready to resuscitate a body assumed to be dead. 'It's not over!' he said. 'The young man has a good move and I could win the game for him.' They returned to the painting and decided to set the position up on a board. Several gentlemen present at the dinner tried to play on behalf of the devil, but Morphy won every time. While some details, including the precise position in the painting, remain points of contention, the historical basis of this story appears to be sound, and its figurative resonance remains: don't give up. The devil may be in the detail, as they say, but we can find him there, and beat him.

The devil also has the best tunes, and this is no coincidence. Any expert will tell you that the sweetest and most soulful rewards of their craft stem precisely from their superior attention to detail. And yet technical details sometimes get a bad press, reflected in the language of not wanting to get 'bogged down' in the details, as if details were the viscous dregs of a swamp where we inevitably get stuck, rather than the small lights on the side of the dark runway that allow the plane to safely take off and land.

In chess, attention to detail is of paramount importance in every position, but it is perhaps most vivid in the technical phases of the game with relatively few pieces, where 'good technique' means being ferociously attentive to the details of seemingly quiet positions, like a lioness keeping a close eye on her cubs when the local hyenas appear to be 'just mucking about' in the vicinity.

Concentration emerges from caring about details. In his classic book *Zen and the Art of Motorcycle Maintenance* Robert Pirsig makes this point clear, when he argues that paying close attention to the mechanical features of the engine of the motorcycle is just as true to the spirit of Zen as the wind blowing through your hair when you ride it. 'That's the way the world keeps on happening,' Pirsig says. 'Be interested in it.'

Magnus Carlsen's style is sometimes called technical, and that is rarely meant as a compliment, because the average player can't understand what makes his moves so effective. He has the best tunes, because he has the best grasp of the details, but only strong players can hear the music.

Carlsen's style is not unique. The former world champion Anatoly Karpov had a similar strength, and some described playing him roughly as follows: 'Nothing happens, but you lose.' The question of what makes Carlsen stronger than Karpov is therefore a good post-tequila, pre-whisky question to ask in the hotel bar at an international tournament, and the answer is not easy, but probably comes down to strength of ego and reserves of willpower, because Carlsen sometimes wins positions that Karpov would not even try to win. Carlsen's concentration is just that bit deeper, revealed in his attention to detail throughout the duration of the game. And when he wins these long games, we don't always detect the moments of insight or flair or finesse. As the cellist Pablo Casals puts it: 'The most perfect technique is that which is not noticed at all.'

* * *

We tend to valorise learning but say relatively little about unlearning, which is unfortunate, because beyond a certain level of ability, one depends on the other. Psychotherapy is an applied unlearning process and so are some forms of cognitive therapy and meditation, but we unlearn whenever we cease to *be* our structures of understanding and start to *have* those structures, to see them and relate to them and begin playing around with them. Much of couples counselling for instance is about trying to articulate and share the experience of daily events that characterise a relationship. The aim is to see a relational pattern clearly enough that we stop being complicit in how it arises; we learn to pretend to be busy when there is too much to do, then we unlearn it and do something actually useful; we learn to defend ourselves from unfair criticism in ways that escalate conflict, and then we unlearn them and choose our tone and moments more carefully.

In chess we learn heuristics like 'Develop your knights before your bishops', 'Don't move your queen in the opening', 'Capture towards the centre', 'Opposite bishops have drawish tendencies' and so forth. Learning these principles and the logics that lie behind them is a necessary part of acquiring chess culture, and I remember feeling strengthened by these kinds of building blocks of understanding – they were something to hold on to. However, at a certain level of expertise these guidelines begin to seem quaint and ridiculous, because every position has such unique characteristics. As understanding grows, one's sense of what works here and now will always trump a preconceived notion. However, there is often a tension between what we think we should do and what we have learned how to do, and it takes courage to trust ourselves to override our own training.

In this sense unlearning involves growing in responsibility. To improve as a player and a person we often need to set aside the familiarity of conventional understanding. To be an expert is to have mastered the canon and refined our practice, but it also means we are not bound to follow the play book as if we had no alternative. True mastery means being present in contexts awash with nuances that demand uniquely appropriate responses.

24. FOLLOWING THE RULES

Whenever I see an illegal position on a chessboard I feel compelled to correct it. When inexperienced players set up the position, the king and queen are often on each other's squares, as are the knights and bishops, while a white square is often the left corner. When I see such things, the feeling I have is not of a teacher wanting to correct a spelling mistake, but more like the melancholy of unrequited love. In most of my life, I am no stickler for rules, but it is the rules of chess that give the game its beauty, intelligence and harmony.

In the summer of 2010, my family sat down to a pub dinner close to a life-size outdoor chess set in Putney, London. There were a group of kids around six years old enthusiastically playing what they thought was chess. They moved whichever piece they fancied and put it on a random square, before saying: 'I win! I win!'

At some moment they absconded, excitedly chasing after each other, and I quickly left our table and went to set the board up correctly. When the renegades returned, the eldest of the group, a girl about seven, started knocking over the pieces one by one. She also summoned a young recruit to go and collect large dominoes and throw them all over the board, completing the transition from harmony to discord.

With a young son of my own at the time, I appreciated that youth and anarchy are natural allies. What upset me was not that kids were being kids, but that they thought they were playing chess. Their idea of the game was the board and pieces, and whatever you chose to do with them. My idea of the game includes the rules, without which you don't get the startling ideas, the gripping tension and the ongoing challenge. This moment is an example of why positive freedom through restricting oneself with rules is often more rewarding than merely having no constraints on whatever you want to do. Rules and restrictions actually make freedom possible. Whether you are a writer or a musician or just doing your day job, creative freedom often evades you unless you can retrace steps to establish some form and limits. The creative spark often waits to emerge on the other side of structural discipline.

I tried to convey a version of this point to one of the young boys who was particularly triumphant about winning. I said: It's good that you won, but you are not really playing chess. He did not take too kindly to this idea, and went off in a strop, complaining to his grandmother: 'That man says I can't play chess.'

The grandmother understood what had happened, and said: 'Be careful, he likes to cheat.' But how can he cheat, I thought, if he doesn't even know the rules? I said I would teach him the rules, and asked which piece he would most like to learn about. He pointed to the rook, and I got him to take the rook around the board in straight lines, praising him as he went. He looked momentarily happy, relieved from the tyranny of unstructured freedom. I wanted to continue, but my dinner was getting cold, so instead I told his grandmother that if he learned the rules, chess would be his friend for life.

The chess world is part of the university of life, and it taught me quite a few things about relationships. In early adulthood one of my main social activities was chess tournaments overseas, and I developed a taste for foreign romances. I had been an awkward spotty teenager with braces and glasses and never quite cool enough to be considered a catch at school, but in my late teenage years I began to look plausible enough to compete in what chess players slyly call 'The B Tournament'. Alas, I was often outmanoeuvred. I remember sitting on a bed with a particularly beautiful Norwegian girl at a tournament in Germany, and gently moving in for the first kiss. With a form of judo diplomacy I'll never forget, she deftly turned her head to the side and simultaneously pulled me closer, before defeating me with a resolutely platonic *hug*.

Soon afterwards I met an enchanting girl on the dance floor at a tournament in Poland and the relationship lasted over a year. It was a fairly typical first love – apparently fated, joyously physical, and emotionally immature. Beyond saying 'I love you', we ran out of things to write in our letters or discuss on the phone (the internet was in its infancy). The long-distance relationship was becoming strenuous, but I was still smitten when she dumped me in a hotel room at Heathrow airport. She was on her way to the world junior chess championships in Calicut, a city in the south Indian state of Kerala. I was heading back to student life at Oxford, single once more.

I sobbed in the shower and sang pop songs heavy with romantic nostalgia to recover. Toni Braxton's 'Unbreak my Heart' and Phil Collins's 'Separate Lives' definitely featured, sometimes accompanied by 'Let it Be' by the Beatles. At the time it was no joke. Our first major breakup is not just the loss of a relationship, but a loss of innocence too. When the first love of our life turns out not to be *the* love of our life, our very idea of love is shattered, and the thought of having to rebuild it is daunting. I called her hotel in Calicut in a feigned attempt to be strong and understanding, wishing her well for her games. There was real emotional pain, but I was also caught up in the delicious drama of it all; with hindsight I was like an actor eagerly playing the part of a rejected lover in the societal narrative of love. I was waking up to the stories we tell ourselves about ourselves, and beginning to notice that they are indeed stories.

Just a few days later I encountered my future wife, Siva, and an uncanny serendipity turned what might have been a passing acquaintance into an enduring relationship. We met at a nondescript flat on the outskirts of central Oxford, where gown becomes town, part of a small group follow-up in the process of learning Transcendental Meditation – I still practise the technique on most days.[20] Siva was a postgraduate student, deeply committed to global justice issues relating to intellectual property law – for instance why the poor often can't afford life-saving drugs because they have been patented by a profit-seeking pharmaceutical company. I was a final-year undergraduate, looking forward to leaving my studies behind and trying to become a chess Grandmaster. Neither of us saw the other coming.

Siva seemed vivacious and intelligently enthusiastic about life. I was not yet ready for a relationship but I was enchanted by her eyes and her voice, particularly the way she pronounced 'wh' as 'v'. In our calls, she would say goodbye by 'keeping the phone' (ending the conversation) so that I could 'work for a vile'. Siva came to Oxford from Calicut.

The Calicut convergence: how improbable that my past became my future in a place where I was not even present. Maybe the relevant variable is not probability, but more like grace. This moment felt like a punctuation mark in my life, a semicolon perhaps. The American writer Lynn Darling captures the spirit of this kind of capricious moment: 'Who we are is a composite of who we might have been refracted through the lens of whom we married.' Siva and I didn't marry for another seven years, and might well not have done, but looking back it feels almost indulgent – a grudging concession to my academic training – to say anything other than that the die was cast at that moment. I feel we were meant for each other, even if I don't quite know what that means.

Those who think marriage is mostly about shared interests and getting along well are probably not married themselves. Whatever makes marriage work is something much deeper and subtler, and perhaps even ineffable. My impression is that good marriages are mostly about two people being optimally wounded for each other. The fable of the deaf man marrying the blind woman captures this spirit. The challenge of marriage manifests as arguments over misplaced shoes, unwashed dishes and forgotten items of shopping, but at heart it is the perpetual reminder that your world is not the only world. As the philosopher novelist Iris Murdoch put it: 'Love is the extremely difficult realisation that something other than oneself is real.'

We have had many joyous and fulfilling moments through many phases of life, but Siva and I have never really been in perfect harmony; we laugh and cry with each other but also at each other. On good days there is a sense of optimal conflict, of obliging each other to bend towards the parts of ourselves that we might otherwise neglect. Seeing the world through the eyes of my wife expanded the world spiritually, politically and personally in a way that made it impossible to view chess – a mere microcosm – as the place I should channel my energy. Siva is maddening sometimes, my war as much as my peace, but I have never doubted that she is my ally. When I am about to go and speak in public we joke that a small version of her will be sitting on my left shoulder, holding on to my ear. We have been talking this way for so long that I find myself looking for her there, knowing she is with me.

Mercifully, Siva is not a chess player, but it was important to me that she respected the game and admired my love of it. In early 2004, when we had temporarily broken up and were separated by several weeks of silence and thousands of miles, Siva came down to breakfast in Bangalore to see her father reading an Indian newspaper, with the sports pages facing outwards, including the headline: 'Rowson wins Hastings'. The Indian press covered the event partly because it is a chess institution, and partly because it included some Indian players. Siva did not want to risk family questions by speaking from home, so she went to a nearby booth and called to congratulate me. I remember the relieved joy at hearing her voice and felt like a lost part of me had returned. I had missed that singular experience of warmth and acute understanding, of being fully heard and deeply known. Sometimes we discover ourselves through the taste of what has been missing. The next time we met I was resolute about getting married, but did not yet have the money for a ring or an idea of where and how to propose.

Even then we struggled to gain Siva's parents' acceptance, partly because we had been on and off for so long without being married and they couldn't understand what was going on. In the UK we have a whole spectrum of togetherness – from date, to item, to couple, to partners, to living together, to engagement, to marriage, and then, quite often, divorce – but in India, mostly, you are either married or you are not. The tension caused by lacking clear relationship status reached its climax on a visit to Bangalore where still being unmarried was making life difficult for both of us. With some help from a mutual friend, I managed to escape from my in-laws for a few hours and take an auto-rickshaw into town to buy one of many impressive rings presented in a briefcase. I paid in cash, mostly with rupees I had earned from teaching chess to some Indian players over the course of my stay.

We flew back to London via Abu Dhabi airport and had an enervating fight about something incidental that was clearly about the underlying issue. Siva was distressed, torn between shouting and sobbing. I had the ring in my pocket and was seconds away from proposing in protest, there and then, but I remembered what it feels like to make a blunder in chess, and managed to hold my nerve. That part of Abu Dhabi airport is possibly the ugliest building I have ever seen. The central construction had a greenish golden hue, a sinister extraterrestrial presence, and it was swarming with international travellers, including those sitting right next to us. With our trays of half-eaten food and announcements overhead about flights departing I am so glad I restrained myself: the relationship might never have recovered. A few weeks later, with the Indian family and Abu Dhabi airport far away, I proposed out in the countryside, surrounded by lush scenery, fresh air and running water.

In 2006 when defending my British title for the third time in Swansea, I had messed up the first part of the tournament. Our plan was that Siva would work while I prepared and played, but the shared creative experience was diffuse and unproductive. Siva set aside the academic paper she was writing to help me concentrate, and did so mostly by attending the last five games in person. Her contribution was not just to show up, but to keep our collective attention on one thing alone. Our commitment to each other was that if she was sitting down and looking at the game (on the demonstration board) I should be too. Knowing she was there, knowing we were in it together, my concentration increased by several orders of magnitude and I won my last four games and retained the title – the final game may have been my best ever. At the prize-giving I gave a short speech where I looked at her in the audience and said: 'I couldn't have done this without you.' I was on the brink of tears because I finally knew what these words meant. The strength of our will and the quality of our attention depends on the love of others.

While Siva helped me grow as a player, it was even more important that she sensed I wanted to create a life outside of the game, and knew I would need help to do so. It had become clearer to us both that while chess was likely to be in my future, my future was unlikely to be in chess. I began research methods training as part of a Ph.D. on the concept of wisdom at the University of Bristol (while living in London) and my income from chess allowed me to live comfortably. I still had a part-time commitment to the game. By thirty I had won a second British Championship title and at thirty-two I was a chess columnist in a national newspaper.

Around then, with childhood at a safe distance, life transformed. I began to outgrow not so much the inexhaustible game, which I still played occasionally, but the exhausting travel and exhaustible world of chess. That world began to be experienced through hotel rooms I didn't particularly want to be in, conversational gambits I no longer wanted to accept – for instance: 'Have you been playing much recently?' In the chess world I began to feel mythic deprivation, sensing that the best stories in life were elsewhere. Professional chess may look like a glamorous world, but for all but the top twenty or so elite players that experience rarely endures. The jokes and stories about the game and the people who play it had once felt so expansive and intriguing, but they began to sound like reheated versions of familiar themes. What was once a world of growth and adventure shrank to a world of winning and losing where I felt I had little more to gain.

Chess, I came to realise, was my alibi as much as my vocation, a viable response to the existential auditing question: What were you doing all those years? Around this time I began to feel I needed a new alibi. The essayist and psychoanalyst Adam Phillips has a beautiful description of this kind of transformative phase of life: 'Growing up is always an undoing of what needed to be done; first, ideally, we are made to feel special, then we are expected to enjoy a world in which we are not.'[21] Chess was still a core part of my identity, and became a precious source of grounding that kept me sane as my life abruptly changed. While expecting our first son Kailash I could not imagine travelling to play abroad as often, and I was also losing interest in chess opening preparation – a serious problem for a Grandmaster who needs to work on the latest developments in opening theory to achieve promising positions from the first ten to twenty or so moves of the game.

The US basketball coach Bobby Knight was right when he said: 'The will to win is not as important as the will to prepare to win.' And I had lost that. But through chess, I had found a great deal more. Saint-Exupéry is also right: 'The only things you learn are the things you tame.'

FOUR

Cultures and Counter-Cultures

Escapism is a trap

I sat in a nondescript hotel room without a view of the water. In 2002 Slovenia felt like a difficult place to be. Outside were the crisp autumnal charms of Lake Bled, but it was swarming with the great and the good of the chess world whom I wanted to avoid. I was supposed to be preparing for my next opponent at the World Chess Olympiad, but multiple parts of my life had collided and I was adrift, saturated and tearful.

I was twenty-five years old, but still felt like I was in the early stages of becoming an adult. There was a laptop and a chess set on a small desk in the corner. These tools had been my professional staples for almost a decade, but I seemed unable to muster the will to use them. I was there to represent Scotland on first board against some of the world's finest Grandmasters, and even Gary Kasparov was in town. Competing should have been a source of pride and purpose and passion, but I could not summon the confidence trick that had shaped my life to that point, could not summon the trick that says: 'Yes! What you are about to do really matters.'

I had flown in to the event from Boston, a few days after it had started, and like a late guest I couldn't find the pulse of the party. I was taking time out of my master's degree and was hoping to complete some coursework in between my games. I had been high on the status of simultaneous achievement and the conceit that I could 'do it all'. Professionally it was hard enough to straddle these two worlds, but the dissolution was compounded by a confluence of events in my personal life. Somewhat absurdly, four irresolute relationships were competing for heart and mind.[1]

I had a fledgling romantic relationship with one of my course cohort back in the US. Alison had driven me to Boston airport and said goodbye with a kiss on the cheek that lingered for thousands of miles. That lightness defined our year or so together, and it was refreshing in the emotionally ambiguous context of my trial separation with Siva; I had called Siva from my hotel phone although she had asked me not to. I knew it was cruel to keep her in my life, but I lacked the maturity and compassion to let her go.

The day after arrival in Bled I had visited the hotel room of a female Grandmaster, Ester, with whom I had recently had an affair. It began at an event in Sweden, then we arranged to play together at a tournament in the former Yugoslavia. I take no pride in this now, and have long since made my apologies, but it feels facile a decade and a half later to blame my younger self for his callow craving. Even in the shadows of the chess world, we were an unlikely couple; she was too hedonistic and I wasn't hedonistic enough. We had always known we weren't compatible, but nonetheless we helped each other move our lives along. In Bled, I tentatively visited her hotel room, but nothing happened. Whatever that was, was no longer.

Finally, my first love, Lisa, happened to be visiting the event. We hadn't spoken for about three years, but we arranged to meet and reconnected as if we had never parted. Travelling from another part of the country meant she had nowhere else other than my room to stay. There was a nostalgic charge, and when our bodies inevitably rediscovered each other it was one of the most heightened experiences of my life. At one point, when proceedings were well under way, Lisa viciously bit my lip with an unbidden erotic intensity I will never forget. We barely spoke the next day, and haven't since.

I was completely lost. In Japanese Pureland Buddhism they speak of human beings as *Bombu* – 'a foolish being of wayward passion'. That's how I felt. My emotional nadir came at an international chess tournament in a stunningly beautiful place. As a chess player I knew that some decisions had to be taken, and the etymological root of decision – to cut away – felt apt. After the charming airport trip, the tortured phone call, the guarded encounter and the overnight stay, there was a strong desire to stop this current, stop this incessant flow of life over which I seemed to have no control. I needed to make sense of what was going on.

It took several months to re-establish direction, but that moment of feeling rudderless was pivotal. I survived the Olympiad without disgrace or distinction, finished my master's degree well, returned to the UK, married Siva and began a Ph.D. in a tentative search for another career. Chess became more like my anchor and less like my sail; an integral part of my identity, yes, but neither my map nor my compass for the next phase of life.

I had travelled far and wide with chess, often to places I would never otherwise have seen. Highlights include the Iguazu falls on the Brazil/Argentina border, the Rocky Mountains in Canada, the Wailing Wall in Israel, a putative remnant of Noah's Ark in Armenia, an artificial castle in Iowa, USA, the Blue Lagoon in Iceland, Gibraltar's Rock and the sublime remoteness of the Faroe Islands. However, I have also spent a huge amount of time in completely mundane places, a morass of airports and roads and walls and tables and chairs. For instance, when I played in the German Bundesliga – a professional chess league – I remember being driven between cities and towns near Düsseldorf airport, and they seemed indistinguishable. On most such journeys I was in the back seat with other chess players, and we would invariably be talking about positions without sight of a board. I also spent many hours alone in hotel rooms where I often felt forsaken by all the communities I was *not* part of. Travel feels less like a luxury when it is a compulsion rather than a choice. The Israeli-Spanish

Grandmaster Arthur Kogan captured it well when he said: 'The dream life gets old.'

Even though I was travelling, my place, my locus of concern, my *where*, was still the chessboard. The chess world was more like a diffuse echo of the board than a particular place where one could rest, and I did not want to live there any more. In this respect I identify with the following extract from the anthropologist Robert Desjarlais in his excellent book *Counterplay*:

> Later, before heading out to my car, I walk through the tournament area. I step past the tournament directors' office, where two men are keeping track of results reported and complaints lodged, past the display of chess books, past the food vendors selling soggy hot dogs and crisp burgers. I stumble around three kids seated on the carpeted floor, placing pieces on a board, and I overhear two men discussing a game. 'That's a nasty pin,' mutters one of them. I stick my head into the skittles room and see pairs of players jousting over rooks and knights, and then walk into the playing hall, where all is quiet and somber and deadly serious, as though a world is at stake. I feel I should be seated at a board as well, fighting it out. But I don't care to be here. Playing now would be like counting pebbles in the sand. I feel discordant, antiheroic. Moments later I'm on the road, heading for home.

I know that feeling. I know the sense of ambling for meaning and connection that is just not there, and that notion of seeming 'discordant, antiheroic'. I have felt a version of this sentiment many times when I – a Grandmaster who is supposed to be full of appetite for the game – feel unable to muster any deep concern for the quality of my moves or the outcome they might lead to. The writer Martin Amis wrote about chess players looking like they were 'defeated in some fundamental way', and I fear I know what he means – the victories being pursued on the board often feel more like a source of consolation than vivacity. However, without any facile rebalancing, I would like to think chess players are also victorious in some fundamental way. After all, we have created a home in a beautiful and beguiling world where our actions at least make sense on our own terms, which is more than many ever achieve.

Chess offers moments of escape, but the experience of escape is also the experience of life as such. Thinking about my chess life, it seems to me there are broadly three ways of venturing into something that helps you get away from something else. At first you feel it is wrong to escape, that you should accept responsibility for your life and take it seriously on its own terms. Then at some point reality becomes oppressive and you need to take flight and refuge in another world – a luxury, if not a necessity. You love this new world because it allows you to think and feel in ways that are not otherwise permissible – you feel freer and more fully yourself. But you also know you don't belong there. That's what I mean when I say escapism is a trap. At some point your whole life catches up with you. You feel less like two whole people in two places and more like one person fractured within one life. But there is a further level of escapism, and the most beautiful: when your reality and your escape from reality become equally real, and one world shines a favourable light on the other, allowing you to appreciate both without fetishising either.

Ultimately the point is to escape from the need to escape, and feel free and at ease wherever you are. But there is no quick way to get there. We have to do a lot of escaping before we become free of the need to do so. In this sense, chess taught me that John Kabat-Zinn's well-known saying is profoundly true: 'Wherever you go, there you are.'

25. BEING A CULTURAL ORPHAN

It is no accident that the most popular fictional character for the last couple of decades – Harry Potter – is an orphan. Nor is it surprising that literary fiction and films have so many characters who have lost their parents or never had them; think of Annie, Oliver Twist, Anne of Green Gables, Batman, Jane Eyre, Frodo Baggins, Tom Sawyer, and almost any Roald Dahl protagonist. While the way we look at the world is heavily influenced by our parents, many orphans have to struggle to make sense of the world entirely on their own terms, which makes for compelling characters and stories. The novelist Hilary Thayer Hamann captures the basis of our fascination with orphans in her book *Anthropology of an American Girl*: 'When you lose your parents as a child, you are indoctrinated into a club, you are taken into life's severest confidence. You are undeceived.'[2]

To be an orphan is to have to make one's own way in the world, and take whatever help you can find in the process. I think of chess as a kind of orphan in that it lacks cultural parents; like an orphan the game is viewed as precious but still nobody really looks after it. People like the game, as they like to read about orphans, but no established cultural form is eager to adopt chess on a permanent basis, and the game remains somehow forsaken. I chime with the journalist and chess enthusiast Stephen Moss when he describes cultural attitudes to chess as 'elegiac'. Many of those who love the cultural contours that have surrounded the game for decades sense that its meaning and mystery and majesty is slowly ebbing away.

Chess falls through the cultural cracks, and lacks a stable cultural category that honours all its elements. Chess is more than a sport but less than *Sport*; chess is educational and educative but not *Education*; chess is full of artistic ideas but it is not *Art*; in many ways chess is scientific but it is not *Science*. On the bright side, perhaps it is precisely this protean quality that makes the game a reliable place to escape to. To put the point assertively, chess cannot and should not be institutionalised. Yet this predicament is problematic because without a cultural category that corresponds to a government department that would naturally fund it, or media section that would naturally report it, the game remains underfunded and under-reported.

Sport says: Your games might feel like sport, but we don't see it.

Art says: There may be art in your game, but we don't get it.

Education says: You might be able to help us, but our timetables are full.

Games say: Nobody else would take you? You can join us, but don't get any ideas above your station; go and sit over there with Monopoly and Scrabble.

It is worth reflecting then on what it really means for chess to be 'part of our culture' in a more general sense. Perhaps chess is counter-cultural in the sense that it needs to remain uncategorised, unadopted and untamed to exert meaningful cultural influence. How else can we explain that chess is so often used as a symbol or metaphor in a variety of cultural forms despite a lack of engagement with the details of the game? Chess *does* something to our shared sense of reality; the game is an active ingredient, albeit a subtle one, in the welter of signs, symbols and rituals we call culture.

First, I think chess symbolises the importance of sublimation. In chemistry sublimation happens when substances change their state (e.g. solid to gas) due to the absorption of heat, and historically the idea was important to alchemists seeking to change base metals into gold. However, I mean sublimation in the sense used mostly by psychologists, which typically refers to mature psychological defence mechanisms, in which sexual energy or anger are redirected towards and through intellectual and cultural activity like chess. Sublimation might go beyond that though; indeed it was one of the main issues on which the two most famous psychologists of the twentieth century, Sigmund Freud and Carl Jung, profoundly disagreed.

The source of Jung's disagreement with Freud stems from their differing attitudes to libido, which Freud understood to be our sex drive, but Jung viewed as something more general, like our life force. For Freud sublimation is primarily about maintaining social order by civilising our instincts: rather than lusting to have sex with someone we cannot permissibly desire, we should channel that energy into, for instance, improving our tennis serve or putting up some shelves. For Jung sublimation is more like a transformational process through which inner conflicts are resolved through symbols of unity that enter our lives as a kind of grace.

For Freudians, chess is therefore mostly a matter of sublimating our patricidal instincts and oedipal complexes; the desire to checkmate the opponent's king is really a sublimated desire to remove our fathers to have direct access to our mothers. For Jungians, sublimation is about symbols which act as 'New content that governs the whole attitude, putting an end to division and forcing the opposites into a common channel ... life can flow on with renewed power towards new goals.'[3] In this respect, I wonder if Freud and Jung might both be partly right. Chess is a transcendent symbol in the Jungian sense, but what it symbolises is close to sublimation in the Freudian sense.

Second, I think chess's cultural function is to be a holding pattern for the idea of formation; not just character formation, but education more broadly conceived as cultivation; chess is a symbol of hard-earned sophistication because the barriers to playing it *well* are high. By symbolising depth and difficulty and struggle in a recognizable form, chess is the symbolic setting for the game of life, the place where our own formation is in question, where we hope our 'form', perhaps our soul, will mature and develop and grow wiser, rather than merely older.

In German Romanticism the term for formation is *Bildung* and the key insight, derived from the ideas of the 3rd Earl of Shaftesbury, is that there is a relationship between our inner formation and the formation of the world outside; our moral challenge is how to work on oneself in a way that helps the world, and vice-versa. Chess speaks to the challenge of *Bildung* because it is a game where system meets psyche, where an improved understanding of the world (the game) can help with an improved understanding of ourselves. Since chess is easy to learn but difficult to master, it reminds us that this process of formation rolls on.

Third, chess symbolises the significance of play, a concept that is often conflated with leisure but is most fundamentally about embodied creative agency. We play in all sorts of ways – chasing, joking, improvising, hiding, learning, simulating, imagining, pretending – and we can play in all sorts of settings. The defining feature of play however is that it is voluntary and cannot be coerced. We play because we can and because we want to. We play because we are free, to discover who we are and who we might be. As the psychologist and play theorist Charles Schaefer puts it: 'We are never more fully alive, more completely ourselves, or more deeply engrossed in anything than when we are playing.' And yet we have lost sight of the importance of play as a disposition, a way of life, perhaps even as a design principle for society, which is why the musician Pat Kane argues that we should replace our fixation with 'the work ethic' with 'the play ethic'. For all its intellectual gravitas and symbolic resonance, chess is about taking play seriously. Perhaps the game's cultural role is therefore to give play its proper due as a moral touchstone, and an end in itself.

26. THE ESSENCE OF SPORT

In the summer of 2012 the Olympics were in London, just a few miles from where I had been living since 2004. Despite being geographically close I felt emotionally quite distant from the event, and I am embarrassed to say that I did not attend. There was no particular reason not to go; I just didn't get round to it. My first son, Kailash, was only three, so it is hard to say what he would have made of it, but part of a father's job is to punctuate the narrative of our children with stories worth telling. Whether we expect to enjoy or remember an event is often less important than the fact we are able to say: 'I was there!'

And yet I was not. I suspect the administrative hassle involved in securing tickets put me off at the time, but that's a lame excuse, and a sign that my mind was elsewhere. Sport is epic, beautiful and glorious, but at the time I was going through a process of escaping from the energy of the sporting world – all that manufactured excitement, all that winning and losing, all those familiar stories breathlessly told. I also felt some mild alienation that stems from my own sport – chess – not being recognised as such by the watching world. And yet, all said and done, I wish I had gone and I am sure I would have loved it. In any case, it is so much better to regret the things you have done than the things you haven't.

Should chess be in the Olympics? Let's seek an answer through an imagined Socratic dialogue between a twenty-first-century Socrates and an impartial Olympic official.

S: What are the Olympic Games?

OO: It's the world's foremost sporting competition, which has been around in some form for almost three thousand years and has gradually become a celebrated international institution.

S: And what is the essence of these Olympic Games?

OO: Well, they are sports rather than games. If we let mere games like chess in, where do we draw the line with, say, draughts, Scrabble and so forth?

S: I see, but what then is a sport, and how does it differ from a game?

OO: Sports are whatever we say they are. There's no non-political definition that everybody will agree with. However, sports typically involve competition that is structured with certain established rules, with a scoring system that is recordable, and that is enjoyed through mass participation.

S: And why does mass participation matter?

OO: It's about status. You can invent a game in your own garden, but to be a sport you have to be recognised by a certain number of people that a sporting institution has to take notice of.

S: I see, and chess? Does it not meet these criteria of structured competition, established scoring and mass participation?

OO: Well yes, and chess is recognised as a sport in many countries that are part of the Olympic movement, including India, France, Germany and Russia. However, for many, sports should be physical: they need to involve the body in some way.

S: I see, and can you play chess without the body?

OO: No, but the physical element of the game is about maintaining concentration and holding your nerve, not using your body as such.

S: I see, and concentration and nerve, these are not important aspects of bodily experience that also matter to other Olympic participants?

OO: They are, but Olympic activities comprise an element of physical skill. It's about showing how the body is used skilfully.

S: I see, and mental and physical skill are fundamentally different?

OO: I concede they are related, sometimes closely related, but spectators can only see what is physical.

S: So chess may involve physical skill of sorts, physiological skill let us say (since it is not directly observable), and such skill is centrally relevant to sport. Chess players fire neurons to think and they expend nervous energy, measurable in raised heart rates; World Championship competitors have also been known to lose significant amounts of weight during their matches; and studies of personality suggest chess players are thrill-seekers who develop testosterone levels during play akin to bungee jumpers. Moreover, a chess player has to control their nervous system in a manner similar to the way an archer has to control their bow – in both cases concentration is the key variable. Considering that all sporting performance arises from our embodied minds, the difference between physical skill and physiological skill appears to be a difference in visibility rather than relevance, would you agree?[4]

OO: Yes, I suppose so.

S: But then if chess has structured competition, established scoring systems, mass participation, and it even involves something very similar to physical skill, why is it not a sport?

OO: Well, you said it. It's the visibility. When people watch the Olympics, they are celebrating the competitive tension, the endurance, the sweet joy of success that can only exist alongside the heartache of failure. It is *seeing* the drama that matters most.

S: I see, and is such drama not also part of the chess experience?

OO: Yes it is, but the audience does not know that.

S: I see, so the reason chess is not an Olympic sport is principally due to a lack of imaginative empathy on behalf of those who have never experienced the game at a competitive level. If they can't see the drama, they can't feel it, and that matters more for sporting recognition than whether the drama is actually there.

OO: That seems to be where we are, yes.

S: Well, thank you for your time. Let's go and watch some synchronised swimming.

27. HUSTLE

I have a friend who never reads or watches anything recommended by only one person, but acts almost immediately on the advice of two or more. He enjoys looking out for such signals and waits for the world to reveal to him what he should do. He says he appreciates books and films all the more when he senses that they are meant for him, and while I am charmed by his methodology, I fear for his sanity.

I thought of him when I started watching *The Wire* on DVD in 2011. The series is a gritty and sometimes harrowing take on the urban drug scene in Baltimore, USA, and is awash with swearing and violence. From that kind of description, I found it hard to imagine I could like it, yet with so many trusted friends telling me I would, I relented, and was pleasantly surprised.

The characters are raw and compelling and their dialect electrically authentic. I remember being irritated to find that audiences in America watched some films set in Scotland, like *Trainspotting*, with English subtitles, but the street language of *The Wire* is also so far from conventional English that I initially had to do the same. Still, in an early episode I knew I had made a good decision to watch when I saw one young drug dealer – D'Angelo – teach two others – Bodie and Wallace – how to play chess. This particular scene is an extraordinary work of art; a beguiling mixture of social commentary, existential despair, youthful hope and dark humour.

D'Angelo describes the king as 'the kingpin' and says that the aim of the game is to protect your own king and get the king of the other side. He says the king can move one square in any direction but that he doesn't have 'hustle'.

There are many worlds within that word: hustle. As a noun and a verb, hustle hints at a relationship between a setting and a plot, a juxtaposition that defines the moral ambiguity of characters in *The Wire*. Describing the king's lack of hustle is a succinct way to say that the king is rarely out on the streets; in professional terms he does not have to solicit clients. The expression also means the king does not directly display *force*, he's not typically *aggressive*, he's not *illicit*, nor *in a hurry*, but equally he doesn't have what you might need to *get things done*. 'Hustle' is sometimes admirable, not least when it seems necessary; the word conveys the spirit of entrepreneurial transgression needed to survive.

The king may not have hustle, but nonetheless he survives for longer than the other pieces by definition. Checkmate – from the Persian *Shah Mat* – literally means the king is dead. 'The man' is therefore the ultimate target of attack, but he is surrounded by people who will give their lives to protect him, and often do. Most chess endgames, when few pieces remain, are characterised by the king suddenly becoming emboldened, partly because with fewer enemies around it is relatively safe to come out 'into the street', but also because there are fewer allies left to do his hustling for him.

The realisation that life-and-death chances are not fairly distributed is what makes the chess scene from *The Wire* so poignant. As the rules of the game are described by D'Angelo, Wallace and Bodie can see their own lives in the game's metaphors, giving rise to an open question of who or what exactly they are living in service of, and why.

Bodie, himself a pawn in the drug wars, points to the pawns, and asks about 'them little baldheaded bitches'. D'Angelo explains that they are like soldiers and shows how they move, saying they are out on the 'front lines'.

Bodie gets excited by the possibility of pawns getting promoted, about becoming 'top dog' if he can 'get to the end'. D'Angelo is quick to disabuse him of the probability of that happening, implying that they often get 'capped' (shot) quickly.

Bodie shoots back that this may not happen if they are 'smart-ass pawns', which he himself later proves to be, surviving and rising through the ranks until series four. Wallace, on the other hand, proved as vulnerable as most pawns do, and died a few episodes later when he was just sixteen after trying to leave the drug scene. Bodie, Wallace's friend, was also his assassin.

The writers loop back to this scene in series four when Bodie is speaking with Detective McNulty and considering his next move. Bodie is resolute about not being a snitch and conveys that he has done everything he was told to do by his bosses since he was thirteen, including killing his friend Wallace. McNulty knows the context and has clearly grown to admire Bodie, calling him 'a soldier', as D'Angelo called the pawns earlier. At that moment, after years of imagining he might somehow escape or transform his fate, Bodie sees the truth of being a pawn more clearly, and realises he is still 'one of them little bitches on the chessboard'. McNulty clarifies: 'Pawns.'

In an early chess manual published around the middle of the sixteenth century, François-André Philidor describes pawns as 'the soul of chess', and this line is widely quoted by chess teachers and commentators because we know and feel its truth. Pawns are not the most powerful pieces, and they are mostly at the mercy of events, but they have a certain amount of hustle and they both set the scene and shape the narrative.

What occurred to me while watching *The Wire* is that most of us are pawns to a greater or lesser extent. We have our moments of power, fame and glory, but we are always potentially alone and vulnerable to forces beyond our control. We are the soul of the game of life, and our lives are precious not in spite of our fragility, but because of it.

28. TRAGIC SAFETY

Chess is sometimes viewed as culturally transgressive. Our game was, for instance, outlawed in Iran until recently because it was considered to be a form of gambling, which was deemed *haram*. However, it takes a special set of circumstances for chess to be considered a threat to public safety.

On the afternoon of 20 October 2011 in New York City, a group of seven men were playing chess at purpose-built chess tables inside a children's play area called Emerson Playground in Inwood Hill Park in Manhattan. According to the New York parks department, there are about 2,000 public chess tables spread across 536 parks. Children in play areas are usually too young to want to play chess, so it is a curious design decision to include the boards near the swings and chutes. Perhaps the idea was that parents or guardians would play each other, but this does not chime with my experience of parenting, because the risk of getting lost in a chess game is that you'll lose sight of your child. Moreover, there was a fence separating the chessboards from the main play area, and on this particular day there were no children around.

While the men were hanging out in that place, blissfully absorbed in evading checks, making captures and pressing clocks, an NYC police patrol vehicle rolled up to the gate of the park. Several officers approached the men and charged them with occupying the area unaccompanied by any children, in violation of a regulation '1–03' about ignoring park rules, in this case a rule meant to safeguard areas designed for children from adult use, and indirectly help to protect children from paedophiles.

The players were summoned to court, to face possible trial. Some settled the case, which meant their charges would be fully dismissed provided they were not arrested in the following six months, but two of the defendants successfully sought a dismissal without any exceptions and won, albeit on the technicality that the arresting officer had referred to irrelevant laws in his paperwork documenting the arrest.

I found this case curiously troubling, because there is a lot going on under the surface and it is hard to fathom what it all means. I am a father and have been a school governor, so I understand that safeguarding children is a duty of paramount importance; system rules that help with that objective are generally welcome. However, we can only do so much to protect children before preventive measures become absurd, undermine our quality of life, and damage the kind of free and trustworthy world that we want to bring children in to.

It is also true that if you have rules, however minor, you had better enforce them now and again, lest the very idea of rules loses its authority. Still, it is vexing to think that seven men playing chess should be summoned to court for what appears to be nothing more than being in a place where children might have been.

The other aspect of this story that is challenging is the suspicion that the officers' actions, their decision to enforce what did not need to be enforced, might have been racially motivated. The comedian Milton Jones, who is white, once quipped: 'I got arrested for playing chess in the street. I said, "It's because I'm Black, isn't it?"' It is hard to say whether that line should be taken seriously in the context of this story, but in my experience of the US East Coast chess park scene, and based on similar experience of others who live there, the subculture is largely African American. Moreover, in this particular case, the player featured in the *New York Times* version of the story, Yacahudah Harrison, is Black and also homeless; he jokes of the chess players taking muffins and jasmine tea rather than drugs, and ruefully describes chess in the context as 'a quiet game that still disturbs the peace'.

On reflection, perhaps this story has nothing to do with chess. The people concerned were not arrested for what they were *doing* at all, but for breaking a rule that actually has a certain soundness in general terms, even if it looks ridiculous when it's enforced. But then is it not also ridiculous to have rules that are not enforced? And the rule to protect children's spaces seems quite reasonable when interpreted wisely.

The story is noteworthy not because it offers clear moral guidance, but because it reveals modern life in all its confusions and contradictions. Law enforcement can turn law-abiding people into law breakers. Child-protection measures risk creating a culture where adults are distrusted for being adults. Race is implicated even when there is no evidence of racism. And chess is often the story even when what happened is really not about the game at all.

This story's quieter tragedy is that the players stayed away, and chess was driven further away from the public realm. The challenge for chess is not to be more popular, because the game is already widely loved. The challenge, particularly in this internet age, is precisely to make the game more visible and public. I am not sure what the final verdict on 'park regulation 1-03' concerning failure to comply with park signs should be, but I hope we will always live in a world where we can assume that it is safe to play chess in public.

29. ELITISM

I do not have many regrets, but occasionally I revisit incidents in my life as a spin doctor, reshaping words and events to present myself in a more flattering light. For instance, in 2001 I played at the Scottish Championship in Aberdeen, and as local boy and tournament favourite I was asked to turn up a little early for one of the rounds to speak to the television media. Alas, I arrived late and flustered, which was ill-fated, mainly because I missed the chance to answer an important question posed by the young female journalist: 'Isn't chess elitist?'

The question is not unreasonable, but there was something about the presumptive way I heard it posed to others that I found aggravating, as if anything that was not instantly accessible must somehow be morally suspect.

The chess player most famous for not being in any sense elite is perhaps John Healy, who wrote a bestselling autobiography called *The Grass Arena* in which he recounts a harrowing childhood followed by alcoholism, boxing, violence and internment. He learned chess in prison at the age of thirty, and stopped drinking because, in his own words, 'Chess is a jealous lover.' He also remarked to a cellmate that: 'It's a pity more people in here don't know the bliss inherent in chess.' His autobiography has been described as a 'savage masterpiece' and is highly recommended.[5]

That said, despite his literary success, Healy remained an outsider. I find it impressive but also tragic that the twice academy-award-winning actor Daniel Day-Lewis wrote the foreword to the 2008 reprint of the book, and yet Healy remains in relative poverty and obscurity, and his attempts to publish other books did not succeed. I do not know the whole story, but Healy's life story is emblematic of many human chess stories; it is a story of intensity, of being lost and found through chess, of feeling that chess ought to be enough to build a life around, discovering that it is not, and then feeling confused because if that game of depth and beauty you excel at is not enough, what else could possibly be? In this respect I find it striking that Day-Lewis described Healy as 'our jaunty gleeful tour-guide and messenger from hell'.

Healy's chess life can hardly be described as elitist, and my missed opportunity of encountering the question – isn't chess elitist? – led me to create an alternate account of history where I answered the question. I arrive in good time, push open double doors with both hands in slow motion, warmly greet the assembled crowd, gently pull on the lapels of my denim jacket, and fix the interviewer with a charming proletarian gaze before answering:

> In all the bad senses of elitism, no. The only entry barrier to chess is that it takes a few minutes to learn the rules of the game, which are no more complicated than the cricket scoring system or the football offside rule. In fact chess is possibly the most egalitarian game on the planet, because regardless of age, race, disability, gender or weather, people can and do compete on equal terms.
>
> The only reason chess may seem elitist in the UK is that we live in an anti-intellectual culture where we tend to be suspicious of people who enjoy thinking in their spare time. But that is our loss,

because chess teaches you that taking pleasure in working things out is not the province of an intellectual elite but the birthright of everyone. Indeed (glancing over at admiring colleagues) in this very tournament we have teenage girls outwitting university professors and builders trouncing businessmen. Chess rewards skill and effort and is thoroughly meritocratic, the very opposite of elitist.

At this point in my memory stream I feel like Superman, and the interviewer turns into an Aberdonian version of Lois Lane. She smiles coquettishly and asks if we might share a rowie sometime – Aberdeen's tough and salty version of the croissant. The idea has some nostalgic allure, so I pause and blink slowly and seductively in her general direction. But then I remember why I am here, and turn towards my board and say: 'Sorry, honey, but I have some pawns to push.'

30. BEING A SUBSTITUTE

You have probably heard of emergency plumbers, but have you ever needed to call out an emergency chess player? One night in January 2012, while sharing dinner with my family, I received a phone call from International Master Andrew Greet, the manager of a team I sometimes play for in the British chess league.

The call went something like this:

'Jonathan, we have been ambushed! Guildford [our opponents the next day] have Nigel Short [former World Championship challenger], Stefanova [former women's world champion] and somebody just saw Vachier-Lagrave [France's top player] in the hotel foyer … I know you said this was a difficult weekend for you, but I was wondering if you might reconsider in the circumstances.'

Ambushed indeed. Normally our team, Wood Green, would be heavy favourites, and would not need Scottish reinforcements, but the presence of three heavyweight mercenaries made us the new underdogs. My presence would strengthen the team just a little bit, and give us a fighting chance. However, it would also mean changing family plans, neglecting my childcare duties and getting up at an indecent hour to catch a train, so I said it was unlikely, but promised to call back after speaking to Siva.

We decided I should play. It was not just that a little extra income feels valuable with a child at home, but more that I have always been very excited about matches like these. They are played over eight boards, and a great deal of thought goes into the team order prior to the game. On rating order of available players, I would have played Black on board two, which sounded challenging, so I negotiated White on board three and we adjusted our board order. Still, after several months away from chess, I went to bed in disbelief that I was being sent into battle the next day.

It turned out remarkably well. I arrived in the spirit of all good substitutes: fresh and eager, hoping to make best use of whatever time remains. I was paired against Tony Kosten, an experienced and dangerous Grandmaster but not a scary monster, and, more importantly in the circumstances, a known quantity. Andrew allowed me to use his computer to do some basic preparation, while watching a somewhat hysterical Sunday morning chat show on evidence for the existence of God. I did just enough work to know what my first move would be, and to give me something to look forward to, before discussing the bigger questions with Andrew.

In the end, I found a clear strategy that gave me a sense of early purpose. My position was not objectively great, but I felt at home with it, which is often just as important. In fact, my opponent quickly became too ambitious and lost his coordination. I responded resolutely and won easily. My game was the first to finish, and I think it helped with team morale. Despite the ambush our team ended up winning comfortably and were again favourites to win the league. Alas, that year we spoiled our chances in the final weekend, which was frustrating for our captain and sponsor, but I wonder how much it really mattered to the players.

My reflection from that experience was that chess-team players care for their team's result in a particular 'as if' way that is consistent with our care for the game more generally. Since the team competition takes place as an aggregate of individual game results rather than as a moment-to-moment coordinated effort, we are always slightly detached from the team performance, which is the setting that motivates us to play better, not really an end in itself. We need the larger team story to find our own individual sense of plot and character, so we are relatively dignified mercenaries who have learned to care about their teammates. But when we show up to give checkmate for money we are mercenaries nonetheless. This same kind of tension is baked into any commercial service transaction: you are paid for your expertise to help achieve a result, but you are also paid to feel allegiance to something other than money.[6]

31. THE IMPORTANCE OF SHAKING HANDS

Like most social rituals, we only start to think about handshakes when there is a breakdown in expectations. Masons do them cryptically with an elaborate twist and grip to communicate membership, and Scouts greet each other with their left hand, signalling courage with the hand closer to the heart that traditionally carried a shield. But mostly we offer our right hands to each other; more or less tightly, more or less fleetingly, and more or less warmly.

At a major tournament in the Netherlands in early 2008 Bulgaria's rising star Ivan Cheparinov refused to shake hands with former World Championship challenger Nigel Short before the start of their game, and this significant non-event, captured on camera and posted online, has been watched by hundreds of thousands.

This particular hand evasion mattered more than most because of a new ruling by FIDE, stating that refusing to shake hands is punishable by default; and when the chief arbiter ruled in Short's favour, he won the shortest game of his career. The decision was overturned on appeal, on the grounds that the FIDE ruling indicates Cheparinov should have been given a second chance to shake hands, after a warning by the arbiter, and this didn't transpire.

The game was replayed on the tournament rest day after a written public apology by Cheparinov. Short was grimly determined, though, and won convincingly, building on his moral victory in style. Afterwards he remarked: 'There is a God, and he is not Bulgarian.'

But why should we insist on a handshake at all? Cheparinov claimed to feel betrayed by Short, who had cast some aspersions on his manager Silvio Danailov, but this seems to miss the point. The handshake is not principally about paying respect to the opponent, but about honouring the integrity of the game. By shaking hands you consent to compete honestly and fairly, even if you feel revulsion towards your opponent, and want to crush them competitively. This sentiment tallies with the purported origins of the ritual, which were about showing your adversary that you were not armed; the little shake we do when our hands clasp may have originally been about ensuring there were no daggers hiding up our sleeves. It sounds far-fetched now, but on this reading, the handshake was a ritual of performative trust between people who had reason to distrust each other.

There is an alternative take, which is that the handshake was initiated by the seventeenth-century Quakers as a social gesture that was more egalitarian in spirit than the bow or removing one's hat, and this makes emotional sense to me. Whether I am playing an amateur or an elite Grandmaster, at the moment we shake hands I feel a sense of moral equality as a human being, even if we are about to witness a significant disparity in chess skill. There may also be a trust issue that is not merely ritualistic, but rather about socio-chemical signalling through smell. Mercifully we don't sniff each other's bums like dogs do, but if you watch the handshake closely, people invariably bring their hands back towards their body with a slight tilt upwards towards their noses, and apparently this unconscious data-collection process is key to making a quick judgment about trustworthiness. However, it is precisely because hands contain and gather so much information that handshakes are one of the worst mechanisms for spreading infectious diseases. Apparently fist bumps and high fives lead to far fewer germs spreading, but the thought of beginning a chess game with either feels somewhere between comical and sacrilegious.

Whatever its social function, the physicality of the handshake also helps prevent the possession of the mind by the game. By touching each other at the beginning and end of the contest, we ground evolved human animals within their shared and mostly peaceful social reality, which is ultimately more real than any simulacrum of war. In the context of violent intentions, the handshake says: We are both human; I know we are about to try to kill each other mentally, volitionally, emotionally, psychologically and competitively, but physically nobody will get hurt.

Refusing a handshake before the game is therefore a premeditated insult, indicating contempt of the opponent and generating enough psychological dissonance to shatter their concentration. To be obliged to shake hands therefore seems reasonable, and it makes little sense if the obligation only truly applies after a warning, because by that stage the psychological and sporting damage has been done.

And yet, if players shake hands because it is mandatory, and not as a gesture of sportsmanship, then something fundamental has been lost. Ideally we should insist on the handshake socially, without having to enforce it legally. The fear of being ostracised by the chess community could be a sufficient deterrent, but it won't always work, if only because I fear we might be too willing to forgive winners, even when they win in an unsporting manner.

And yet we don't really have a choice. When we are *forced* to do something that has value because we *choose* to do it, we denature the act. Much is lost when we turn social norms into legal rules more generally, as the politician and academic Michael Ignatieff discovered when he spent two years touring the world in search of some kind of moral unity in a globalised world. Ignatieff found that the apparent source of unity, the human rights framework, was not perceived to be a global ethic at all, but more like a liberal elite project. That may be unfair to the considerable gains made over many years by human rights campaigners, but while something is gained by having rights in law, something is lost too.

Ignatieff found that what was universal was an appreciation for 'the ordinary virtues' including generosity, compassion, forgiveness, tolerance and mercy. What seems to matter to people is that they are free to give and receive these kinds of virtues on their own terms, and not through any set of codes or rules, but based on relationships and judgment and feelings in context.

Of all Ignatieff's research on the subject of morality, the detail that made the deepest impression is that his mother was completely unsurprised by her son's findings about the ordinary virtues being more important than any totalising system of law and morality. She summed up her view with a profound statement: 'My idea of heaven is a place where all dislike is purely individual.'

32. MEN AND WOMEN

The question of how men and women differ and why it matters is too big to address comprehensively here. However, since chess is associated with intelligence, and since we struggle to speak constructively about how men and women differ in their interests and aptitudes and barriers to full participation in all aspects of life, grappling with what we know about women in chess is prismatic for the quality of our public conversation.[7]

To put the premise forthrightly, *in general* women do not appear to like chess as much as men, and do not seem to be as good. For instance, on the rating lists of most countries only 2–8 per cent of players are female, and there is rarely more than one active female player in the world top one hundred players.[8] A similar male preponderance applies in mathematics, physics and engineering too, though notably not in life sciences.

Chess players speak of the importance of 'keeping the tension' in certain positions, allowing the complexity of the position to breathe even when it is hard to handle, because we lose resources and squander opportunities if we simplify matters too quickly. The need to keep the tension applies here too. People are inclined to say 'Men are just better at X' or 'Women are more interested in Y' or 'Our brains are different' on the one hand; or 'You cannot generalise' and 'It's all socially constructed and political' on the other, all of which is *partly* true.

The overarching view I have come to is this: men and women are different, but the nature, meaning and implications of those differences should not be decided by men. Biology matters, but in a human context biology is never just biological, because what biology *means* is typically social, cultural, political and historical in nature. Facing up to that conundrum is tense, as a complex chess position is tense; it is not clear what should happen next, nor how we can simplify matters.

When I look at recent public debates by leading academics in the field, for instance between Cordelia Fine, the author of *Delusions of Gender*, who understands the neuroscience but emphasises social construction, and Simon Baron Cohen, author of *The Essential Difference*, who understands the social construction but emphasises the neuroscience, I notice that their disagreements are mostly about finer points of methodology rather than world views. Fine puts it dryly in her final word on one of their written exchanges in *The Psychologist*: 'I hope that readers are not disappointed by the remarkable de-escalation in the Battle of the Sex Differences being staged for their entertainment.'[9] Hope for a richer discussion lies in realising that the gender question is fundamentally epistemic in nature; it's about how we see, perceive and understand the world, and how diverse ways of knowing manifest in our capacity for societal flourishing or breakdown.

Getting the method and spirit of that conversation right is a formidable design challenge, because the issue is emotionally loaded and our sense of what is normal in public life has mostly been shaped by men, and that bias remains baked into our language and expectations. The task is to speak in good faith without being too worthy, to recognise power imbalances without becoming a crucible of victims and villains, and to offer insight that brings about a better integration of our public and private realms in a way that speaks to the major economic and political challenges of our time.[10]

OK, but how?

One of my favourite facilitation techniques is the controlled explosion. Everyone begins the session by articulating all the words and arguments and stories and sources of evidence that really annoy them, and which they are likely to react to emotionally. The point is to purge the fuel for reactivity in the room, in a way that helps people to speak freely and listen deeply afterwards. We need this kind of approach because most related public discussions struggle with vested interests, unconscious biases and emotional reactivity taking over. The terms we use risk sounding coercive because of how they have been interpreted and deployed in the past. 'Biological difference' is a case in point, as is 'time of the month', 'natural' and 'emotional' – all terms for which we need a controlled explosion. Getting that kind of dross out of the way is essential.

The next controlled explosion would be about disarming truisms and detoxifying terminology. Men and women are alike in more ways than they are different, and they differ within their own sexes more than between them. While 'man' and 'woman' refer to relatively uncontroversial biological differences like men having greater upper body strength and women being able to bear children, male/masculine and female/feminine refer to sociocultural judgments about corresponding qualities of heart, mind and temperament, with related social expectations that vary historically and culturally. It should be noted that much of this language is currently in flux as social discourse expands, for example by integrating transgender and non-binary individuals' reports of their experiences.

In that loaded context, William Blake's celebrated line 'to generalise is to be an idiot' sounds right, and yet, by its own definition, it is an idiotic thing to say. We need in fact to *welcome* generalisations, but always on the shared understanding that they have qualifiers and exceptions.

My offering to one of the latter controlled explosions would be to admit that women have become so fundamental to my sense of self, quality of life and political hope that if I have a bias on the question of how men and women differ it is self-consciously in favour of women. This bias might be related to my formative years. I was mostly raised by a single mother, though I never thought of her as such because she was so good at building alliances. My mum kept our home life afloat, accruing and paying off debts of necessity and tending to tragic family illnesses while succeeding professionally and staying positive. Her spirit of joyful resilience stays with me.

I would also confess that becoming a father has changed my view of gender relations. Parenting is only one sphere of life, but it is prismatic for the issue at hand. I believe the main challenge for men having children is not so much becoming a father, but becoming a better husband (or partner) to a mother. The direct relationships with your children may well be joyous, however exacting the daily tasks may be, but your relationship with your partner is changed fundamentally in ways that are not always acknowledged publicly; more precisely, as different kinds of competence become evident, power relationships alter. Every family is different, but the fate of many men is to suddenly find they are co-parents with a mother who naturally, or so it can seem, assumes the role of *primus inter pares* – 'first among equals' at home.

Having responsibility for a household with children in a school community places both parents at the mercy of events. The challenge is not so much multitasking as adapting to new kinds of questions we have to ask of a domestic ecosystem that is suddenly much more dynamic: What is there to eat? Not just for me, now, but for four of us, three times a day, for the whole week? Who needs my attention most at the moment and how can I best offer it? Should we rearrange those doctor's appointments, and how do I establish which future dates are available for us? Why hasn't the broken vacuum cleaner been collected for repair yet? Is there unfinished homework I need to know about? Should we have more coffees and arrange more play dates to keep the social pulse at school alive? What needs to be cleaned, ordered, sorted, paid, fixed or cancelled most urgently? Why is our eldest son waking up so early? And then there is a similar set of questions the next day, and so it goes on. I confess I often fail to ask such questions, but becoming a father has made me more aware of the social and emotional consequences of that failure.

Orchestrating this dynamic domestic context with grace is important and undervalued work, and it is unrelenting. Many men cannot handle the pressure and abscond one way or the other, either because they are incompetent or irresponsible, or just because they can. Women, however, are less likely to even feel that they have that option. I have spoken to many committed fathers who experience a similar realisation through co-parenting: women have qualities of heart and mind that we need more of in public and private spheres of life; those qualities are not just about multitasking but the disposition to view social, emotional and administrative responsibility as part of the main curriculum of life, rather than things to get out of the way before getting back to work or play. It is no revelation to say so, but it bears repeating: women sustain and renew the world every day with forms of skilled, unpaid labour that are taken for granted by society.[11]

With the controlled explosions out of the way, a helpful way to deepen the discussion is to think of humans as bio-psycho-socio-spiritual beings, in which distinct but related aspects of our nature are always influencing each other. To say that men and women are different is not merely to say they are biologically distinct and everything else is socially constructed, because you cannot separate those things so easily. Men and women are bio-psycho-socio-spiritually different in ways that we cannot easily discern without acknowledging and changing power relations; it's not just that the issue is complex, it's that how we describe it is charged with moral and political significance.

We are biological in the sense that our embodied minds have evolved with some species-specific needs and traits that influence how we think and what we prioritise. We have psychological depths and quirks because we are encultured over many generations, embedded in webs of value, meaning and purpose that transcend conscious reasoning and shape automatic behaviour. We are also deeply social, having evolved through and for social cooperation within small groups, and we are always influenced by relationships of some kind, including technologies that increasingly define and shape social life. And we are also ensouled, at least in the sense outlined by the atheist neuroscientist Nicholas Humphrey, who argues that humans live in 'the soul niche', where niche is an ecological term – the environment to which we are adapted: 'Trout live in rivers, gorillas in forests, bedbugs in beds. Humans live in soul land.' Humphrey adds that 'soul land' is a territory of the spirit, and that this is not only where humans live, but also where they give of their best.

With this fuller context, we can return to how the gender issue plays out in the chess world. From a bio-psycho-social-spiritual perspective the notion that women's lower aptitude for chess is *just* biological ceases to make sense, but the claim that biology is not relevant at all looks equally foolish.[12]

The contention that women are psychologically not as well suited to chess also feels mostly false. Perhaps the main counterpoint is Hungary's Judit Polgar, who has defeated world champions and was ranked eighth in the world in 2005. Her example alone makes it look unlikely that there is any insuperable barrier to a woman being the best human player. That said, there is some lateral corroborating evidence to support the *possibility* that there are psychological differences in play. For instance, while men and women have the same average levels of IQ, there is greater variation in distributions in men. The psychometric measure of IQ is 'what the tests test' rather than reflecting the fuller societal notion of intelligence, but on this specific measure men are slightly more likely both to be intellectually challenged and more intellectually advanced; this *could* be obliquely relevant to male dominance at the highest levels of chess. Other lateral findings include men generally having greater spatial orientation, which might have some relevance to chess, as might relatively high levels of aggression.[13] While some would view such findings as indicative, they could also be seen as overinterpreted, and they don't prove anything decisive in the context.[14]

The sociological explanation for gender differences in chess is more compelling but less than fully convincing. Male dominance emerged for historical reasons relating to who was encouraged to participate in social activities like chess, and then perpetuated itself through a vicious cycle of exclusion in which the lack of female players created a relatively unwelcoming culture for them, which was then reinforced by gender stereotypes and expectations. Due to these effects, the pool of talent became much smaller in early adolescence, as women felt relatively isolated and found other interests, and then statistically the chances of rising to the top were diminished.

This sociological account implies that, given the opportunity and with the culture changing accordingly, women would play as much as men and become as good. That idea chimes with a formidable body of research by the neuroscientist Lise Eliot showing how imperceptible differences between boys and girls become larger and entrenched through cultural reinforcement, when they might be eliminated entirely if cultural expectations were different.[15]

If that were the whole truth, we would expect rating gaps to reduce as participation increases, and we don't find that. Moreover, even if you consider a country like Georgia, where women's chess is culturally valued and their participation is around 30 per cent of the total, you still don't find the gaps in ability closing. [16] No doubt boys are supported and encouraged to play chess in ways that girls are not, but it looks like the game does not hold the same degree of interest, with the same amount of intensity, for reasons that are not merely sociological. Perhaps the most pertinent question ever asked on this matter came from the anthropologist Margaret Mead: 'Women could be just as good as men at chess, but why would they want to be?'[17]

Chess takes a lot of time and energy for uncertain rewards. To get really good at chess you have to really care about the game, often to the exclusion of other things. And the question we don't ask enough is: Why should you care? As George Steiner wrote, the enigma of chess is that it is both 'fundamentally insignificant and enormously meaningful'. It is in these terms that I interpret Mead's question: women *could* be just as good at chess as men, if they were willing to suspend their disbelief about what really matters. That they may be less inclined than men to do so could suggest that, from a bio-psycho perspective, men may be *relatively* predisposed to seek out meaning in the game of chess, while from a socio-spiritual perspective women may be relatively predisposed not to, perhaps because they have a superior grasp of its ultimate insignificance.

If this exegesis on women in chess seems elaborate, it is worth remembering what is at stake. Sexism is brutal and endemic in some places and subtle and pervasive in others. Unequal participation and achievement in chess is a small example within a much larger phenomenon that includes unequal opportunity and pay in the developed world, unequal access to education in the global south, and that's before we mention widespread domestic violence and rape as a weapon of war. Any apparently innocent conversation about gender roles carries the heat and weight of those kinds of structural and actual violence, and any constructive conversation has to both address and transcend them. We need a more effective integration of our public and private realms and roles. As women and men begin to be able to talk about their differences in aptitude without coercion and with light rather than heat, our social norms could start to shift, including patterns of status, achievement and cultural reinforcement at a time when we need to move beyond status-seeking competition as our pre-eminent value.[18]

Getting this conversation right might be pivotal to how we reimagine society in a time of ecological crisis, where we need to adapt and transform our ways of living and knowing to survive. In that context, making better sense of the real rather than presumed differences between men and women is not just a parlour game; it is a new frontier for civilisation.[19]

FIVE

Cyborgs and Civilians

Algorithms are puppeteers

There is a story of Mahatma Gandhi boarding a train that had just started to pick up speed. When one of his sandals fell off in the process of embarking, he instinctively removed the other one and threw it down, so that somebody else would find them, and have a pair to wear. No despair at the loss, no befuddlement, just a clear action grounded in compassion for a person in need whom he had not yet met. Many of us might see the wisdom in the act, but only several moments later when it would be too late.

My Ph.D. thesis was a sustained reflection on what we can learn from that kind of story, of which there are many. The aim was to consider wisdom not as a folksy construct relating to sage advice, but rather to try to understand how we might better become ready, willing and able to help others in complex or charged situations. Most doctorates have a clear, narrow and specific research question within a single discipline, but I had no appetite for that. Through chess I had already tasted domain-specific expertise and shared it widely in writing; and what I really wanted to understand was the broad transdisciplinary question of what it means to become wiser. The thesis involved lots of reading and conceptual wrestling, and trying to make sense – partly through my own meditation efforts – of what exactly is supposed to transform through spiritual practice. In the end my examiners were satisfied. My main supervisor, Professor Guy Claxton, remarked that while he had hoped my thesis would become more like a carefully curated wedding cake, he was happy that I had produced such a delicious bowl of spaghetti.[1]

In the summer of 2008, I was a few months from finishing the thesis. As fellow doctoral survivors will know, it's not easy to write between 80,000 and 100,000 coherent words that represent something resembling a contribution to knowledge. But I was in the home straight, and had set 5 November 2008 as my delivery date, partly because this was the day Barack Obama was expected to be elected the first African American president. I figured if I was going to be distracted by the political drama of the time – which I was – I should also be motivated by it. I was not yet aware that I would be a father the following year, but it was in that life context of beginning to detach from the chess world that I had the privilege of helping world champion Viswanathan Anand prepare for his match with Vladimir Kramnik.

Kramnik is figuratively and literally a Russian giant who dethroned Gary Kasparov after his twenty years at the top. Anand won the official World Championship in a tournament format around the same time, but years of tedious chess politics meant that these two players had never met in a match. When it became clear that the chess world was going to get the contest it wanted, I offered my services to Anand. I was a strong middleweight Grandmaster rather than a heavyweight, but analytical help is about more than chess strength. Unlike many hired guns, I had some lateral perspectives on chess, an easy rapport with Vishy, and I genuinely wanted him to win. The plan was to offer a few opening ideas for him to develop and some speculative psychological insight for him to ignore.

I was also eager to participate in preparation at the very highest level. I had no experience of World Championship preparation, but I had read descriptions of other matches from the seventies, eighties and nineties. Most of those matches were in pre-computer or early computer days, and what I assumed might be a slight shift in emphasis was much more fundamental. I imagined that the training would be part over-the-board analysis session, part inquiry into the psychodynamics of competition, and part *Rocky IV* training montage, where Sylvester Stallone lifts huge blocks of wood and runs through the snow. I expected the training to be roughly 20 per cent physical, 20 per cent psychological, 30 per cent joint analysis over the board and 30 per cent on the computer.

In fact, the work was about 95 per cent on the computer, and virtually all of that time was spent trying to help Vishy form new ways of achieving good positions in the opening phase of the game. Just as finding a needle in a haystack is easy, if you have a metal detector, finding an important new chess move is easy, if you have the right software. Analysis engines can give an immediate numerical assessment of what is happening in a position, including which move is best, who is better placed and by how much. These engines are our guide, and Grandmasters are like knowledgeable and eager tourists, asking informed questions to yield unconventional insight.

The camp, as chess players call their training venues, was Vishy's main European base, a smallish two-bedroom apartment just outside Frankfurt in Germany. The only sign of chess as such was a half-forgotten set on a coffee table near the window. I was accompanied by the Danish Grandmaster Peter Heine Nielsen – Vishy's long-term adviser, now working for Magnus Carlsen, and the former FIDE world champion Rustam Kasimdzhanov, who hails from Uzbekistan but had been resident in Germany for several years. The three of us got on well and stayed at a nearby hotel.

In general the morale of the group was high, and during breaks we watched comedy clips on YouTube. On most days there was a group jog in the morning including some steep stairs, but it was a little ad hoc, and then there were some musings about match strategy over lunch, which we usually ate in a Thai restaurant about ten minutes away. *The work* however, happened as the four of us sat around the same table in our own worlds for several hours in a dimly lit room late into the night. The scene was like a Silicon Valley incubator house: humanoids with transfixed faces lit by the glow of computer screens. Onlookers would not have been able to guess what we were doing in that room.

We typically listened to Coldplay from Peter's computer, a benign cheering hum with occasional blasts of euphoria, which grew on me. I introduced the Israeli vocalist Yael Naim to Kasim's delight, though Vishy protested when I tried to play Tracy Chapman for the second time. I made just enough warm drinks for the team to remind ourselves we had bodies, but stopped short of being a *chaiwala*. I noticed that at the end of each day Vishy would eagerly go to the kitchen to clean up and thereby unwind from the chess and his computer screen, which I came to realise were more or less the same thing for him.

Mostly we followed the best ideas according to the analysis engines with what Vishy joked was 'space-bar preparation' – when the analysis engines are synchronised with the position you are navigating, rather than move the pieces on the screen with your mouse, you press the space bar to keep the engine going down the line it deems to be most accurate for both sides, while watching it unfold on the position on the screen. It is a kind of thinking, I suppose.

You do pause occasionally to consider alternatives the computer might have mis-assessed. Humans are much weaker than computers now in general, but they operate differently, so you develop a feeling for where the computer's evaluation function (who has the better position, by how much) or horizon (how far ahead it looks) might not capture something a Grandmaster can. Periodically you add a little textual comment for the next person who may build on your work and then email the analysis to the group.

We did debate contentious ideas and assessments of particular positions over the table, but mostly this was a prelude to stress-testing ideas in more depth with the computer. We would go back and try a range of plausible ideas and watch to see if the evaluation changed; a signal to look further for hidden details. At one point, feeling frustrated with my inability to make a dent on a particularly solid line, I got up to consider an idea on the actual chess set at the far end of the room under the main window. I remember Peter smiling at me sympathetically but also incredulously, as if to say: 'If only it were that easy.'

Preparing with a world champion for a World Championship match was precious to me not because it was extraordinary but because it was mundane. I saw the grind behind the glory. I witnessed the monotonous practice that precedes the magical performance. I was there when the groceries were bought and the dishes were washed. There was no heightened drama, just slow-burning determination, gentle discipline and professional friendship. The experience was precious in the way that going on a pilgrimage or running a marathon can be precious. It was a short pause in everyday existence, and a memorable plunge into another stream of life.

As for my contribution, I'm fairly sure I did not do any harm, and may even have helped a little. Vishy won the match decisively, not least because the team as a whole (which included some other Grandmasters from India and Poland) succeeded over several months in developing a completely new repertoire for Vishy as White, based on a different first move – 1.d4 rather than 1.e4; the queen's pawn two squares forward rather than the king's pawn. That small difference entirely changes the nature of the game, creating different pawn structures calling for different strategies, and circumventing much of the opponent's preparation. An analogy would be a tennis player going into training for several months and emerging capable of serving well with either hand; a capability he only reveals in the final match against an unsuspecting opponent.

We succeeded in keeping that crucial first-move surprise a secret on the basis of personal trust, without any heavy-handed non-disclosure agreements, which is impressive given the high stakes. It was also clear to me that Vishy is impressively organised, and manages to generate an arsenal of chess information that is codified, relevant and valuable. So I was transfixed and impressed, and intrigued by the whole process. But at a professional level I was more alienated than inspired. This screen and data-intensive process was not chess as I have come to know and love it. It felt like work and it felt like the future, but not, I hoped, my work, or my future.

To give an illustration of how far the experience deviated from my expectations, I was in two minds about whether even to bring my computer to the training (a basic Sony Vaio laptop I had used for years). Very soon after arrival, before a pawn had been pushed, Vishy asked me: 'How many cores do you have, Jon?' (I prefer being called Jonathan, but had never told him this.)

'Oh, I'm not sure,' I said, which was clearly not a reassuring answer. Vishy talked me through finding the relevant details on my computer. When he saw it on my screen he paused ruefully and said: 'Oh, Jon has only one core.' Kasim and Peter looked at each other, a little troubled. I had no idea what was going on, but it was as if I had arrived at the border to a new country, only to learn that my passport was not valid.

Vishy looked mildly ruffled but said it did not matter, because it was possible to connect to online analysis engines – a mysterious notion at the time because I had never done that before, but it was a source of hope too. Alas, I then had painfully mundane problems relating to getting the wi-fi to work, and realised I was slowing the team down. I maintained a professional face, but inwardly I was approaching one of those childlike moments of absolute humiliation.

Mercifully, everything was soon sorted, and it was like finding water in the desert. For the first time I started looking at positions with a four-core analysis engine (which, at the time of writing a decade later, would be considered pretty slow). Your cores are about your processing power, and speed matters because it saves a lot of analytical time. The faster the engine the quicker it can search ahead and determine which lines are good and bad before you get there manually. That filter helpfully narrows your own search process down to only those lines that are worth pursuing, and before you know it you can tell which opening lines are critical and ripe for analysis, and which are in some sense solved. That's important for the team because you can all trust each other to be looking at lines that matter; you know that if you're asked a question about a position it won't be a waste of time. Tactical details that arise almost by force several moves downstream are often hard to see coming for a human, but they are spotted almost instantly by the computer, changing the evaluation of that line before you need to explore it. It was only because I was literally up to speed with the others that I could enjoy several productive days at the camp. But I will never forget that feeling of being an analogue creature, floundering in a digital world.

33. HUMAN ERROR

Those who *enjoy* being humiliated by artificial intelligence might like to know that modern chess-analysis engines have witty names like Houdini, Stockfish, Fritz, Komodo, Rybka and Shredder. These engines will not only beat you mercilessly, but talk to you while they are doing it.

For those who associate chess with carbon life forms pushing wood, the dominance of these silicon monsters might come as a bit of a shock. To give an indication of their role, almost every active player in the world now uses them to analyse positions, and it would feel irresponsible for me to annotate games for an audience without consulting an engine first (although I sometimes do it anyway, on request).

Some consider the chess strength of these machines depressing, and a further indication, as if we needed one, that humans are not as intelligent as we like to think. However, we should reflect on the fact that these machines are slaves to their algorithms, designed by us for our own entertainment. You may not like losing to them, but they do not enjoy beating you. They compute rather than *think*, and do not even know that they are playing chess. If these thoughts don't console you, you can always outsmart the computer by turning it off.

Humans are good at many things, but one of the things we are best at is designing machines that are better than us at one thing in particular. The advantage humans have over machines is not cognition, it is consciousness. Unlike the literally senseless algorithm, we can experience the excitement of thinking, the enchantment of beautiful geometries, the buzz of competition, and offer the game our unrequited love.

When Deep Blue beat the reigning world champion Gary Kasparov in 1997 I was in my first year at Oxford, and since I was 'the chess guy', everybody kept asking what I thought about the news. Naively in hindsight, I kept saying that the result was an anomaly and that Kasparov would probably win a rematch. In fact, the computer's emerging supremacy was such that within a decade it became obvious that human–machine matches would soon be a waste of time.

Around 2006 was the last time humans could give a dignified account of themselves against the best computers. World champion Vladimir Kramnik played a six-game match with Deep Fritz in Germany, and showed that it was still possible to 'outplay' the machines, but that actually beating them was another story. The essence of the challenge was that while computers would make imperceptible errors that you have to work very hard to exploit, they no longer made really huge blunders, as even the very best humans still do.

These days we no longer even expect the best players to out-think the computers strategically, never mind beat them. There is almost nothing we humans can do on the board to any competitive effect that a good programmer with a Grandmaster consultant can't help the computer to do too.

Back in 2006 there were two moves that summed up the tragicomedy of humans trying to defeat the machines. Against the course of play, Deep Fritz suddenly threatened checkmate, but this was missed by Kramnik because it was almost incidental, based on an unfamiliar pattern in which a knight supported the queen giving check, but from a square where you would not typically expect it to fulfil that function. During a game, we can never see positions without prejudice, literally without prejudging in some way. In this case Kramnik's perception was coloured by familiar patterns and events from earlier in the game. The knight in question had travelled far, dealing with unrelated issues in different sectors until it found itself capturing a rook, normally the highlight of a knight's career, except in doing so it incidentally controlled a decisively important square.

Kramnik had played very well until this point, and probably thought he could now create a winning endgame by force. He would have been caught up in his own exquisite narrative of events, peppered with concepts like outside passed pawn, bishop versus knight, back rank, queen exchange, so he played his well-motivated move confidently, picked up his cup and headed towards his designated rest room. Thousands of humans watching live online were completely aghast, because they could see what had happened.

In response, the computer silently registered the input. There was no shock, no body language, just an abrupt change in evaluation.

Checkmate.[2]

I had used a computer to prepare and to analyse my games since about 1997 – already quite late – but I had never really identified with computer preparation, nor did I see it as an integral part of the game. For most elite Grandmasters however, it is as if half their brains are in their laptops. Chess, like the world at large, is now an increasingly blurry combination of human and machine.

Like many, I do what I can to stay technologically competent, but I miss the analogue world. I miss the centrality of the wooden board and pieces, the authority of the books, the pioneer experience of creating what appeared to be new knowledge, and the humility of rarely being absolutely sure of anything. Chess is not what it used to be, but then neither are humans.

The cognitive scientist Andy Clark describes humans as 'natural-born cyborgs'. Most of us are not literally cyborgs because cybernetic organisms have mechanical and biological parts, but we live in the early days of wearable and immersive technology, virtual reality, big data and deep learning, and having digital chips inserted to measure bodily functions is no longer science fiction.

The boundaries between organism and machine are increasingly blurred, which poses questions about many things, not least the nature of human identity and creativity in a world saturated with data and algorithms. Clark asks us to see ourselves as cyborg systems, in which the boundaries of the self include the systems we use. On an extreme version of this view, a hard-drive crash is comparable in its impact on our normal functioning to having a mild stroke.

How do we make sense of this liminal predicament? On the one hand I feel the need to honour and protect the analogue with a few pen portraits below of particular people whom I have come to admire, but I also recognise that the digital is not only here to stay, but is also inexorably changing the world, and not necessarily for the better. President George W. Bush once said, 'I know the human being and fish can coexist peacefully,' and one would certainly hope so, but when it comes to how technology functions in our world, I am not so sure.

Technology is not all lights and gadgets. The word stems from the Greek *tekhnologia* – systematic treatment of an art, craft or technique. There are 'technologies of the self', described by the French theorist Michel Foucault, and most technological change is actually socio-technological in the sense that technology shapes and is shaped by particular kinds of human uptake. In this respect the defining theme of this chapter was initially going to be 'The muse loves the machine'.

I was charmed by the idea that what chess had taught me about the technology–human interface is that the creative, poetic and transcendent parts of ourselves might not merely make peace with the algorithmic and data-driven direction of society, but actually learn to love it. The contention was that we might become more deeply creative and psychologically integrated if we accept that we have always been cyborgs of sorts (a stick is a *natural* object and *mechanical* tool) and we could therefore learn to trust technology as a humanising force. One particularly beautiful game made me feel this way.

34. THE AESTHETICS OF CYBORGS

If you could know how and when you will die, would you choose to? In many stories protagonists who have gleaned the details of their own demise gain courage in dark situations from knowing that their time has not yet come. Perhaps to wake up to the precious time we have, it is not enough to know that we will die at some indefinite point in the future; perhaps knowing the moment of our death would have some added value, making it easier to live without fear or anxiety.

Alas, unless we believe in prophecy, or have dabbled in just enough philosophy of physics to think the future may already have happened, we are unlikely to have such self-knowledge. However, there are many similar forms of knowledge that are based on the past rather than the future, whereby we know from memory that we thought or felt something, but can't always remember why. This is also a kind of liberation, because it channels our attention in a particular direction.

The simple compass reflects this profound truth. If you know one thing, which way is north, you can piece together the other things you have to know to get to wherever you have to go. This is also why detectives pay attention to tiny details. Sometimes a small piece of knowledge leads inexorably to a vision of how all the other pieces fit together.

Chess Grandmasters now have a similar experience on a regular basis. Quite often we have prepared a particular opening several months previously, checked the findings with a reliable computer and established a conclusion about which lines are good or bad. Such processes help you at the board even if you only remember the conclusion, not how you reached it.

Knowing what the conclusion is makes it much easier to find the supporting arguments. Alas, in real life this fact is abused by many, politicians included, who are often guilty of what is known as 'confirmation bias' – not balancing arguments to establish the truth but selectively choosing arguments to support a preconceived decision.

In chess, we have to be more objective, and knowing the evaluation of a line is now one of the main fruits of preparation, allowing you to remember or even recreate the details at the board. In January 2013, in a spellbinding tactical masterpiece that is one of Vishy Anand's finest-ever games, the world champion was relying on home preparation, but he remembered or recreated the powerful moves himself at the board, buoyed by the confidence that he knew they were there to be found. You might call it a *cyborg aesthetic* in that the game required human and machine intelligence, and personally I think it was no less beautiful as a result.[3]

On reflection though, the message that the muse loves the machine does not ring entirely true, because the muse fears the machine too. Humans can make use of computer technology to be more creative, and solve problems, but that is not the whole story because it is silent on questions of power and influence, of unknowable observers and unconscious manipulation. The techno-optimist talks of solving problems, but often forgets to ask: Whose solutions? Whose problems?

In a Dublin youth hostel in 1992 I spent a few hours analysing an adjourned position with a young Englishman, Demis Hassabis, who seemed like any other teenager at the time. I was fifteen and he was a year older, though I knew he had been a chess prodigy. Adjournments rarely happen these days, but back when people were less busy, we would often pause games on one day and start them again on another. In this case Demis had an extra pawn, but it was difficult to convert because it was doubled and his opponent's queen was so active. I am not sure why a Scottish player was helping an English player in a team competition, even when his opponent was German, but I think we both just found the intellectual challenge intriguing. We spent a couple of hours at least trying to conjure a breakthrough with various elaborate schemes, but without success. The position was drawn, and Demis could not make any use of the work we did together the next day.[4]

In 1992 the internet was barely known as an idea, Google did not exist and even the best chess computers made elementary errors. I did not stay in touch with Demis, but he clearly spent the next few years well. He did not forfeit any time becoming a titled chess player of any kind, though he almost certainly could have. Instead he turned his aptitude for games into a passion for gaming, studied what he needed to know about the brain to grasp some of the finer details of memory, thinking and learning, and he is now a millionaire doing fascinating work as CEO of Deep Mind, which is owned by Google and at the frontier of research into artificial intelligence. In December 2017 Alpha Zero, a game-playing artificial intelligence created by Deep Mind, took computer chess to an entirely new level.

Alpha Zero taught itself from only the basic rules using a process called 'the general reinforcement learning algorithm' and defeated the best existing chess engine of the day – Stockfish 8. Alpha Zero became the strongest chess entity in the world from scratch not by using masses of data or through Grandmaster input, as had been the case with computer chess until then, but just by using an algorithm designed to help the program learn from its own games against other engines; the program kept playing opponents at a similar level to optimise learning opportunities and progressed step by step. If you have a way to connect results to changing evaluations to choices of moves and then you can play millions of times and learn something from every single game, you can quickly know what you need to know to play brilliant chess.

The newspapers reported breathlessly that Alpha Zero had taken only a few hours to go from knowing nothing about chess to being the strongest program in the world. In some places four hours was quoted, in others nine or twenty-four, and the reason the numbers vary is that the hours are not really the relevant variable. Deep Mind used 5,000 gizmos known as tensor-processing units (TPUs) which are specifically designed to accelerate neural network learning machines like Alpha Zero. With that processing power they quickly generated the millions of games that were 'digested' and evaluated so rapidly. Then they used sixty-four slightly different TPUs to further train the neural networks. When you realise that multiple learning systems were running in parallel, the rapid ascent from zero to world-beating within a day is still extraordinary, but less unnerving.

As the old puzzles put it, if it takes one man a hundred hours to build a wall, how long will it take a hundred men? Or to use a more appropriate analogy, if you heard of someone who could juggle twenty-four balls without dropping any, you would not believe it, unless it turned out to be a particularly agile octopus with the requisite breathing apparatus and impeccable tentacle-to-eye coordination.

Some of Alpha Zero's games were mesmerising. Concepts describing thought processes are anthropomorphic, but Alpha Zero has what looks like ferocious attacking instincts combined with unnervingly deep positional understanding. In one game the program sacrificed an important pawn, what we call 'a protected passed pawn' because it has real chances of being promoted later but remains protected by its brethren pawns. That sacrifice was so long-term that even Vishy told me he was shocked by it. Demis himself described Alpha Zero's style as 'Alien … like chess from another dimension'.

When considering critiques of technology there is a risk of confusing pertinent political awareness with reflex technophobia. I don't know exactly what is happening inside technology companies like Deep Mind, and I am sure there are many people there, including Demis, who believe technology can and should be a force for societal good. It is a complicated picture though, because technology companies work on different things for different reasons, and there are so many imbalances of power and information and technological unpredictability that we cannot be sure that even the best of intentions will lead to good outcomes. The challenge is not just that the technology is not always under control, but some of it is so opaque even to its own designers that the very idea of control becomes fanciful. The law of unintended consequences holds sway.

As Frank Pasquale puts it in the book *The Black Box Society*: 'We have given the search sector an almost unimaginable power to determine what we see, where we spend, how we perceive.' When we think about the impact of technology in general terms the biggest question to ask of any given product or service is not therefore how interesting it is, but rather: who owns this, what do they want from it, and what kind of person does it want and need me to be?

Gary Kasparov fell into precisely this trap in his 1997 match with Deep Blue. The strongest player in the world was excited about the scientific experiment and the drama of the human encounter with the machine, but IBM, who owned Deep Blue, were squarely focused on winning, and rewarded with a massive increase in their stock price when they did. Even in his recent book *Deep Thinking* I don't think Kasparov has grasped what really happened, perhaps because doing so would be too dissonant with his broadly libertarian and capitalistic sensibilities. As I argued in my review of that book, the main lesson from the match was the one Kasparov didn't seem to want to learn, but humanity should: commercial interests and the public good are by no means always aligned.[5]

One of the biggest challenges of the twenty-first century is how to deal with the fact that private actors now control the public realm. We have seen the effects of how social media, psychological profiling based on data analysis, targeting messaging and network effects can directly lead to surprising and often unwelcome political outcomes. We also know that our attention is fractured by updates, messages and notifications like never before. We have gained much, but we have to remember what we risk losing.

What follows was first written long before iPhones and MacBooks were ubiquitous. It feels dated because it is dated, but it's a useful nostalgia trip. There was a time when it was not self-evident that computers would overtake humans at chess, and much else besides.

35. SIMPLICITY IS NOT SIMPLISTIC

If you were paying attention in the UK in 2007 you would have noticed ads for Macintosh computers, where Macs were presented as the cool, user-friendly alternative to virus-prone, cluttered PCs.

Back then I thought that Macs were somehow quaint and outdated, and that people who used them just had awkward contrarian temperaments. But then my wife bought one, and

I quickly sensed that there was a higher form of intelligence in the home. Or rather, another one.

Macs are simple by design. They are not simple as noughts and crosses is simple, but more in the way that $E=MC^2$ is simple – vast complexity reduced to a few simple operations. Using a PC, you get used to highly counter-intuitive ways of computing, and second-guessing tortured logic.

With Macs, you can do so much so easily that you come to understand why the American polymath and poet Oliver Wendell Holmes said: 'I would not give a fig for simplicity on this side of complexity, but I would give my life for the simplicity on the other side.'

Still, I am not a total convert because Chessbase, the dominant chess software company, does not cater for Macs, and there are still some things that a chess player can only do on a PC. Moreover, although I am no longer Macophobic there are times when it leaves me feeling lost, or yearning for a right click. At such moments my wife tells me that Mac is too clever for me, or worse, that it just doesn't like me. I was therefore delighted to recall my encounter with the Mac's built-in chess program back in 2007.

Given that the program was built for a general audience, I imagined it would not be as strong as the best analysis engines of the day, but every part of a Mac is clever, so I knew I would have to muster all my anti-computer wiles to 'earn its respect'. My task was not made any easier by the sneaking suspicion that my wife, who watched the game so eagerly, wanted me to lose. That wish was part of an in-joke of me and the Mac not being compatible, because while my wife 'got it', being oh so intuitive and intelligent, I could not possibly be worthy, being oh so clunky and conventional.

As it turned out, I mercilessly crushed the machine. And not with a hammer. I made a deft positional pawn sacrifice which gave me complete strategic control of the game, then I patiently manoeuvred and ganged up on its weak pawns, which I gradually picked off. It was vintage anti-computer chess from another era.

With a vanquished Mac and a tempered wife, for that moment, and perhaps that moment alone, I was master in my own home.

I share all this now mostly for nostalgic reasons. I am part of the generation for whom computer supremacy was neither a given, nor a foregone conclusion. We were genuinely unsure for a long time whether computers could 'think' with the sophistication of Grandmasters. They can, and do, albeit differently, and they often make us look pretty stupid these days. Which is what made that gratuitous domestic victory so sweet, and worth sharing with posterity.[6]

If one problem with modern technology is ownership, another is speed. Technology used to change between generations – for instance vinyl records were gradually replaced with CDs which were gradually replaced with digital music, but now technology is changing within generations, with significant developments sometimes occurring within the same year. While some technologies remain remarkably similar – aeroplanes have barely changed in decades for instance – many are changing so fast that we are losing our sense of being able to understand and control the world around us. And there are dizzying emergent properties when technologies combine; for instance if and when artificial intelligence, synthetic biology, virtual reality, robotics and quantum computing get together, I don't think I really want to be there, if only because life as we know it will be in question.

The Swiss playwright Max Frisch described technology as 'the knack of arranging the world so we need not experience it'. At first blush that sounds amusing, but it has a sinister edge. We are all at risk of what the philosopher Langdon Winner refers to as 'technological somnambulism', whereby we become tools of our tools, in that they start to shape our behaviour to such an extent that we are effectively sleepwalking. The source of the risk that we will be put to sleep and stay there is not technology as such, however, it is algorithms.

In his book about the near future *Homo Deus*, Yuval Noah Harari contends that 'algorithm' is arguably the single most important concept in our world. He defines an algorithm as a methodological set of steps that can be used to make calculations, resolve problems and reach decisions – it is not the calculation as such, but the method followed to reach the calculation. Harari adds the twist that organisms are algorithms; in our sensing and feeling even humans are effectively algorithms with methods for the calculation of odds relating to our survival and interests.[7]

I am not so sure. I don't think it makes sense to think of humans as algorithms as such. We appear to have consciousness and free will that is constrained but not determined, and we can write our own code, change our methods and thereby change our calculations. If we are algorithms, we are reflexive algorithms where causes and effects influence each other in unpredictable ways, which is not really an algorithm at all. However, our lives are increasingly intertwined with algorithms, including codes that turn data into options that are so finely attuned to our algorithm-*like* automatic behaviour that we stop thinking altogether.

Many don't see this kind of development as problematic, because it can free up mental energy for more interesting work. If I walk into a room and it already knows I want to turn the lights on and open a window, and it does it for me, isn't that a good thing? Maybe. Maybe not, because it inures us to our loss of agency. It is a certainly a risky thing, because algorithms don't merely take care of simple automatic behaviours but increasingly structure our choice architectures (framing what our options are in ways that make some more likely) and shape political and economic outcomes. The algorithms may at first be created by humans, but they increasingly learn and update themselves. That kind of machine learning is a scarier prospect than most people realise. Unlike human learning, which is slow to spread, when one machine learns something, everything sharing the same code learns it immediately as well.

My experience helping a world champion prepare gave me direct experience of how algorithms could gradually take over. The threat is not that computers will become conscious and some kind of superintelligence will emerge and destroy humanity – though that possibility is real. The more credible threat is that our imaginative capacity will shrink because the algorithms will keep presenting us with our own hall of mirrors and we'll forget there is a world beyond our own techno-social algorithmic echo chamber. That is why I refer to algorithms as puppeteers, with ourselves often acting like unwitting puppets. The algorithms themselves may not have any ill will or even any particular strategy, but as we become increasingly subject to what they decide we should look at or hear, we will have to fight to remain free.

We should remember *Pinocchio*, Carlo Collodi's tale of the misbehaving wooden puppet who wanted more than anything else to be a real boy. The marionette had to shake off his original 'algorithm' to become free. Although basically good by design, he was highly suggestible to bad influences, lacked self-control and had a tendency to lie that made his wooden nose grow longer. It became clear to him that if he was ever going to become a boy he had to grow wiser, better and kinder than his previous self to do so; his main challenges were to work, be good and to study. By doing so, rather than cause his father problems, Pinocchio begins to provide for him, becomes of service and transforms himself into a real boy as a result.

Looking back on the formative experience of World Championship preparation, I can't help but think of sitting in a dimly lit room pressing the space bar as a kind of virtual reality, and a form of bondage rather than freedom, no matter how fascinating the developments we were witnessing on the screen. Whether the algorithm is a chess-evaluation function, a targeted commercial advert or a selected political message, we risk becoming somebody else's puppet, unless we can become our own puppeteers. As creatures of habit, we are vulnerable to manipulation, but as autonomous agents we can, in principle at least, become our own puppeteers, at least often enough to feel like we are a puppet of our own choosing. Like Pinocchio, we may have to choose a particular kind of freedom rather than merely doing whatever we want to, but we can transcend the algorithms that shape our lives.

36. PULLING THE STRINGS

Who is pulling the strings? In politics we cannot always see the true source of power behind political actors, and we do not always want to. Yet sometimes we end up suspecting something, or perhaps even knowing it, but not really being allowed to act as if we know. Few things are as socially complex as an open secret. When you're surrounded by people who share knowledge of an important fact, but also understand that nobody can speak about it safely, you have little choice but to develop code words to communicate.

At the Chess Olympiad in Yerevan, Armenia, in 1996, I was only nineteen years old, and for most purposes a grown-up, but I remember one evening I felt distinctly out of my depth. I had never been very interested in chess politics, but it always looked like a mess: the top players never seemed happy, there were breakaway organisations and widespread allegations of corruption. So when an entirely new figure appeared on the scene promising to bring lots of money to the game and sort everything out, chess players were keen to hear more. That figure was a then thirty-four-year-old charismatic Buddhist millionaire with political connections in Russia. He was already president of the relatively underdeveloped Russian Republic of Kalmykia, and in his campaign to become president of that region he had promised 'A mobile phone for every shepherd'.

One night after dinner the Scottish contingent of twelve players and officials had an appointment to meet this new candidate for the FIDE presidency, Kirsan Ilyumzhinov. He was surrounded by what looked distinctly like a crew of bodyguards, and while my memory may be embellishing based on my feelings at the time, I think they may have been armed. In any case there we were, in a large hotel conference room with all the trappings of power, in effect being lobbied for the single vote of our federation. There was no direct request, just a general get-to-know-you schmooze fest. He gave each of us gift bags including caviar and vodka and a comic book about his own life story; honest gifts perhaps, and by no means a bribe, but conceivably a step in that direction. I threw out the book because it was so clearly propaganda, and I don't remember eating the caviar, but I still have the vodka unopened at home, waiting for the right moment to drink it. I don't know how Scotland voted that year, but I know that meeting made it more likely we would at least consider Kirsan. With hindsight it was a model of how political influence in any domain operates: a seductive combination of charisma, charm, hope, fear and promises. In theory our federation held the power, but in that room it felt a lot like Kirsan was pulling the strings. A few days later he was elected as FIDE president by a landslide and remained in power for more than two decades.

Malcolm Pein is a very different kind of political operator, but he is an influential and respected figure in the chess world. As well as being a competent player and successful businessman he is a columnist for the *Daily Telegraph*, organiser of the London Chess Classic, one of the most prestigious events in the world, and as indicated previously, he is director of the flourishing Chess in Schools and Communities charity. He also has a wicked sense of humour, and something resembling 'the common touch', which is invaluable for a game often wrongly perceived to be elitist.

In the summer of 2013 I was glad to see Malcolm interviewed in the world's pre-eminent chess magazine, *New in Chess*, and particularly struck by his answer to the question: 'If you could change one thing in the chess world, what would it be?' Malcolm's answer was: 'The Muppet.'

Not just any old Kermit, but *the* Muppet. Somebody in Malcolm's position could not affirm the fact, but I suspect he was referring to Kirsan Ilyumzhinov. Kirsan had long since been the main barrier to chess getting the kind of profile it deserves. If he merely spoke of being abducted by aliens we might have found him charmingly eccentric, but when he also made a virtue of extending friendship through chess to Colonel Gaddafi, Saddam Hussein and other notorious autocrats, we simply could not attract the kinds of sponsorship our game would otherwise warrant. To illustrate, I know a former senior executive at a major global bank who loves chess, and would gladly have made the internal case to give significant support to it, but he told me that Kirsan would be toxic for any major brand.

Kirsan was re-elected twice by a majority of FIDE member countries, but the nature of the voting system is democratic in only the most simplistic of ways. 'One country one vote' means that smaller nations hold disproportionate power, and the lack of electioneering rules has led to allegations of questionable forms of persuasion. Kirsan put on the record that 'paying for votes is not allowed by FIDE and by its members', yet any chess politician has to operate in a grey area between the retail politics of spending plans that will attract votes, and specific spending promises that might elict them.

But if Malcolm did mean Kirsan, why call him The Muppet? It is an affectionate insult. Biting, but without bitterness. Kirsan is always smiling, genuinely loves chess and seems somewhat oblivious to the way he might be perceived in the West; in fact he shares some of the characteristics of the forty-fifth US president. It is hard to feel real enmity towards Kirsan, and yet it was also widely understood that as long as he was there, chess would continue to underachieve.

Kirsan was ousted as FIDE president in 2018 after facing sanctions from the US Treasury for his apparent support for the Assad regime in Syria, and after gradually losing political support in Moscow, which always felt like it might have been the source of Kirsan's power – controlling the chess world is a useful part of Russia's soft power and international influence. In the 2018 FIDE presidential elections, Malcolm Pein stood as a candidate for deputy FIDE president, on the presidential ticket of the incumbent deputy president Georgios Makropolous from Greece, but he lost out to a strong campaign from Arkady Dvorkovich, who had been Russia's deputy prime minister since 2012.

So much for chess politics. No Malcolm, no muppet, but the Russian hegemony continues.

37 · THE ANIMAL INSIDE

Humans are more like animals than algorithms, but algorithms have power over us partly because we are animals in denial. It is because we are strangers to our own organismic natures that we struggle to understand how easily we can be manipulated by machines. If we knew our own minds better, we would not be so susceptible to the kinds of adverts based on psychographic profiling that make us more likely to buy something or vote for somebody. Mostly we are creatures of habit who live to eat and drink, bond, mate, build our habitats and protect what we value. We are therefore vulnerable to others telling us how to live because the part of us that is animal is very suggestible indeed. We need to know ourselves biologically to understand ourselves psychologically. Paradoxically, we need to realise we are animals in order to become fully human.

While playing twenty questions in a French evening class many years ago, my group decided our subject should be Winston Churchill, but when the questioner came back in the room we were immediately thrown by their first question: 'Is it an animal?'

Most of our group said *non*, but I confused everybody by saying *oui*. Yes, of course it is an animal. My logic was simple. Churchill was human, humans are animals, QED. But I was overruled. For most people, humans are animals in the way tomatoes or avocados are fruits. We humour the idea as a fact, but don't accept it as a reality. On this account, humans are merely like animals, which explains the popularity of the question – if you were an animal, what kind would you be?

This question is meant to be a conversational gambit, a playful talking point, and nobody is supposed to have an answer ready for it. However, when asked in 2013 on internet television, Magnus Carlsen did not hesitate: 'A crocodile. It seems to have a good life. A crocodile just lies there and relaxes, and it can more or less kill any other animal. Crocodile without a doubt.'

In that statement, you can glean Magnus's inner strength. There is no 'Who am I?' neuroticism, just a good old-fashioned answer with a clear justification. Magnus would be a creature who knows what it is, does what it likes and has nothing to fear.

Soon after he said this, back in 2013, the crocodile was about to face the Tiger of Madras, Viswanathan Anand. While the crocodile went into the match as favourite, almost a hundred rating points ahead, the tiger was on his home turf, canny enough to keep a safe distance from the crocodile's mouth, and wily enough to wait for the moment to attack a weaker part of the scaly anatomy.

This was not the first time the chess world had considered creature comparisons. Kasparov was once called a gorilla by Nigel Short, while Karpov was 'very like a fish' according to his rival Victor Korchnoi, but more often compared to a boa constrictor, squeezing the life out of his opponents.

England's Michael Adams, a mainstay of the world top twenty, has been nicknamed by Russian rivals 'the spider', for the way he subtly weaves positional webs around his opponents. My favourite animal line, however, comes from the legendary American, former world champion Bobby Fischer, who made reference to his absent father as follows: 'Children who grow up without a parent become wolves.'

In the first round of the Sinquefield Cup in Saint Louis, USA in 2013, Magnus the crocodile faced former World Championship challenger Gata Kamsky, who could, in this context, be considered a hippo; extremely powerful and dangerous but somewhat languid, and certainly vulnerable to a sudden crocodile attack. As one might expect, the first phases involved a lot of waiting around, balefully sizing each other up in shallow waters. The hippo made the first lunge, but the crocodile elegantly swished to one side, and bit back with decisive force.[8]

Whether we consider ourselves to be like crocodiles, spiders, gorillas, fish, snakes, wolves or hippos, or something else entirely, we are the kind of creature who can imagine ourselves being another creature, and that is precious. But we now live in a world where algorithms combine with psychographic methods (inferring what you are like as a person from what you like online) to determine your personality profile, which may not be an animal as such, but will be a version of yourself that is treated as relatively stable, and one thing rather than another. The risk is that we are sleepwalking into a world where we are figuratively viewed as fish and therefore given water, even if we want to be a gorilla, or viewed as a hippo and therefore given mud, even if we want to be a spider. We will need all of our imagination to find a way to change the systems and structures of information that are shaping our world. Somehow we need to preserve a fluid sense of who we are in a data-driven world that perpetually reinforces one idea of who we are to serve somebody else's interests. So if we have to choose, we should perhaps consider being Proteus, the mythological sea creature who could change form at will, and was very difficult to catch.

38. VEGETARIAN EATS TIGER

Serious chess players spend a lot of time away from home, and the accommodation at tournaments is highly unpredictable. In Canada in 2000 I had a resplendent serviced apartment designed for a family of four all to myself, while in Denmark in 1996 I was offered a sleeping bag and a judo mat and directed to a dimly lit sports hall which I shared with twenty others.

On that occasion I protested at first, but underestimated my adaptability, because when I got used to the idea it became a rewarding and memorable experience. The Spartan environment brought out the best in the strangers who suddenly had to share their space, and it was in this environment that I met Tiger Hillarp Persson from Sweden.

Tiger is of course a great name, but some carry it better than others, and although he doesn't wear face paint, or sharpen his nails, I have always felt Tiger embodied his name rather well. For instance, at the event where we first met, his shoes collapsed, and rather than rush to buy new ones he started walking around barefooted, leading to a dramatic improvement in his results.

Tiger has typically enviable Swedish features and strong board presence, and these factors, combined with the name and the bare feet, generated some sort of aura, bringing him confidence and luck, a result way beyond expectations, and a big enough prize to buy several good pairs of shoes.

A couple of years later, an anonymous sponsor arranged a match between me and Tiger in Edinburgh which I won comfortably, mainly because I was better prepared. I had not eaten meat for decades and the British broadsheet newspaper *The Daily Telegraph* pounced on the opportunity for a pleasing headline: 'Vegetarian eats Tiger'.

Not long afterwards, Tiger started another winning spree, becoming Nordic champion and winning a Grandmaster event in York. At this stage the prize money was rolling in, and while walking around the ancient city I remember Tiger murmured something about buying a boat, but he also knew that there might be a 'backlash', and there was.

In the subsequent years Tiger's playing style matured, and although his form has fluctuated, and he is sometimes too creative for his own good, he has established himself as a strong and dangerous Grandmaster who can win in all sorts of footwear.

When I visualise Tiger I see him with shoes on, and walking, a symbol of freedom and direction and spaciousness – he is somehow 'out there' in my mind, even if the reality may sometimes be different. In early 2016, while visiting Stockholm for work I called him in Malmö (about 300 miles away) just to say hi from his home country, Sweden. Was he on a boat? Was he walking? No, he was playing another board game, Go, online. Although he was pleasantly surprised to hear from me you could tell that he was conflicted and needed to get off the phone. He later emailed to apologise, which he didn't have to do – I already understood.

Like Grandmaster Stuart Conquest, Tiger has become a psychological reference point for me. Both are good friends of a similar temperament and ability, so when I find myself regretting my decision to leave competitive chess behind, or lament that I am no longer travelling around and playing, I ask myself: would Stuart or Tiger say I have made a mistake? In both cases the answer is invariably no. And yet they appear to have such freedom, and all those blissful hours with the beautiful game of chess. I live with these doubts that I might have been more fulfilled had I chosen a similar direction. I doubt it, but without being able to live another life to allay such doubt, how could I ever be sure?

39. CONFIRMATION BIAS

There is a story of a man who kept cracking his fingers. His friend asked him why he did it and he explained that it kept the elephants away. When his baffled friend said: 'But there are no elephants,' he replied: 'You see, it works.'

When we are invested in an idea, latching on to supporting evidence, however spurious, is a deeply ingrained human trait. Indeed, research on thinking skills reveals that we are much better at finding arguments for our own point of view than considering counter-arguments that might challenge it. This finding applies regardless of measured intelligence level or years of formal education. Rationality is mostly not like a mediator who seeks resolution of conflict, nor an impartial adviser who wants to understand both sides of a case before making the best decision. Rationality is more like a lawyer whom we pay to represent our desire to hold on to our current opinion.[9]

I wish I could say that chess can help to counter this problem, but it is not clear that it can. Research published at University College Dublin in early 2009 does suggest that Grandmasters behave like natural scientists while considering their moves. We seek to disprove (falsify) our favoured ideas while amateurs seek to confirm (verify) theirs. In this respect we are true to the philosopher Karl Popper's criterion for Science. We don't say, in the manner of a certain American president: 'What a great player I am, what a great move this must therefore be, look at all the reasons it's so great.' We do say: 'After rapidly narrowing down options, I need to check them against the best responses of my opponent before deciding which looks least likely to be refuted.' Seeking falsification is a very different mindset from seeking verification, and a much healthier way to think and live, because we deepen our appreciation for reality when we allow it to subvert our desire for it to be a particular way.

Alas, this form of thinking expertise, so much needed in the world at large, may not transfer very well beyond the domain of competitive chess. A case in point is Azerbaijan's elite

Grandmaster, Shakhriyar ('Shakh') Mamedyarov, who plays brilliantly but once displayed shocking confirmation bias by accusing an opponent of cheating on the basis of 'evidence' that was not much better than that of the elephant-fearing man above. There have been many such examples, but in this case the gap between the strength of the player and the quality of his general reasoning was disturbing.

At a high-level international tournament in Moscow in March 2009, Mamedyarov, playing White, became suspicious when his Russian opponent Igor Kurnosov, a strong Grandmaster but not yet world class, took his jacket from the back of his chair and left the board regularly between moves – the jacket could potentially contain a computer or communication device of some kind. Chess analysis engine apps on mobile phones can rapidly evaluate any chess position with a high degree of accuracy and suggest the best moves in chess notation (the first line of the reading). If you are even close to your opponent in strength you only need to consult such a device at one or two critical junctures of the game to make a decisive difference to the result.

Mamedyarov's suspicions grew when Kursonov turned down his draw offer, and he completely lost perspective when his opponent kept playing strong moves, enough to defeat him in a mere twenty-one moves – a rare occurrence at this level. Mamedyarov published an open letter accusing his opponent of cheating and withdrew from the tournament, later producing 'evidence', namely that his opponent's moves corresponded to the first choice of what was then the favoured chess analysis engine, Rybka.

If you start with the assumption that Kursonov was cheating, the circumstantial evidence seems strong, but when you are not invested in any particular outcome the case dissolves. First, it is not unusual for players to leave the board between moves, and we know that Kursonov was a chain-smoker who had to go outside to smoke (in winter, when a jacket comes in handy). Second, although Kursonov was lower rated than Mamedyarov, he was very strong, young and growing in confidence, so if he liked his position it is not surprising that he might turn down a draw offer.

Third, the moves he played do not look particularly difficult to me, and you would expect a Grandmaster in form to find them. The forces were in close contact, a symphony of attack and counter-attack, and the position was dynamic in nature, and thematic for that opening variation. All Kursonov's choices were moves I could imagine myself playing on a good day – they were not counter-intuitive ideas that only a computer could justify with algorithms; they flowed from standard tactical and strategic themes that just required confidence and vision to enact. Fourth and finally, the correlation with Rybka's moves depends entirely on details of processor speed and the duration of search. And even if you could control for those technical factors, on the sixteenth move Kursonov actually plays a slightly inferior move, compared with the engine's suggestion. That's a telling detail; from the perspective of verification the approach is: look at all these great moves he played that were the same as the computer – he must be cheating. But from the perspective of falsification the question is: how many bad moves were made that would suggest he may not be cheating, and this potentially critical inaccuracy was a case in point.

To any fair-minded person considering the evidence impartially, the accusation against Kursonov seemed completely unjustified. But in response to an open letter by Kursonov reiterating the facts of the matter, Mamedyarov did not back down. Instead he published a second letter explaining that he had examined Kursonov's games in the rest of the same tournament and found similar correlations with analysis engines that he considered strong evidence of cheating, when in fact they were spurious. Mamedyarov had completely lost the plot.

I think the heart of this story lies in a detail that has been mostly overlooked. On move fourteen Mamedyarov, playing White, offered his opponent a draw. As we have seen, a curious feature of competitive chess is that in most tournaments we can offer to cease hostilities at any time. We do not know exactly why Mamedyarov offered, but sometimes stronger players feel vulnerable and use their reputations as a kind of shield, allowing them to escape prospective harm. But Kursonov declined, even though the position was about equal at that point and Mamedyarov significantly outrated him. In chess tournament practice that is not particularly shocking, because sometimes we just feel like playing regardless of the odds or tournament context, but it was nonetheless audacious and a form of insubordination; it would be like a recently qualified army officer saying to a decorated general or colonel: 'No thanks, I don't want your advice.'

To experience that slight, and go on to lose ignominiously must have been humiliating for Mamedyarov. I imagine this perceived betrayal of appropriate conduct sent his ego into a tailspin from which it could not recover; indeed his very next move was the blunder that led to his downfall. We are much more swayed by our egos than we like to admit. We forget that most animals operate within strict hierarchies and honour codes that they live and die to defend. Perhaps what Kursonov did was not just win a game of chess, but violate Mamedyarov's status and self-concept. It appears that he created cognitive dissonance in Mamedyarov's mind that could be resolved in one of two ways: fully accept that he had been outplayed and that he was perhaps neither quite as strong nor quite as revered as he imagined, or decide that such a thing could not possibly have happened by normal means and then cobble together 'evidence' to back this comforting conclusion.

He chose the latter approach, and his reputation suffered. However, time heals. Mamedyarov remains much loved as a chess player for his pugnacious attacking flair, and he has been ranked as high as number two in the world. Kursonov faced a different fate. He climbed up the world rankings over the next few years to reach just outside the world top fifty, but on 8 August 2013 he lost his life tragically, knocked over by a car while crossing the road in his home town of Chelyabinsk. He died at once, at the age of just twenty-eight. He was one of Russia's most promising Grandmasters and by all accounts dearly missed by his colleagues.

The alleged cheating story gradually dissipated, but it coloured the careers of both players over the following few years. When the news of Kursonov's untimely death broke on Russian chess sites,

Mamedyarov was one of the first to react on Facebook, where he lamented: 'God bless you. I am very sorry.'[10]

40. WATCHING

In March 2014 I was sitting at home in London with some tepid coffee and a computer, relying on a webcam in Siberia to watch an Indian national hero muse over his next chess move against a Russian cricket fan. At the same time I was listening to Denmark's finest player and his Lithuanian wife, a Grandmaster with an ambrosial voice, politely and enthusiastically responding to the suggestion of 'Scotland's strongest player', which they had just received from me via Twitter.

I was watching not one position but several, and doing so in multiple modalities. I was observing the moves but also the facial expressions and body language of the players, and was thinking my own thoughts, but also listening to commentary and updating my perspectives in response to the moves as they were played. And then I was writing out my own ideas, sharing them with thousands of others, and waiting to see how they were received. The experience is technologically enhanced, socially engaging, emotionally volatile, aesthetically pleasing and intellectually intense.

On the back of my suggestions, people from all over the world were telling me why I'm mistaken, or suggesting that what I propose wasn't really my idea because the online analysis engine suggested the same thing, which is sometimes a coincidence but, I confess, not always.

I tried to stay focused on the position, but it's fun to be part of a global conversation about poetry in motion; four live games between the best players in the world, given extra significance because they would help determine the next World Championship challenger.

Those who say that chess is not a spectator sport are partly right, however. The game doesn't really come alive in this way for those who merely watch, because they search in vain for a simple plot or a clear score line. You really do need some proficiency in the moves and motives to get excited by the vector of possibilities. But when you have that capacity to take imaginative and empathetic flight, chess is your friend for life, and there is no better spectator sport for completely absorbing your attention.

At one point on the same day, it became clear to me that Vishy Anand, who was leading the event, was about to sacrifice his queen. For a variety of reasons, which are strictly between me and my five female psychoanalysts, I have always been too relaxed about sacrificing my queen, and tend to overvalue other pieces and undervalue queens, so I was openly enthusiastic about Vishy's decision. Most chess players are biased in the other direction, however, and many tweeted to ask: 'What on earth is going on?' The truth is that it was just another transformation that didn't really affect the balance of the position, and the game was soon drawn.

But there we all were, in this new networked society. A global conversation about an international event, with human insight enhanced by technology. I felt giddy, and the affordances around me – the screen, the keyboard, the portals to the other worlds – were all there for me. I was happy, I think, because I was both puppet and puppeteer.

SIX

Power and Love

We need to make peace with our struggle

In the summer of 2005, shortly before travelling to the Isle of Man to defend my British Championship title, I was contacted by the journalist Hugo Rifkind, who wanted to write a profile of me for the Scottish edition of *The Times*. We got along well and I was impressed by the piece published a few days later. It included one particular line that I was proud to see myself in: 'He wears his obsession lightly.' About ten years later I read one of Hugo's now regular columns in the main edition of *The Times* which I picked up in a cafe on holiday in Cornwall. For a long time *The Times* was the UK's paper of record, and reading the column evoked some status anxiety – Alain de Botton's term for the experience of getting too little love and attention from the world at large. I felt this way not because the column was good, but just because it was good enough to be in that particular paper.

Feeling uneasy about your love from the world is a real form of suffering, however petty and narcissistic it appears on reflection. In this case, the repetitive inner monologue went something like this: this talented contemporary of mine is reaching an audience of hundreds of thousands from a prestigious platform and I am not. Have I spent the last decade well?

My chess star had faded. The thing that was supposed to give me that coveted love from the world was somehow part of my back-story and I could not rely on it any more. To think of my chess career evoked regret as much as pride. I might play again, but in a chess sense I was never likely to rise in the status charts. If I was going to receive that kind of 'love from the world' again it would have to come from elsewhere, or perhaps I could mature and see through the need for it. There are certainly days where I feel I have managed that. I feel less envy now, less desire to be anybody other than myself, and more forgiving of the decisions I have made. But I do not for a second doubt the hold that status anxiety has over us, nor its volatility – envy often pounces on us like a stealthy predator, destroying our peace of mind.

On the other hand, when I felt this tinge of status anxiety it was not as if I had wasted my time since leaving chess behind. I had started a family, written widely for newspapers and magazines, finished a Ph.D. and achieved widespread influence and respect in policy research, grappling with the major challenges of our time, not least climate change. I was on the BBC *Today* programme and BBC *Daily Politics*. There was lots to be proud of, but at that moment it all felt insubstantial. Hugo was writing and connecting in a straightforward way that made sense and conferred status. What exactly was I doing?

At the time I was on holiday in St Ives. I had become fond of Cornwall and was there with Siva, Kailash (then six) and my father, whom I was treating to a short holiday. My dad is a retired art teacher and still practising artist, but his life has been defined by having schizophrenia for as long as I can remember. He lives alone in a ground-floor flat near the centre of Aberdeen and is often lonely. But he is also a great survivor, and a care-in-the-community success story. He has a good and gentle soul, but his mind is ravaged by a toxic cocktail of paranoia and hypervigilant identity maintenance, fuelled by an inability to filter perception properly – he is often inundated and overloaded with meaning.

On that holiday we had BBC news playing on the television while preparing dinner, and my dad was sitting by the window, looking out over the sea but periodically glancing back towards the kitchen to ask us a range of meandering questions. Meanwhile, the former Foreign Secretary Malcolm Rifkind – Hugo's father – was being interviewed on television about recent international events, in this case I think about withdrawing British troops from Afghanistan.

We come to know ourselves in apparently insignificant moments like this. Whatever status anxiety I had about the respective profile of myself and Hugo at the moment completely transformed, as if it was a kind of tonic that needed to be handled in the right way. Suddenly I felt enormous gratitude for my life, and compassion for myself and my father. I looked at the two respective dads, one a pillar of the establishment and expert commentator on national television; the other glad to have company, enjoying reprieve from his madness and solitude 700 miles away.

I found myself smiling inwardly for days afterwards, and now think of that experience as 'my Hugo Rifkind moment'. The experience had nothing to do with Hugo personally, whom I still enjoy reading and follow online, but through a chance sequence of events I felt renewed affection for my father and the life that he and I have endured and enjoyed. Through that affection, a keener sense for the absurdity of my own identity maintenance emerged, as did the tragicomedy of life more generally.

Our lives are of course more than our family circumstances, and our fate is not determined by the success of our fathers. And yet it helps to notice, with gratitude and forgiveness, the formative circumstances that are uniquely our own. Success, after all, is not what one has achieved in life, but what one has overcome to achieve it.

41. CHANGING NAPPIES

Displaying a remarkable sensitivity to context, Kailash Hamish Rowson came into the world on 1 May 2009, International Labour Day. This was a joyous time for the family, but our bundle of joy was a bundle of other things too. Nothing adequately prepares you for becoming a father, but my chess experience proved surprisingly useful in my new role as nappy-changer in chief.

1) Preparation: it is crucial to have some background knowledge of the 'opponent', not only from sensory feedback around the relevant area, but also by considering recent sleeping and feeding activities. More practically, is he warm enough? Are the nappy bags, cotton pads and tepid water all close at hand? Psychological preparation is also vital, so I would give Kailash a little pep talk, and ask for his forgiveness in advance.

2) The opening: the first stage of the game, involving removal of lower parts of clothing is usually straightforward, but you have to contend with some determined wriggling, and I would often find that I am outnumbered, with two hesitant hands wrestling four unpredictable limbs.

3) Deft manoeuvring: lift baby gently and fold outside part of nappy on top of soiled part so that baby's lower cheeks rest on relatively clean surface.

4) Prevent unnecessary counterplay: hold both legs in the air with left arm.

5) Activate your pieces: reach for the cotton pads with right arm, dip in tepid water from newly designated nappy cup.

6) Simplification: gently but firmly remove all the mustard-like substance, regardless of whether it looks French or English.

7) Exchanging to win: deposit mustard-covered cotton in nappy sack, followed swiftly by old nappy. This can be tricky if the bag is not open, so ensuring that is now part of my preparation (see stage 1).

8) Establish positional control: place fresh nappy under lower cheeks and release legs.

9) The decisive attack: swiftly position nappy with wings at rear, remove covering tape and close nappy, ensuring that good plumbing guidelines are followed, with potentially leaky apparatus pointing towards the toes.

10) The endgame: cover baby with clean clothes, and carefully lift with both hands while supporting head.

In case that sounds too easy, chess has also taught me that plans have to be constantly revised, and if the baby starts peeing in the middlegame, any stage between 3 and 8, your best defence is to laugh and reset the pieces.

The juxtaposition that defines the vignettes in this chapter – power and love – is perhaps not as self-evident as the others, but it is just as fundamental. I was introduced to the idea that power and love can and should inform each other when I was asked, with just a few hours of notice, to chair my first public event in front of about 200 people at the Royal Society of Arts, in early 2009.

Adam Kahane was the speaker; a formidable social-change theorist, facilitator and mediator who had just published a book by the same title – *Power and Love* – reflecting on his experiences working with companies like Shell and countries in transition like South Africa. The contrast that defines the book stems from many sources, including the theologian Paul Tillich, but it was brought to public attention in a tight and exquisite formulation by Martin Luther King Jr in his 1967 address, 'Where Do We Go From Here?':

> Power properly understood is ... the strength required to bring about social political, and economic change ... One of the great problems of history is that the concepts of love and power have usually been contrasted as opposites – polar opposites – so that love is identified with the resignation of power and power with the denial of love. Now we've got to get this thing right ... Power without love is reckless and abusive, and love without power is sentimental and anaemic ... It is precisely this collision of immoral power with powerless morality which constitutes the major crisis of our time.

I have used this quotation many times in my writing and speaking since. I suspect I already sensed the core sentiment from my experience of playing chess, where a love for the game's beautiful ideas has to coexist with an aptitude for the game's brutal battleground. Making peace with our struggle means coming to terms with the fact that you are always on a battlefield of sorts, but there is always beauty where you are if you allow yourself to see it.

When Leonard Cohen sings about leaving behind your idea of a perfect offering he reminds us that the aim is not so much to find our way to the end of our plot, that utopian place where we finally win on all fronts and thereby find peace. No, the aim is to rediscover the setting in which such plots are conjured. It is only through a heartfelt encounter with your current context that peace will be found. Over the years, chess taught me to make peace with struggle in this way. To choose chess as a form of life is, after all, actively to choose to struggle – to seek out resistance with the express wish of overcoming it. The game does have a 'will to power' aspect, whereby you seek to dominate and ascend and conquer, but that is not all that is going on.

There is also the simple love of playing, and the delight and beauty of the unexpected ideas that lie waiting for you, like fireflies arising from the bushes. This is illustrated in the Hollywood film *Innocent Moves* starring Ben Kingsley and Laurence Fishburne, in which a young American chess player is supported by his father to become a better player. Distantly inspired by the search for Bobby Fischer, who had disappeared at the time, the film does a good job of capturing the tension between the hunger for power and the need for love. On the one hand the young boy, Josh, needs to be turned into a winning machine to make the most of his potential – that part of him is pushed by his chess trainer. But it becomes clear that his character is altogether more creative and compassionate, and he only plays chess well when his love of life – the part of him fostered by his parents – and love of the game coalesce.

42. GRATITUDE

How do you give thanks to somebody who has inspired you? You might try to meet them, shake one of their illustrious hands and tell them with trembling lips – tearful eye to nervous eye – that they have changed your life for ever.

While such expressions of gratitude can be heartfelt, and nourishing for both the giver and receiver of thanks, the deepest way to thank somebody for inspiring you is to inspire them right back. There is a famous saying to capture this idea: the best teacher is not the one with the most students, but the one who creates the most teachers.

My wife Siva brought an article in *The Hindu* newspaper home from a trip to India in the summer of 2012 because the story was so striking, and expressed in quintessentially Indian English:

> Ever since five-time world chess champion Viswanathan Anand got back from Moscow after his triumph over Boris Gelfand in the 2012 championship, he has been grandly felicitated for this achievement. There was one more felicitation function on Saturday, but this one, like nothing he had ever experienced before … Dr Agarwal's Eye Hospital felicitated Anand by committing to perform 100 free cataract surgeries for poor patients … every year.

Such a gesture goes beyond any 'grand felicitation', and surely left Anand in no doubt that his work over the chessboard has a direct impact on the lives of people less fortunate than himself.

To inspire literally means to give breath or life. There are 18 million blind people in India, 55 per cent of them due to cataracts, an eminently treatable condition, and a hundred people a year were given their lives back, not directly because of Anand's chess, but because the chairman of a chain of eye hospitals, Amar Agarwal, wanted to say thank you in a way that kept the inspiration alive.

Of all the meditation techniques I have experienced, gratitude meditation made the deepest impact. After settling down the breath, you begin by silently and inwardly thanking the people who helped bring you into the world, then your parents for looking after you when you were helpless, your teachers, your doctors and nurses, all your friends and relatives, and after several minutes of reflecting on just how much you have to be grateful for, you may well find yourself welling up with tears. If that happens, think about the people you want to thank, and consider how you might pass on the gratitude in a way that shows the depth of your appreciation.

43 · BAD CHOCOLATE CRISPIES

After a period of working too hard in the early autumn of 2013 I went shopping with my four-year-old son Kailash, and promised him we would make some sort of cake when we got home. I didn't have the energy for a three-tier Victoria sponge, so I bought a hundred small cake cases, butter, cornflakes and white cooking chocolate, and told him we would make 'special chocolate crispies'.

Alas, I forgot the golden syrup that holds it all together, so when we got home I was hoping he might forget the deal, but no. Kailash kept pestering me to deliver on my promise and I eventually had to say: 'I'm really sorry, Kailash, but we don't have syrup so we can't make good chocolate crispies.'

He said: 'Daddy, if we can't make good chocolate crispies, let's make bad chocolate crispies.'

The statement felt almost constitutional in its authority and I was humbled. Liberated from my syrup-deficit mentality I hugged him tightly and immediately set about the task, repeating his emphatic suggestion with joy.

We proceeded to melt some butter in the only clean pan available, to which I added some sugar, on the pretence that I was 'caramelising', and though I knew I was meant to use a separate bowl to heat the chocolate, I chucked that into the pan too, along with a few sultanas, but swiftly turned off the gas before anything exploded.

We shifted the goo to a bowl, added cornflakes and stirred together triumphantly with a trusty wooden spoon. As chocolate crispies go they really were pretty bad – too much butter, incongruous sugar texture, tentative chocolate taste, insufficient crispiness, errant fruit, and so forth – but we were nonetheless very proud of them, and it was definitely the highlight of the day.

This episode reminded me of an early encounter with the Scottish International Master Mark Condie, when I showed him a game I lost. I proceeded to account for my decisions as if they were all entirely justified. At one particular moment, my reasoning was something like: 'I knew the best move was X, but then I didn't like the position, so I decided to do Y instead, in the hope that he wouldn't see Z, but he did, and that's why I lost.'

Mark's response was: 'You've got to play the best moves, man.' The 'man' made an impression at the time, perhaps because I was only fifteen, but the enduring lesson was that sometimes you have to make do, even if the resulting position, or chocolate crispie, wasn't originally what you had hoped for. Or, in words attributed to Theodore Roosevelt: 'Do what you can, with what you have, where you are.'

44. COMING OUT OF HIBERNATION

In October 2006, on Mount Rokko in western Japan, thirty-five-year-old Mitsutaka Uchikoshi tripped and lost consciousness. He survived in cold weather without food and water for twenty-four days. The best available evidence suggests his survival was only possible because he fell into a state similar to hibernation. He suffered severe hypothermia, multiple organ failure and extensive blood loss, but he retained normal brain function, avoided dehydration and lives to tell the tale.

Hibernation makes sense if you are an animal relying on food stocks that run low in winter, and amounts to lowering your metabolic rate, slowing your breathing and dropping your body temperature.

Something similar happens in certain forms of meditation, and scientists have long suggested that there may be a continuum of forms of hibernation, with human hibernation being both conceivable and potentially very useful for treating various diseases, interstellar travel, or if you just want some time out.

To be clear, I am not saying that humans can hibernate, but as autumn makes way for winter, people feel like doing less, sleeping more and staying indoors, and you can feel that this time of year should be relatively inactive. Yet it does not feel that way, with November for instance often having little daylight but being an acutely busy period for people at work, shops already abuzz with abundant artificial light. There is a figurative dimension to hibernation too, though. Sometimes we don't want to shut down our whole life, but we do need to shut down parts of it, to focus, or prevent system overload.

Towards the end of 2012, after some lacklustre play in the British chess league, I had the feeling that almost every chess player has when life challenges are compounded by listless moves and disappointing results. I momentarily wanted to stop playing, wondered what the point of chess was, asked myself why I cared so much about it, and so forth. In short, I felt like putting the part of me that is chess player into a prolonged hibernation. Several years on, I am still in that state, and happily so, but I'm also looking forward to the chess player inside waking up and finding that it is spring again.

45. BEING AT HOME

Among the sweetest moments in the *Lord of the Rings* film trilogy is a conversation between two travel-weary disoriented hobbits. Frodo notices Sam is still carrying salt from the Shire and asks what he plans to do with it now they're in a barren wilderness near Mordor. Sam expresses a forlorn hope that they might have had some roast chicken at some point. Frodo smiles at the optimism, but adds appreciatively that he understands why Sam has the salt, which is a symbol of home.

In December 2012 I remembered this scene while watching *The Hobbit – An Unexpected Journey*. The defining feature of hobbits is their love of home. The only moment in the film where I felt moved was where Bilbo Baggins realises that it's through his own love of home, his books, his armchair, and his garden – that he appreciates the deep need of the dwarves to end their experience of exile.

The main protagonists of the Christian nativity story are also refugees, and it's perhaps no coincidence that Christmas is a homecoming in a broader sense; rediscovering a deeper and richer idea of home, and inviting others to share in the love of people and place that shapes it.

Like most professional chess players I used to spend large parts of the year away from home, so I valued it then as I do now, more perhaps than those who have never had cause to miss it. At first travelling was an exciting part of the job; it felt thrilling to find myself in Brazil, Israel, the Faroe Islands, or wherever else I would not have been had the relevant chess action not been there too. In that sense, I felt I belonged away from home.

But I began to tire of the need for regular travel. Until you are about thirty, a relatively nomadic existence seems glamorous. You get to 'see the world', 'broaden your mind', 'meet lots of different kinds of people', 'learn about other cultures'. There is truth in all those clichés of course, but untethered freedom grows wearisome, and hotel rooms begin to feel like jail cells when you have nowhere else to go.

Now that I'm a bit older, I would emphasise a familiar point. The value of travel is at least partly about helping you to appreciate home. This point applies literally in terms of travel but also figuratively in terms of the experiences and activities that give us a sense of belonging. Chess itself is a kind of home for me – a place where I feel welcome, and at relative ease. And I feel I know and appreciate it so much more now that I no longer live there.

The point is not just that 'absence makes the heart grow fonder', but rather that absence allows you to relate to something you were previously defined by. Only by *relating to* worlds like chess can we feel generosity towards them and wholehearted gratitude within them. You grow through being at home, but unless you leave home you can't really grow beyond it. Having done so, you look back, and find that you are still there, but now you are elsewhere too, and potentially everywhere. The experience of home is particularly joyous when it is something you feel you have, but you will never know that feeling if your home is all that you are.

46. SOFT POWER

Once you have been introduced to the idea of 'soft power', you can never look at a Hollywood film or an Olympic medal in quite the same way again. While hard power is about guns and gold, soft power is about attracting attention, projecting strength, and wielding cultural influence to help you get what you want. Building soft power is a peaceful form of struggle, a way of trying to win without violence.

'The American dream' is part of America's soft power, exerted daily all over the world in formulaic films, attracting envy and economic migrants. China's spectacular Olympic ceremonies in 2008 were only incidentally entertaining. Their main purpose was to announce to the world: 'We are the new superpower,' thereby giving China extra leverage in their global economic and political negotiations.

Soft power is important, despite being intangible. For several decades, chess was used as an instrument of soft power by the Soviet Union, to portray superior intellect and willpower. When Fischer played Spassky in 1972, no less than Secretary of State Henry Kissinger got involved to ensure that Fischer would compete and win. No shots were fired, little money changed hands, but in terms of soft power it was a resounding victory, because the Soviets could no longer use chess to claim that their system produced the best minds.

In 2010 world champion Viswanathan Anand was a quintessential reflection of India's rising soft power. He represented India's global elite – skilled, mobile and rich. Anand stated in *Time* magazine that it was particularly good to have an Indian world champion, because the game originated in India.

This genesis story is also part of India's soft power, alluding to their great cultured past, as outlined in the introduction. We can trace chess to *chaturanga*, an eight-by-eight board game played in India in the third century BC, and there are references to the game in the great Indian epic the Ramayana.

However, some historians in China claim the game as their own. For *chaturanga* they have derivatives of *xiangqui*, instead of the third century they claim the second, and in place of the Ramayana they refer to striking parallels in the *I Ching*, one of the oldest texts in the world, with sixty-four hexagrams corresponding to sixty-four squares, and yin and yang to Black and White.

Chinese investment in chess has paid off handsomely, and they are now one of the strongest chess countries in the world. In 2014 their team won the Chess Olympiad in Tromsø, Norway, the equivalent of an Olympic gold medal for the country as a whole, and they repeated that feat in Batumi, Georgia in 2018. India are not far behind, and both countries have considerable strength in depth, not unlike their economies.

Whatever one thinks of the Chinese claim to the origins of the game, I hope soft power is used for a greater purpose than to increase material gain in the form of economic growth. Classical Chinese civilisation was about so much more than that. Some say the very idea of soft power originates with Lao Tzu. He once said something that would be timely today if only we could hear and heed it: 'The soft overcomes the hard. The gentle overcomes the rigid. All of us know this to be true, but few can put it into practice.'

47. HIERARCHY

In India, when one greets a respected elder of almost any kind – teacher, uncle, auntie, doctor, father-in-law, priest – it is customary to bend down and touch their feet, which they typically respond to by touching your shoulders or head. There is no cultural instruction manual or signposts on the street insisting that you do this, but whenever friends and family gather the Indians I am with seem to do it instinctively. At such moments I feel conspicuous not just because I don't bend down, but because I don't want to.

Pranama in Sanskrit means paying obeisance or bowing down, and can be literally translated as 'very bending'. *Pranama* is a kind of voluntary submission, and therefore quite difficult for a Westerner to play along with. At first blush the custom looks like an acceptance of hierarchy: a performance that affirms there is someone present who is fundamentally more worthy of respect than you. My liberal sensibilities don't like it because it feels like communitarian coercion, and my egalitarian instincts don't like it because it seems to celebrate hierarchy. Above all, my ego doesn't like it, because it suggests I am not the centre of the universe, but that, of course, is the whole point.

It is no accident that the body movements involved in Islamic prayer involve similar kinds of prostration, nor that images of intense Christian prayer often feature people on their knees with their hands together, as if pointing upwards. The point is not just that the state of your body affects the state of your heart and mind, but that it takes physical effort to shift our default setting of pride towards humility, so that we can emerge in a new state of body and mind characterised by trust, confidence and peace. When the ultimate battle in life is for the health of your soul, it is such a relief to surrender.

On more recent trips to India, I have found *pranama* quite easy to practise, and don't feel I forfeit anything that is really worth holding on to in the process. The performance of mutual respect is beautiful, customs contain wisdom that reason can't always decipher, and hierarchy is ultimately diaphanous – you can learn to see through it. There are of course oppressive hierarchies. Our history is defined by stories in which the premise is that everyone should know their place. Still, nature is rife with natural hierarchies of predators and prey, and human flourishing depends on growth hierarchies; the capacity to improve and perform at anything is not shared equally, and life would be the poorer if it was.

The chess world is profoundly hierarchical, as almost any sporting culture is, but the hierarchy is a necessary part of a game that involves keeping score. The young child learning the moves is no less worthy of love and respect than the world champion, but it is no bad thing that she is motivated to play less like herself and more like Magnus. As a young child I was fascinated by the rating system and wanted nothing more than to climb right to the top of it. 'What's your grade?' is the question of choice on meeting a new chess player, all the more so if you suspect they are good. When you hear the answer you don't make a moral judgment, but some kind of domain-specific pecking order is firmly established. I used to calculate my rating with a pen and calculator regularly to see where I had reached, and I know players who recalculate their rating today with online software, after every single game. Losing ten rating points, the maximum serious players can lose in one game, has been compared to losing a pint of blood, while gaining ten points is like noticing your muscles getting bigger.

Status is not mysterious, but it is somewhat stealthy. We talk about it all the time, but rarely explicitly. There is a joke about a criminal on trial being asked why he robbed the bank. 'Because that's where the money is,' he said. Similarly, if you ask people why they want to go to a famous university, why they wear designer clothes or why they want that promotion at work, the spirit of the answer may be similarly direct: 'Because that's where the status is.'

Being higher up on a hierarchy in any walk of life confers status. That's just a fact of life, but it's also a public health issue. We know from studies of social primates, and from our own experience, that social status depends on how much autonomy we have in life, which is partly a cause and partly a consequence of how much attention we receive. Any parent will know that most children crave attention, and no wonder: they want to be seen, to feel safe and valued, and to know what they are supposed to do. Those feelings engendered by benign attention have adaptive value; they help us survive and thrive, and they co-arise with neurotransmitters that make us feel good.

The world authority on these matters is Professor Michael Marmot, who coined the term 'status syndrome'. After controlling for genetic factors and social environment, our health is most closely tied with our social status. His book on the subject is based on more than three decades of research that began with studies of civil servants in Whitehall in the 1970s. These studies showed that even among white-collar employees with steady jobs there is a clear social gradient in health. To put that in perspective, our bosses are likely to be healthier than us and to live longer simply because they are our bosses, and Oscar winners tend to live four years longer than other Hollywood actors. The key variable is not money but status – how much autonomy you have and how much attention you receive.[1]

As previously discussed, chess is a status-conscious world in which one's rating is a clear marker of your place in the social hierarchy. Chess ratings begin around 600 and go up to about 2880. From personal experience I can attest that it is not unusual for chess players to walk through a door in order of rating. We may not do such things consciously, and there are always other social factors in play, but we retain some tacit awareness of the amounts of respect people are worthy of based on their rating. In this respect chess status is a bit like the British class system, which is intuitive to those in the know, but full of cryptic clues to those who are not.

The statistical details of the rating system are complicated, but 'the K-factor' of our rating is the multiplier that influences the volatility of the rating system. In May of 2009 the World Chess Federation was on the verge of doubling the K-factor so that the rating system would become less conservative. That would have meant that while I would previously only gain five points by beating someone with the same rating, I would soon gain ten. That may not sound terribly exciting to non-chess players, but as a political metaphor it is a kind of revolution; it means that it would suddenly be easier to abruptly shift the social pecking order.

In the end it did not happen, but that kind of tweak, for which the real-world parallel would be like a progressive change in marginal tax rates, would increase social mobility. Being able to rapidly shift one's social standing is an antidote to hierarchies that have grown sclerotic or oppressive. On the other hand some hierarchy may be necessary for social order, and complete social mobility could mean cultural chaos.

This is challenging terrain, but it reminds me of the evolution of my feelings towards *pranama*. When you kneel down to pay respect by touching an elder's feet, they touch you back as a sign of affection. At that moment of reciprocal gift exchange I don't tend to feel I have been coerced. I feel like I have chosen to momentarily submit as part of a broader and deeper freedom. And when I stand up again I know I can decide whether or not to do it the next time.

Not everyone is so lucky, I know, but hierarchy can be a game we willingly play rather than a rule we have to follow. Social hierarchies and levels of social mobility are political issues and public health challenges that lend themselves to questions of macroeconomic policy; that's important work, which I am glad is not my job. In the meantime, perhaps the best we can do is to make peace with our struggle with hierarchy through the way we pay attention, offer affection and show respect.

48. RACE, COLOUR AND CREED

While teaching chess in primary school I was once asked by a ten-year-old boy whether chess is racist, because White and Black are supposed to be equal, but White always gets to move first. The boy was white and he was playing Black, and I think he was joking, but it was one of those serious jokes that have to be handled with care. I said no, chess is not racist, not least because some of the best and most celebrated players in the world today are Chinese or Indian, but I also said it was a good question, because we can learn a lot by looking at the history of the rules we take for granted.

For starters the pieces are not always strictly white and black and are sometimes more like cream and red or ivory and brown. You could also ask the same question of why, in mathematical graphs, the Y axis is vertical and the X axis is horizontal: 'they just are'. The deeper point is that until the late nineteenth century there was no convention about who moved first, and the players would just agree at the start for one side to kick things off. That custom becomes problematic when you organise tournaments, because the side that moves first does have a slight advantage, and it is difficult to formalise a fair process for every player without specifying colours connected to the first move.

Since it has to be either White or Black that moves first, you have to choose. (In draughts – which Americans call checkers – the convention is that Black moves first.) The convention that White moves first in chess seems to have been established at some point between 1830 and 1870, which in global historical terms is a time of widespread colonialism and slavery; that correlation may lack causation, but the question requires further historical study.

Racism can be violent, toxic and perniciously subtle. In 2017, as part of my open society fellowship research into human rights, I visited Goree Island off Senegal, a key transit point in the Atlantic slave trade, and now home to a memorial museum that has been visited by numerous heads of state, all saying some version of 'Never again.' Goree is a notorious tourist trap, and I struggled to find an emotional response to what I was being asked to imagine because the experience felt curated. Nonetheless, the sense that the stone cages I entered were once crammed with men, women and children who were brutalised, bought, weighed and sold was unnerving. I was supposed to feel shock and horror, and there was some of that, but mostly I was struck by how little we learn about the scale and monstrosity of slavery at school, in the UK at least. The brutality and darkness of the slave trade makes it difficult to attend to all the energy and emotion evoked by race in a tempered way, but we have to try, not least because the underlying logic was capitalism at its most insidious.

Today racism is at once everywhere, because every place has some kind of racial history, and yet nowhere, because we sometimes make the mistake of thinking that history remains in the past. Racism is being chained to the bottom of a boat surrounded by your own vomit and faeces, taken to the other side of the world to be whipped within an inch of your life, until you submit to being someone else's property and tool. Racism is also the bus driver who says hello to everyone boarding except you, the immigration officer who asks more questions than they have to, or the shopkeeper who seems reluctant to check the back of the store to see if they have what you want in stock; I have been with or near Siva in all those contexts and many others. In fact we have been in an interracial relationship for so long that we have forgotten that is what it is, but the world finds ways of reminding us. The darkest chapters of racism are hopefully over, but the disposition to be racist and the experience of racism have not been extinguished. The case for vigilance is strong.

While walking around the streets of Aberdeen as a child in the 1980s I rarely saw anybody who wasn't white, but I would occasionally see stickers on lampposts and billboards saying: 'Free Nelson Mandela'. I had no idea who Mandela was or why we should free him, and when I heard he was in prison in South Africa it made even less sense. I am grateful to my Modern Studies teacher at Aberdeen Grammar School, Mr Gordon Hutcheon, who introduced me to the notion of apartheid or 'separateness' and explained what it meant in practice. He helped me understand why the story of Nelson Mandela was not about a single person in jail, but a touchstone for the conscience of mankind.

At a time when South Africa was explicitly segregated on the basis of race, the majority Black population were often oppressed and sometimes tortured or murdered. Nelson Mandela campaigned for many years through peaceful means, but when these efforts were met with further oppression he became more militant and was eventually arrested for treason.

He spent over twenty-seven years in grim conditions in prison, mostly on Robben Island, but the psychological and emotional work he did on himself in that time made it possible for him to eschew the hatred and revenge that was feared as the inevitable outcome of his release, which eventually happened in 1990. In prison Mandela completed a law degree by correspondence at the University of London, he learned Afrikaans to improve rapport with his captors and the minority rulers outside, and when he despaired at his treatment he read himself poems, not least W. E. Henley's 'Invictus', which includes the lines: 'I am the master of my fate. I am the captain of my soul.' Mandela's story of hard-earned forgiveness led a divided society towards reconciliation; it was his heroic capacity to remain free while captive that kept South Africa from civil war.

I sat my Higher Modern Studies exam in 1994, and was an avid student of a subject unfolding in real time. Mandela is affectionately known as 'Madiba', from his Xhosa clan name. I remember him being interviewed on BBC *Panorama* a few days before South Africa's first fully democratic election, in the context of pervasive assassination threats to the prospective first Black president.

Right at the end of the programme he was asked: 'Are you a brave man, Mr Mandela?'

He replied: 'There is a saying in my village, that the family of a brave man cries every day, and sometimes it is not wise to be brave.' Then the resounding *Panorama* music came on, and I welled up with tears, because I so much wanted him to live, and to lead a unified country that had once seemed impossibly divided.

Mandela was political in all the best senses of the term, and his story is one of the things I feel a sense of duty to pass on to my sons Kailash and Vishnu, because it shaped the political consciousness of my generation. Mandela's life does not merely serve to illustrate the power of forgiveness and reconciliation, but also offers a taste of political hope. He showed that victory against the odds is possible.

In this sense Mandela was a fighter. A great humanitarian, no doubt, but his humanity came from going through and reaching beyond the violent impulses within us, not by skirting around them. It is not said enough that Madiba was also a pugilist who loved boxing. Although he advocated non-violence, he lived in a context where innocent people were being shot in the street, often for little more than the colour of their skin. Madiba did not therefore rule out the need for arms as a last resort: 'For me, non-violence was not a moral principle but a strategy; there is no moral goodness in using an ineffective weapon.'

There is no record of Mandela applying these fighting instincts to chess, but he once gave the Queen the gift of a South African chess set during a state visit to the UK in 1996. When I think of what Mandela's story has to offer us through the lens of chess, I would say patience, because he was in jail for a long time; courage, because he had to believe in himself and his ideas when the position was hostile to both; and imagination, because he had to see several moves ahead to a position with new rules, new pieces and new powers, while trusting that he could somehow keep control.[2]

Nelson Mandela died on 5 December 2013. He was ninety-five years old. I admired him and maybe even loved him, but when I heard the news my main feeling was joyous relief. I had seen the signs and heard the song 'Free Nelson Mandela' so much as a child that the very idea had entered my soul. I felt in death, after a life's struggle with psychological and political freedom, he was now spiritually free, living on in the hearts and minds of millions. His was an extraordinary and inspiring life, and a courageous and enduring contribution to humankind.

Nelson Mandela made peace with his stuggle, and we all have to do that on our terms. On reflection, while one of many reasons to write this book was to share my deep love of chess, another was atonement. My chess career was characterised by significant success that fell short of complete fulfilment. Ever since I started a professional life outside of chess I wanted to finish this book to be at peace with the relationship between my past and my future.

In almost any endeavour, just below the celebrated exceptional players there is an army of the frustrated excellent. Their stories have value, especially when it comes to lessons for how to live well, because most of us do not achieve all our aims in life. The challenge is somehow to achieve peace of mind in the context of regret; knowing you could have achieved more combined with the forgiving conviction that you did what you could in the fuller context of a human life. You notice the dissatisfaction and look it squarely in the eye, smiling, but you don't run from it or pretend it's not there. I think of the desired emotional equilibrium in question as a quest for *successful underachievement.*

I certainly did not push myself as hard as I might have. I am probably Scotland's strongest-ever player, but with all due respect to fellow Scots, in chess terms that is a bit like being the highest mountain in Kansas. I was joint winner at the 'World Open' in Philadelphia in 2002, which sounds good, but it was really just an international open tournament where I was one of about ten strong players on 7.5 points out of nine when the counting stopped. And while it took some dedication to win the British Championship three times in a row from 2004 to 2006, in those years the world-class English Grandmasters didn't play. I never threatened to be the very best British player, and I was never world class.

This sense of partial fulfilment is neglected at a cultural level. We tend to focus on those who achieve everything they set out to, with perhaps a nod to the agony of failure, as if competitive experience was a binary affair. We don't look very deeply at a much more common experience of significant success laced with a mild sense of failure, but most of the people I know suffer from it.

'I think you should let it go,' people say. Or: 'You achieved so much more than most.' Such generic advice has a corrosive impact because it attempts to silence a living part of the psyche. Those unfulfilled parts of the constructed self are the sites of Buddha's second noble truth – craving, a root cause of suffering. Craving is an integral part of our continuing project of identity creation and maintenance; the stories we tell ourselves about ourselves. To threaten the legitimacy of that self-ing process risks opening up an existential abyss.

The idea of successful underachievement is conceptually neither here nor there, but emotionally it is everywhere. Many prefer not to engage with it, but rather to reassure you about the absolute and unimpeachable value of your existing achievement, or play down the importance or relevance of what you wanted to achieve. The fear seems to be that if the apparently successful own up to this nagging sense of underachievement, everyone will be reminded of unfulfilled dreams. It is not quite a cultural taboo to go there, but it is easier to downplay the importance of goals or to imagine they might yet be achieved than it is to accept what is more often the truth: Yes, those goals mattered. And yes, you only partly succeeded. Which means, yes, you also failed.

Although it may seem strenuous to go there, there is a deeper success available to us when we confront that pain. After a little struggle to settle into the experience, we can see our unease and observe it, gently and kindly. Writing this book has helped me understand that the mild pain of regret won't go away, but

I welcome it now as something uniquely my own. Your regret offers you the kind of deep friendship you can only have with your former enemies. As Francis Spufford puts it: 'We are a work in progress. We will always be a work in progress. We will always fail, and it will always matter.'[3]

SEVEN

Truth and Beauty

There is another world, and it's in this world

Between leaving school in Aberdeen and beginning university at Oxford I spent a year in one of Scotland's most notorious neighbourhoods, Ferguslie Park in Paisley near Glasgow. The area was more like a housing sink estate than a park; a place of high crime, high unemployment and high drug use. I remember going to the doctor's surgery for some immunisations before travelling to play in the World Under-18 Championship in Guarapuava, Brazil. The doctor seemed astonished that somebody playing chess, about to travel to Brazil, might exist in the neighbourhood. 'What's somebody like you doing, living here?' he asked.

I was living with my first main chess coach, Donald Holmes, who no doubt had good reasons for staying there, perhaps to get on the property ladder – I don't think I ever asked directly. It was important for me to be somewhere other than home in my first year of adult independence. I needed to focus on the game, which meant creating distance from friends, and getting closer to the small but supportive chess community in Glasgow.

I never felt particularly unsafe in the neighbourhood, but I didn't exactly blend in either, and actively avoided conversations, walking swiftly whenever I was out on the street. I kept myself to a strict routine of chess study and swimming. I would do several lengths of the local pool with chess daydreams in my head, for instance the glory of winning tournaments with perfect scores and the unfolding narrative of how I became world champion. As I sliced through the water with the front crawl my ego was wild, raging, totally out of control. The extent of my craving for chess success only became clear when I swam. It was almost like I had an amphibious alter ego. Thankfully, the walk back from the pool took half an hour, and as long as it wasn't raining, by the time I reached home I was usually back to normal.

Every month or so I travelled abroad for a tournament, but mostly I was by myself, pretending to be committed to chess, but secretly sad to be missing out on the parties back in Aberdeen. I grew up through the process of commitment and detachment. I remember it as an important and defining year, though not a particularly happy one. One Sunday Donald brought home two girls after his weekly visit to church. They were friendly, roughly my age, and I was glad for the company, but I was also disconnected; my life of chess study and foreign travel made it hard to even want to connect.

Still, I remember the conversation vividly. When the subject of chess came up, one of the girls – I remember her only as the one who was *not* about to study dentistry at university – asked Donald why he liked chess. Without hesitation he said: 'Because it's beautiful.'

The girls laughed nervously, but Donald was completely serious. He held his ground and they took the point. I was impressed because I knew what he meant, but until then I didn't have the courage and maturity to speak in such terms. It is beautiful! That's why I was there. That's why I was devoting so much of my life to chess.

About four years earlier Donald had shown me what is sometimes called 'The Game of the Century', between Robert Byrne and Bobby Fischer, played in 1956 when Fischer was only thirteen. It is an extraordinary creative achievement, full of geometric wonder and precise calculation. The game illustrates perfectly the former world champion Mikhail Botvinnik's statement that 'Chess is the art that expresses the science of logic.'[1]

Intellectual beauty is the lifeblood of chess rather than something that occurs as a one-off historic event. World-class games are replayed thousands of times to open-jawed amazement. But there are beautiful ideas permeating otherwise unremarkable games between players of all abilities. What makes the beauty of chess ideas not merely interesting, but also important, is that beauty and truth are so closely intertwined. If an idea does not 'work' it might be impressive, or even aesthetically appealing, but it can't really be beautiful.

The perception of intellectual truth and beauty, in chess at least, is not relative to the subjective intent of the players, but to aesthetic qualities of the ideas that feel more objective. My personal experience of chess beauty is that it is relative only to the rules of the game that give chess ideas their meaning. This is what I mean when I say chess taught me that 'there is another world and it's in this world'. Chess beauty always felt to me like it was both humanly constructed *and* as if it came somehow from beyond, speaking the ineffable language of the fabric of reality.[2]

There is a particular quality of experience that marks out beautiful ideas – it's a sense of rightness amidst contention: of order amidst chaos, of simplicity on the other side of complexity. Mathematics shares this feature of perception with chess, and perhaps also music: the gap between being almost right and being totally right makes all the aesthetic difference in the world.

We are approaching deep philosophical waters here, full of contention about the nature of beauty and whether reality is fundamentally physical. Do some features of reality, for instance human consciousness or mathematical laws, transcend the physical in some way?

I cannot be sure. What I can share here is that my experience of playing chess makes me think that Plato – the philosopher who argued that beauty shapes the world we know at a deep level and can act as a guide to perceptions of ultimate reality – was at the very least on to something. In fact, this chapter was nearly called 'Plato was on to Something'.[3]

The rules and ideas that define chess were created by human beings, and the game also has a particular history, evolving to its current form. It is also true that our appreciation of beauty can be seen as an emotional response to knowing that something makes sense, or works. In all these senses, chess is clearly 'of this world'. However, chess retains mystical allure because it is characterised by being uncannily attuned not just to our intellects but also our souls. It is no accident that the game has thrived for about 1,500 years.

The search for moves in chess feels fundamentally aesthetic in nature. We are hunting for something that looks right and feels right and we are thereby drawn towards some ideas, and repelled by others. Perception is inherently evaluative. Chess players are like sniffer dogs, except that what we are trying to sniff out is what works, and we know when we have found it. Good moves have the qualities of truth and beauty; they are discoveries of how things are, and how they should be.

49. THE NATURE OF INTELLECTUAL BEAUTY

BBC Norfolk interviewed me before the start of the British Championship in 2007. I was asked to ignore the video camera and a fluffy grey microphone, and instead focus on the interviewer, a sunburned stranger in his late forties who wanted to know why I played chess.

A quick scan of his bemused expression told me that he genuinely wanted to know. It seems he had observed the tournament hall, did not 'get it', and was hoping I might explain why so many people had congregated in his part of the world, only to collectively disappear into a dimension of it he did not understand.

I answered, to his eyebrow-raising surprise, that chess is beautiful, channelling the boldness of my chess teacher Donald Holmes from years earlier.

I said that while thinking about chess we are transported to a realm of exquisite patterns and hidden relationships that are endlessly stimulating. I also spoke of the addictive tension that builds from the first move, and rises and falls in synchrony with the succession of mini-battles that characterise a single game. The interviewer was clearly impressed, and told me that in twenty years of sports journalism he had never heard such an answer.

However, the lady who ran my B&B told me that although the interview came across well, the main theme of the feature was the one the journalist had planned all along: look at all these chess eccentrics who are impossible to comprehend.

Chess journalism is a cliché-fest. Even very competent writers and broadcasters struggle to do anything other than follow a very narrow script relating to intelligence, difficulty, thinking ahead and so forth. The challenge is that to have proper curiosity about anything, you need to know at least something, so that the question of what you don't know carries some value. In this context, I think one challenge for chess is to make sense of what might be called invisible beauty, because it clearly intrigues people. Not the familiar beauty of how things look, but the hidden beauty of how things work.

One suggestive example is a simple number trick based on the idea that nine is a selfish number, in the sense that it insists on recreating itself: 9+9=18, 1+8=9, 9+9+9=27, 2+7=9 and so it goes on; the nine refuses to go away 9+9+9+9=36, 3+6=9 etc. I find this trick charming because it points to an underlying harmony that feels meaningful, even if it may not be.

As long as the appetite for such invisible beauty is suppressed, I believe chess will remain a societal snack for a minority with the acquired taste. Moreover, perhaps the undervaluing of invisible beauty has wider implications, for instance in the decline in people studying sciences at university. Beauty is one of those words like love: we should use it more often, but only when we mean it.

50. FINDING BEAUTY IN BEAUTIFUL PLACES

On a holiday in the backwaters of Kerala in southern India in 2004 one of the group we were travelling with was lying on a hammock, reading a book. The scene was postcard-perfect, with tranquil water beyond the hammock, palm trees in the distance, some lush foliage and a setting sun. The man appeared to be in paradise, but I had my doubts. I approached and asked if what he was reading was any good. 'No,' he said. 'It's bloody awful.'

Outer beauty experienced through the senses and inner beauty experienced through the heart, mind and soul are different things. They do intersect, for instance when we feel awestruck by nature, but we find it much easier to talk about what *looks* beautiful than what is beautiful. I am often asked for instance about my favourite chess sets, but rarely about my favourite chess moves. I would much rather play a beautiful move on an ugly set than an ugly move on a beautiful set. In the first case, the action would feel closer to the truth.

What makes a move ugly is often simply that it doesn't work very well, but often moves that can be justified on logical grounds still violate our sense of order, harmony and purpose. We know more about what makes a move beautiful, and on this matter I am indebted to Jonathan Levitt and David Friedgood for the wonderful exploration of chess aesthetics in their books.

A curious thing about chess beauty is that it is rarely just given. We don't often say: look at that position, how beautiful! More often the beauty is latent and creeps up on us, and appears as a kind of revelation, and we can sense these revelations long before we can grasp them. There is a scene in one of the Jurassic Park movies where a *Tyrannosaurus rex* is provided with a goat in his cage, carefully supplied by means of a secure crane. The observing palaeontologist looks troubled and says: 'The T-rex doesn't want to eat, it wants to hunt.' Chess beauty is a bit like that too – we don't so much want to see it, we want to find it.

My personal experience of searching for truth and beauty simultaneously over decades made me highly receptive to theories of chess aesthetics, which Levitt and Friedgood encapsulate in four main elements:

Paradox is the source of surprise, because it usually involves the breaking of rules and the subversion of conventional material values. It is paradoxical for instance to block your own pieces while trying to checkmate the opponent's king, just as it might be paradoxical for a murderer to deliberately ensure that their gun is unloaded while trying to kill somebody in a movie.

Depth is about non-obviousness and subtlety, usually in the context of a strong mysterious move that reveals its purpose several moves later. In life in general, the philosopher Isaiah Berlin suggests that our struggle to convey complex ideas is related to the challenge of depth:

> The notion of depth ... is one of the most important categories we use. Although I attempt to describe what profundity consists in, as soon as I speak, it becomes quite clear that no matter how long I speak, new chasms open. No matter what I say, I always have to leave three dots at the end. I am forced to use language which is, in principle, not only today, but forever, inadequate for its purpose.[4]

In chess there is no equivalent of dot, dot, dot because as long as the game continues there is always a next move, but there are unfathomable depths. A chess idea is deep when its purpose can only be discovered by looking towards resources hidden in the future, which allows us to bring back futuristic knowledge to adjust plans in the present.

Geometry is the most tangibly visual of the elements, where the visual element is not so much the arrangement of the pieces but the vividness of the relationships between the pieces, the lines and the squares. Geometric beauty is a feature of great photographs and paintings, a function of how lines, curves, spaces, colours and light intersect. In chess the pieces do some of this geometric work, but there is also a purposeful underlying logic that accentuates the experience.

And *flow* describes the fluency of movement from one stage of a position to another, and the way the tension of the position is carried by the twists and turns of the logic. Flow is always at least partly about our experience of time; the chess experience cannot be understood without the cadences of rhythm and tempo; we look at a static image, but our minds are full of movement and narrative;

this happened, and then this happened, and then *this* happened and you won't believe it but *this* happened too!

Each of these elements – paradox, depth, geometry and flow – are relevant to any situation where an organism is trying to make sense of features in their environment that their autopilot is not capable of grasping – they contain clues to help us to find out what is going on and what it means for our next move in every sense. Chess beauty does not therefore stem from sensory stimulation, but it does disclose the underlying logic and harmony of the world, and hints at what it might mean for our life.

Many chess examples include all these elements of beauty. The thing that made the deepest impression on me about Levitt and Friedgood's book *The Secrets of Spectacular Chess* was the commentary of the authors on one particular example that was a stunning illustration of chess beauty: 'If you have never seen this study before and fail to find it exciting, our only advice is to give up the game. You will have no future in chess!'[5]

51. THE TYRANNY OF NUMBERS

Numbers can be beautiful, but sometimes they are tyrants, wearing us down. Whether you are a political party supporter facing up to bruising election results, a thirty-something fearful of becoming forty, or perhaps your fixed-term mortgage is coming to an end and interest rates suddenly matter much more than you ever imagined they could – in all cases, numbers are rarely simple, or benign. At such times it is salutary to remember Einstein's sage advice: 'Not everything that can be counted counts, and not everything that counts can be counted.'

Of course, Einstein was by no means averse to maths, and numeracy is more important than ever, so the point is not to disregard numbers, but to keep them in perspective. We should learn to respect and understand numbers, but at the same time retain the power to question their relevance, and never give them sovereignty over our thoughts and feelings.

This attitude to numbers is one of the many things I learned from chess. In fact, in my experience the defining feature of a Grandmaster is their ability to count accurately, but then to see beyond the numbers to what really counts. The reason this feat is so challenging is that, as we have seen, soon after we learn how the pieces move we are taught their approximate material value, and these values get so deeply lodged in our psyches that we forget they are approximations.

Although the values of the pieces (i.e. pawns one, knights three, etc.) hold up as averages across millions of games, we always play one position at a time. So the difficulty is learning how to apply the general values to specific positions. For instance, we don't usually count the king, but in an endgame an active king is often worth more than a bishop or knight, and while two rooks add up to more than a queen, very often the queen is better if she has things to attack and the rooks are not coordinated. Chess is very easy to learn but extremely difficult to master, because counting is never enough, and good judgment requires years of practice.[6]

This sensibility of respecting numbers as heuristics – guides to action – but resisting the idea that they are accurate or fundamental is more important than ever. Today we are living in what Frank Pasquale calls 'A Black Box Society' – a society where a black box full of numbers about you is being crunched and decisions are being taken on that basis: 'Reputation. Search. Finance. These are the areas in which Big Data looms largest in our lives. But too often it looms invisibly, undermining the openness of our society and the fairness of our markets.' This lack of visibility is critical, argues Pasquale, not least because we are vulnerable to it: 'Presently, a falsehood in a single large database can percolate into dozens of smaller ones, and it is often up to the victim to request corrections, one by one.'[7] As the saying goes, technology is never neutral but often indifferent.

The challenge of misusing data is troubling enough, but the more fundamental problem with numbers is with the fetishisation of measurement, particularly when we seem to be measuring the wrong things. In 1968 Bobby Kennedy famously said that our main societal measure of progress, gross domestic product (GDP), 'measured everything except that which makes life worthwhile'. The economic historian Dirk Philipsen gives a more forensic analysis, arguing that this touchstone of public debate is quality-blind, people-blind, ecosystem-blind, justice-blind, complexity-blind, accountability-blind and purpose-blind.[8]

GDP is merely the most prominent example of measuring the wrong things. As the philosopher Zachary Stein puts it, we are overattached to a particular view of the world:

> Measurement instruments and techniques will be built that appear to deal in realities but instead deal in demi-realities. Truncated representations of complex phenomena are taken as sufficient and revelatory when they are, in fact, insufficient and misleading. This is worse than flying blind, it is flying blind when you think you are seeing clearly.[9]

How, then, do we get beyond the numbers? Is there a way to live that is relatively free from rampant data capture, insidious surveillance and delusional measurement? Well, yes and no. The problem is not with numbers or data or measurement as such, it's about how meaningful the numbers are, who rightly owns the data and how wise and discerning is the decision to measure anything, and then when measurement is sought, how inclusive a view of life does it reflect? There are radical approaches like coming off social media and changing your smartphone (which is really a pocket computer) to a simple phone, but given our current direction towards greater quantification, measurement and surveillance we need a more fundamental reckoning about the kind of civilisation we are creating. In the meantime, remember that numbers should be our servants, not our masters.

52. LUCK

Luck is no less mysterious than beauty. There is extraordinary depth to the idea of luck, which you cannot fully grasp without understanding systems, complexity, causation and counterfactual realities – and who can do that? Luck is so mysterious in fact that it sometimes feels intensely meaningful. As Milan Kundera puts it in *The Unbearable Lightness of Being*: 'Chance and chance alone has a message for us. Everything that occurs out of necessity, everything expected, repeated day in and day out, is mute. Only chance can speak to us.'

According to the nineteenth-century American philosopher and poet Ralph Waldo Emerson, only the shallow believe in luck. Perhaps he is right, but even those who don't believe in luck are often forced to reflect on it, and may merely know it by another name. Emerson added that the strong believe in cause and effect, but we never really know which causes lead to which effects. In this sense, perhaps luck is just a necessary and comforting word for things we can never fully understand.

But is there luck in chess? I believe so, and I don't think there is anything shallow about it. We are not at the mercy of dice or cards, but any seasoned player, if they are honest with themselves, knows what it feels like to be lucky. It usually occurs when you suddenly have a crucial resource in the position that you didn't foresee, or when you make a good move for the wrong reasons. Or you could look at it in a more entertaining way, like the Norwegian player Jim Loy: 'There is luck in chess. My opponent was lucky that he was playing against an idiot.'

There is something about familiarity with luck that allows you to generate it in your favour. You might think that if you can create it, or work for it, then it's not really luck, and technically you may be right, but that is not how it feels. I think the best players all approach the game with what might be described as 'confident uncertainty'. We know our strengths, but we respect the depth and complexity of the game, and sense that we are never fully in control. This state of mind leaves you receptive to incredible opportunities, and allows you to stay focused even when things go wrong. As the Russian Super-GM Bareev put it: 'There is always luck in the air, and one has to grab it.'

One of my most palpable experiences of luck came in a game against the English Grandmaster John Emms at a tournament in Gibraltar in 2004. I had been comprehensively outplayed and my position was lost, but I resolved to confuse my level-headed opponent as much as possible before giving up. I played a few speculative moves that he should have dealt with by allowing a certain amount of mess, but in his effort to keep things completely under control, he allowed me to complicate matters further. Then he panicked and missed a critical move that allowed me to defend and attack simultaneously, and then he completely lost the plot and I went in for the kill. To win the game felt quintessentially lucky, and yet I felt proud of myself because by resisting in the way I did, at a psychological level I provoked his unforced errors.

The mystery lies in that apparently straightforward advice. Some live as if expecting to get lucky, and thereby attract their luck. Others live as if luck is unreal, but still look lucky to others. Luck is ultimately unfathomable, but nonetheless real. So the next time you hear somebody say that the best players are always lucky, give them the benefit of the doubt.[10]

53. THE LOVE OF WOOD

What is the genesis of a chess Grandmaster? 'It all starts with the love of wood,' said the Dutch Grandmaster Jan Hein Donner. He argued that this love underpins the exquisite tension of the game, because we have a tactile urge to reach out and touch the wooden pieces, but we know that such a movement is sacred and irrevocable in the context of the battle. Our need to endure this suppressed urge may be why the prospect of the next move is always so exciting, and the 'touch-move' rule – whereby if we touch a piece with the intention of moving it we have to do so if legally possible – is held so dear.

In cities, most of us are surrounded by wooden furniture and at least some trees, but we tend not to give wood as such much thought. In the winter of 2014 I had a family holiday in the Blackwood Forest in Hampshire, where Donner's thought came back to me. We were surrounded by the sights, smells and sounds of various kinds of trees, including the unnerving sound of them falling to the ground in a storm. We also started walking with sticks through choice rather than necessity, and deep in the interior of the woodland we left samples of gratuitous wood art from the surrounding sticks and branches, just for the love of it. Wood is pleasant to touch, beautiful, aromatic, and so easy to shape for both practical and aesthetic purposes that it's amazing we take it for granted.

Most chess players are not frustrated carpenters however, and most games of chess are now played with plastic boards and pieces, or on computer screens. I am not sure how much this matters. If you think chess is just about the mind, and little to do with the body or the senses, perhaps not. But I wonder if we should take Donner's point more seriously. Is there some natural affinity between human beings and wood that is fundamental to the charm of the game? While chess can be played with a variety of substances, including entirely in our minds, there is deep satisfaction in connecting the beauty of our thoughts with figures that are worthy of them.

Vision is considered the key quality of a chess player, but I wonder if touch in particular and our embodiment more generally might be more important than we have thought. The experience of concentration does involve the body being situated in particular spaces and places. Yoga speaks directly to the importance of that idea because it was traditionally about stilling the body so that we could achieve one-pointed focus of the mind without distraction. In chess, concentration arises from less austere bodily commitment, but it is still fundamentally about physically and mentally 'being there' at a particular time and place.

The postures of the top players vary enormously, but most chess players move around quite a bit, both at the board with legs shaking or cheeks being scratched, or away from the board, nervously glancing backwards at symbolic battlefields of our own choosing. We also introspect in a visceral way, checking in with our hunches, our gut feelings and the vision both of the eyes and the imagination. And of course we move the pieces with our hands, described by the scientist Jacob Bronowski as 'the cutting edge of the mind'.

The tactile aspect of the game is not at all trivial; it is part of the charm of 'being there' at the chessboard. We know that the neural connections between hands and brain are significantly more numerous and elaborate than other points of contact within the body. No surprise then that young players are often seen with extremely jumpy hands while playing chess. As a youngster I used to play with my hand moving towards the pieces and away again as a chicken might peck for grain. But one day a friendly opponent looked me in the eye, smiled, and said: 'You can always sit on them, you know?'

54. KEEPING IT REAL

How many legs does a dog have if you call the tail a leg? It's not a trick question, but in case you think it's too easy, keep in mind that it was posed by Abraham Lincoln. The answer is not five, but four, because 'Calling a tail a leg doesn't make it a leg.'

The importance of Lincoln's steadfast realism is highlighted by the writer Philip K. Dick: 'Reality is that which, when you stop believing in it, doesn't go away.'

But is it good for us to 'keep it real'? Could any of us get through the day without a little pinch of self-deception, a few grains of denial, perhaps just a wee dram of delusion?

Most of us do defy reality in this way, and perhaps that's no bad thing. The expression 'depressive realism' refers to the clinically established fact that those who suffer from depression often tend to have a more objective grasp of reality than those who don't.

A review of the relevant studies in 2012 found that, on balance, those with a propensity for depression often have a more realistic perception of their reputation and their capacity to control events than those who are not depressed. They also tend to have fewer self-enhancing biases, including the optimism bias, the trait that leads us to congratulate ourselves for saying the glass is half full, even when it's 58.3 per cent empty.

I have close family members with serious mental health problems, so I don't want to treat the issue frivolously, but perhaps we can speak of some milder forms of depression as a kind of 'denial deficit disorder'. Imagine the dystopic scene in which a tanned suburban psychiatrist flashes a radiant smile to his highly intelligent but somewhat despairing patient: 'The trouble with you, my boy, is that you need a bit more denial in your life. These pills should do the trick.'

These thoughts were prompted by an interview with Vladimir Kramnik in 2013, just after he had shared first place with Magnus Carlsen in the Candidates tournament in London, but lost out on becoming World Championship challenger due to the vicissitudes of the tiebreak system. He discussed the new challenger's qualities at length, and I was particularly struck by the line: 'That's the way he is. Cold-blooded, rather pragmatic, somewhat melancholic even.'

Somewhat melancholic? At first blush this sounds strange, because even then the future world champion was energetic; he smiled, laughed, enjoyed his success, and appeared to have a balanced personality, grounded in the support of a loving family.

But I know what Kramnik means. I played Carlsen and have watched him in person. He does have a latent lugubrious quality that manifests in his facial expressions and body language while playing. Perhaps this quality is merely a function of being highly objective for too many hours of his life, but I believe it may go beyond that.

Carlsen is not an idealist or a performer like Kasparov, who loved the narrative, the drama, the quest. Magnus just wants to win. So while there is plenty of creative amplitude in his play, the underlying motivational vector appears to be relatively sombre and flat. It does not appear to be doing him any harm.

55. THE THINGS THAT MAKE SENSE

In the autumn of 2013, I had an experience common to many people in their mid-thirties: overload. On most days I would get to the end of a whirlwind of activity and feel like my life was living me, rather than the other way round.

The problem with overload is that you don't have time to make sense of what is happening to you. There are too many things to do but no time to do the one essential thing: figure out why you are doing them.

Chess is not just one more thing to do. It's like a pit-stop, a time out of time to heal oneself through a few hours of dedicated sense-making. Sublimation is the psychological term, which, as already indicated, might be one of chess's major cultural functions. Chess helps to channel the turbulence of our existential plight into a purpose that makes sense, through creative, constructive and meaningful ideas. The game makes sense partly because it's cathartic and redemptive.

Of course none of this happens consciously. While I was growing up, it's not as if I knew I had a problem to which chess was the solution. It just so happened that at a time when I desperately needed things to make sense, the structures of the chess world – the rules, the ratings, the rook manoeuvres – offered that experience in a way that the world outside did not. And so I studied almost every day, and travelled for hundreds of miles to test myself against worthy opponents. It never occurred to me to ask why I was doing it.

An analogy that comes to mind is a scene from the 1989 film that made Tom Cruise famous, *Born on the Fourth of July*. The character Ron Kovic returns from Vietnam disabled and completely disillusioned, unsure of who he is or what he's living for, and at one particularly low point he reflects with his friend Charlie about the fact that he had a family and God, and more generally things that made sense; things he could count on, before becoming so lost. He finds himself eventually, through anti-war activism.

The truly wonderful thing about chess is that, ultimately, you can count on it to make sense. If you spend enough time with a position, the truth will reveal itself to you, and usually in a way that leaves you feeling momentarily like you know where you are in the world.[11]

56. THE MIDDLE WAY

For many years playing a chess tournament meant escaping to another world. I savoured the single-minded focus on the game, including a steady daily rhythm of preparing, playing and analysing. I would often season this tempo with my own disciplined practices, including yoga, meditation, long walks and herbal teas.

By December 2012 that was no longer my life. I was competing in the London Chess Classic Open while staying with family at home. I was playing reasonably well, but my identity as a Grandmaster was already in tension with my responsibilities as a father, husband and householder. It is possible to coexist in these two very different worlds, but not easy, and I was learning to accept that trying to achieve my prior standard of discipline was unwise.

Part of me wanted to ascend to the roof terrace and pay obeisance to the rising sun with twelve *Surya Namaskars*, before preparing oatmeal porridge, solving a few tactical exercises and getting stuck into three hours of intense opening preparation on Chessbase, but the reality was rather different. I woke from a disturbed night in gentle desperation for a coffee that I barely had time to drink, negotiated various timings with Siva, and then wrestled with Kailash, who never wanted to wear his gloves on the way to nursery, despite the freezing cold. I got a walk of sorts on the way back home, and felt ready to get focused, but then I thought: Who's going to clean the kitchen? Call the childminder? Buy the Christmas tree?

For many, competitive chess fulfils a similar function to spiritual practice, because it is a place where the quality of our thoughts and emotions is reflected back at us. Preparation is therefore partly about conditioning your nervous system for the delicate balance of imperious desire and contemplative restraint. Magnus Carlsen is celebrated for his ferocious willpower, but he would not be the world's highest-rated player ever without the scrupulous objectivity that is the true wellspring of his strength.

Like any sports star, Magnus has a large team to keep the hassle of the real world at arm's length. For my part, I was glad to have a busy working wife and a gloveless pre-schooler. I was also inspired to think that Buddhism recognises my predicament of the perennial human challenge.

It was once thought that you had to choose between the ways of the world and the ways of the spirit, but Buddha taught that the best path is 'the middle way' in which you negotiate your spiritual practice, whatever that may be for you, in the context of your earthly commitments.

In Buddhism the middle way is not a compromise but a commitment. The path is in 'the middle' not in the sense of the middle of the road but more like the middle of the tennis racket. This idea is that your duties and pleasures in the world are not obstacles to spiritual growth, but opportunities to deepen the meaning in our lives, if you get them in the right kind of broader, deeper and fuller perspective. As an approach to life, the middle way is not necessarily Buddhist, but it is detailed most tangibly as the eightfold path that we should attempt to walk: right view, right intention, right speech, right action, right livelihood, right effort, right mindfulness and right concentration. In each case the notion of 'rightness' is not moral judgment relating to the avoidance of transgression but a path that acts as both the means and end to the forms of life that are most worth living. What happens when you try to walk that path is not necessarily that you grow happier, but life does become more deeply meaningful.[12]

Looking at life through the relationship between truth and beauty in chess might seem an abstract concern, but grasping the generativity of this relationship is invaluable for societal purpose and educational design. Indeed, the central argument of Friedrich Schiller's *Essays on the Aesthetic Education of Man* from 1795 seems more relevant than ever.

Schiller argues that we have to cultivate an aesthetic appreciation of the world to rise above biological conditioning and emotional reactivity; only then can we make sense of the world on our own terms in a way that is judicious. In that sense, aesthetic appreciation for intellectual or artistic beauty 'restores us', as Schiller puts it; it makes us less suggestible by grounding us in reality and orienting us towards truth. Or, to put it more simply, the best route to truth is via beauty. Perhaps our challenge in a 'post-truth' world is less about fighting for facts, and more about cultivating the kind of refinements in perception that allow us to remain mindful of beauty while we think logically. There is a game that helps with that.

My chess experience tells me there probably is another world in this world, and that other world is defined by truth encountered through our aesthetic sensibility. Such sensibility is natural and lies latent within us, but it needs to be cultivated through arts, broadly conceived.

Schiller puts it poetically: 'As noble Art has survived noble nature, so too she marches ahead of it, fashioning and awakening by her inspiration. Before Truth sends her triumphant light into the depths of the heart, imagination catches its rays, and the peaks of humanity will be glowing when humid night still lingers in the valleys.'[13]

EIGHT

Life and Death

Happiness is not the most important thing

One must be light like the bird, not like the feather.
Paul Valéry, French poet

The driver who picked me up from Tel Aviv airport had tears on his cheeks as he drove to my hotel. It was 4 November 1995. A few hours previously, Israel's Prime Minister Yitzhak Rabin had been assassinated. The fragile peace process, neither the first nor the last, looked unlikely to hold. Such moments leave an imprint on your soul. Since then, news items about Israel and Palestine have always been coloured by that weeping taxi driver – a normal human being despairing at the futility of death in an intractable conflict.

I was in Israel for the European Junior Championship, and although the tournament proceeded as planned, the opening ceremony was cancelled the next day. One minute I felt bewildered to be at the epicentre of a reverberating world, where a global statesman had been killed; the next minute I was back to sublimated geopolitics, myself the assassin, thinking mostly about how to kill the opponent's king. That experience with the sobbing taxi driver was a moment of intimacy and resonance that had enormous human value. Such memories bring quality to life but they have nothing to do with 'happiness'. Chess taught me that whatever makes humans tick is something other than happiness, however cleverly it is defined.

Happiness, according to Professor Paul Dolan's lucid distillation, is 'the experience of pleasure and purpose over time'. This definition captures much that gives life value, but not courage or sorrow or redemptive pain or so much else that matters. Even on this relatively inclusive and precise notion of happiness, I don't think it is our ultimate motivation. Humans are much too complex, restless, dark, impish and transgressive ever to feel at ease with enduring feel-good purposiveness alone.

There is much more of value in life than merely being happy. The essayist and psychoanalyst Adam Phillips puts it like this:

> Happiness is fine as a side effect ... It's something you may or may not acquire, in terms of luck. But I think it's a cruel demand. It may even be a covert form of sadism. Everyone feels themselves prone to feelings and desires and thoughts that disturb them. And we're being persuaded that by acts of choice, we can dispense with these thoughts. It's a version of fundamentalism.[1]

Chess is not so much a path to happiness as a ritual where we free each other from the pressure to be happy. If you walk in to your average chess event and look around the room you see humans, mostly male, in physically awkward positions, straining to make sense under competitive tension and high adrenaline. Chess players tend to look absorbed, but also very tense, and they voluntarily place themselves in that state for hours at a time, decades at a time. Whatever we are seeking, it is not about being happy.

So what then might it be? We have already considered the importance of struggle to human life, and that is part of it – the need to test oneself. But again, why? There is also an attempt to create and experience meaning – the mattering that matters, but asking for the meaning of meaning is no joke – we need to figure that out before we can say meaning is more important than happiness.

The journalist Emily Esfahani Smith, author of *The Power of Meaning: Finding Fulfillment in a World Obsessed with Happiness*, defines meaning as a combination of belonging, purpose, self-transcendence and self-authoring. These four pillars are the structure for the kind of life in which we can grow. I am not surprised that chess is implicated in each of these pillars. There is a community where we feel belonging; there is purpose through battles to be joined and won; there is transcendence in the experiences of flow and the sublime; and we can build our identity around the stories we tell about our games. However, I suspect that even this sophisticated view of meaning may not be the heart of the matter when it comes to ultimate purpose.[2]

Clearly chess is *about* many things, but ultimately I think it's about trying to purge what the Buddhist philosopher David Loy calls ontological guilt. Ontology is the study of what exists or is real, so addressing ontological guilt is not about the old-fashioned idea of sin as moral weakness, but rather about overcoming our sense of not being entirely real, our sense of *lack*.[3] As long as we are caught up in a battle we care about, as we are with chess, we can feel that not only do we exist, but that we matter too. Milan Kundera captures this motivation with a celebrated contrast in *The Unbearable Lightness of Being*:

> The heavier the burden, the closer our lives come to the earth, the more real and truthful they become. Conversely, the absolute absence of burden causes man to be lighter than air, to soar into heights, take leave of the earth and his earthly being, and become only half real, his movements as free as they are insignificant. What then shall we choose? Weight or lightness?

The experience of having children is a good example of the initiation into the contrast between a life that is heavy rather than light. When prospective parents ask me whether children make us happy I am inclined to say no, not happy as such. They often look shocked, but I believe the decision to have children is about making ourselves real through responsibility and joy and meaning, not happiness – it's not about feeling good on a moment-to-moment basis. Children don't make your life more or less happy necessarily; the dial of pleasure or pain can turn either way, and very often does within the space of a few minutes. Tickles and hugs and radiant smiles are part of the pleasure, but there are also phones placed down toilets, random acts of violence against siblings, anxious visits to accident and emergency after head bumps, getting them to eat, to sleep, to play nicely, to learn … it is a glorious challenge and a joyous struggle, and the experience is intensely meaningful and rewarding. But happy? Not as such.

The deeper point is that children make your life *heavier* in a way that is experienced by most people as good. Children give your life depth and definition and responsibility. Being a father to Kailash and Vishnu has been the greatest blessing of my life, and I sometimes find myself welling up thinking of what those relationships mean to me: the intensity of the attachment, the unexpected moments of joy, the gift of being needed and valued and known: Daddy? Daddy! Daddy. And yet the joy is deep because the struggle has been intense. There have been years of exhausting manual and emotional labour, the impossible task of keeping them completely safe and the latent shame of feeling you might let them down.

While choosing children is choosing 'weight' in Kundera's sense, I now think choosing chess is ultimately about choosing 'lightness'. Kundera's distinction is based on a reflection on Nietzsche's theory of eternal return, which suggests that if time is cyclical and the universe reconstitutes itself over aeons of time, each moment is unbearably heavy because it will be repeated eternally. While if time is linear, each moment is light, never to be repeated again. Neither idea is literally true, but this notion of each moment being light because it will never happen again reminds me of chess. We know the game will soon be over. We know we set the pieces up and start all over again. Life, however, need not be like that.

The tragedy of chess is that many use it to make themselves real and add depth and definition to their lives, but the game is not ultimately fit for this purpose. However culturally resonant it may be, it remains a game within the game of life, not the game of life itself. Chess almost serves as a viable world of its own, but it cannot give us what we really seek, which I would say is the experience of being real that arises from realising we are not real in the way we previously thought we were. As the psychotherapist Carl Rogers puts it: 'The curious paradox is that only when I accept myself just as I am, then I can change.'

What chess taught me, through contrasting the intense drama of the game with the relative monotony of life, is that beyond pleasure, purpose and even meaning, we have a deep need to make ourselves feel real. We do that through creating things where we can be sure the mattering matters, like chess games, but also like sport, art, music, and through any responsibilities we undertake, including our commitment to our relationships. Our sense of self is constructed by the need to defend the reality and importance of whatever we have created, including our chess positions. That process of creation and construction is poignantly human, because it is so fragile.

Many people intuit the contingency of our existence and the lack of a stable landing platform for our experience; this is known in Buddhism as *anatta* – no self – and is now a mainstream view in Western philosophy and neuroscience. Even if we are not Buddhist nor even particularly philosophical, we can still sense this unreality within and glimpse, on reflection, how flimsy our process of identity construction can be. 'I am this' and 'I am that', we say, but we don't notice that we are the kind of being who says I am this and I am that. The Self may be a necessary and functional illusion in constant flux, held together by memory and storytelling. Your felt sense of 'I' matters emotionally, psychologically, socially and legally, and it helps you get through life, so don't leave home without it, but our 'I' may be the pattern that connects what is real in our life, not the reality itself. 'Why are you unhappy?' asked the Taoist teacher Wei Wu Wei. 'Because 99 per cent of what you think and what you say and what you do is for yourself, and there isn't one.'

I am not sure where I stand on this matter. We are all in a process of being and becoming in perpetuity, and it seems to be the experience of meaning created through the interplay of self-creation and self-transcendence that makes life worth living. There are certainly days when I feel like the sense of self is a kind of illusion, and the boundaries between myself and the people, objects, memories and associations that make up the self are blurred or non-existent. There are other days when the self feels fundamental, and precious because it is unique. On those days I feel part of a process of individuation, collaborating with a universe that is making myself *more* real. In this respect I am moving closer to what some interpreters of the Kabbalah in the Jewish mystical tradition call our 'soul print' or 'unique self'.[4] The pathway to becoming real appears to be *both* about an experiential grasp of the illusion of selfhood and a sense of deepening individuation. Paradoxically, we become real when we stop pretending to be real, and we are most fully ourselves when leave our idea of ourselves behind.

Chess can help with this process, but it is just as likely to be a trap that keeps an unreal self in perpetual check. I know many chess players whose lives have become stuck and increasingly unreal as it became harder to maintain the confidence trick necessary for games of chess to constitute reality, to matter. In my teenage years chess helped me to escape the emotional demands of the world that were otherwise *too real* to cope with. In my twenties, chess was often an alternate reality, but I felt more fully myself there than in the putative real world where I had yet to find a place. In my early thirties, I mobilised enough willpower and discipline to keep the meaning of chess alive. However, by my mid-thirties this effort was already becoming strenuous, and it was only because I had education and relationships beyond the chess world that there was a path back to reality defined by a certain amount of 'weight', without which I fear life might have become unbearably light, and increasingly unreal.

That is my story, and by no means the only way chess and life shape each other. For many individuals in different cultures with different economies and chess traditions, the game may offer a 'weighty' pathway of meaning and purpose and growth necessary to create a stable sense of self, before the question of deconstructing the self or transcending it even arises. It may also be true that the Buddhists overstate their case, and we have something resembling unique selves or immortal souls after all. I really don't know. What I do know is that in psychological and spiritual terms we have to be somebody before we can be nobody. And in my experience, the best nobodies often turn out to be somebodies after all.[5]

57. ONE MOMENT IN TIME

Woody Allen's stand-up scenario called 'Down South' imagines him unwittingly stumbling into a Ku Klux Klan gathering that he had assumed was a fancy dress party. This unfortunate predicament heightens when the Klan realise he is not one of them, and begin to tie a rope around his neck. The audience is invited to share in Allen's dying thoughts. He says his life passed before his eyes and he gives details of his school in Kansas, his swimming and fishing, and his love for a particular kind of catfish dish. And then Allen realised that he didn't recognise these things from his own memory at all. He was going to be hanged in two minutes and the wrong life was flashing before his eyes.

I love this scenario for the absurdity and the desperation. The least we can hope for is that when our time inevitably comes, then the right life will flash before our eyes. If lives do indeed flash, I imagine some of what flashes before my eyes will be chess games. I don't think I will remember tournament victories, trophies or prizes, because they all blend into each other after a while. But games where we really felt like we excelled leave an imprint on our souls. There is some sort of self-overcoming involved, a mastery of the intellect and will, a deep wellspring of strength that feels personal and precious. Those moments are also characterised by the right kind of exhaustion in which you are not tired, yet you feel a rewarding emptiness that comes from knowing you have given everything you have.

Such games are rare. They may happen only every few years or so in a chess player's career, and personally I can count them on one hand. I thought of this phenomenon when watching a dazzling display of my lifelong friend, one of England's finest Grandmasters, Luke McShane, in 2012. He defeated the then world number two Lev Aronian with a level of power and panache that he will not forget, in a game that made me think of Kasparov at his best. When we look back at such games the memory is somehow crystallised. It is not this move or that move, or even this result or that result. The abiding sensation is a moment in time where we felt profoundly alive.[6]

Whitney Houston spoke to that sense of maximum vitality when she opened the 1988 Olympics in Seoul with her song 'One Moment in Time'. It was described as 'a majestic carpe diem chest-thumper' by *Entertainer* magazine, and the video of the song ends with the Olympic cauldron blazing. 'One Moment in Time' is often played alongside sporting montages, and has a triumphalist spirit, but it has hidden depths too, because that desire for one moment in time is a longing for eternity.

Eternity is often thought of as a particularly long period of time, but it can also be seen as a *single* moment that is infinitely extended in time, a perpetually present moment. In this sense, eternity is about the embrace of timelessness and time, a backwards glance to the big bang, and a perennial creation story. We resonate with the desire for 'one moment in time' paradoxically because it's a moment outside of time too.

There is a story of a mystic speaking with a nihilist. The latter laments that there is no meaning to hold on to in life, because nothing is permanent and everything is constantly changing. 'That's right,' said the mystic with emphasis, '*constantly* changing.'

58. HOTEL BREAKFASTS

One ordinary Sunday morning in the autumn of 2012 I was gazing out the window of a large conference-style breakfast room in a conference-style hotel near Reading. I was looking for inspiration but couldn't find it, because while the scenery was verdant and expansive, I could barely see it through the drizzle and fog. At that moment it struck me, like unsettling news from a polite doctor, that I had been playing the 4NCL – Britain's team chess league – for fifteen years.

I looked down at the trusty fried egg on my plate, accompanied by two glistening hash browns and a small puddle of baked beans. This hot food before me, which had once been a symbol of professional on-the-road freedom, now represented, by my rough calculation, my seventy-fifth hotel breakfast in this particular chess event.

I searched for kindred spirits in the faces of fellow chess players, hoping for a nod or wink of solidarity to signal that they felt the moment too. Perhaps they also sensed that our lives are cages of our own making, built by the need for identity and locked by the force of habit. But no, they mostly looked relatively contented, sharing stories of yesterday's game, and thinking ahead to today's.

The faces were very familiar, somewhat older, and, though I had no real way of knowing, not obviously any the wiser. After all, they, like me, were still travelling away from home with a curious sense of purpose, to honour a generic venue with two creative battles, recorded in algebraic notation. They, like me, were hoping for an affirming social experience on the Saturday night, and no doubt also expecting far too much from their hash browns on the Sunday morning.

The closest parallel is the 1993 film *Groundhog Day* with Bill Murray. In that wonderful film, highly recommended as an illustration of spiritual growth, the protagonist is trapped in the same place on the same day, repeated indefinitely as he wakes up to the same radio announcement: 'It's Groundhog Day!' He breaks out by transforming his outlook, developing himself, helping others, and finally winning the affections of the woman he had previously merely desired, but gradually chooses to love.

I wasn't quite up to that scale of liberation, but after breakfast I put my hood up and went for a walk in the rain, phoned some loved ones and tried to muster willpower for the game ahead. Unfortunately, the morning's revelation was just too intense, and I could not shake the unsettling feeling that my game did not really matter. I really did try to fight, but played without sufficient distinction to defeat a young International Master from Canada, fresh from his first-ever 4NCL breakfast.

I noticed a game on the same day that contrasted with my own lacklustre display, and it reminded me of the beautiful and original combinations hidden in the game for keen eyes to find, even when our minds lack the vitality to execute them. Scotland's Graham Morrison, who was probably on his fiftieth or so 4NCL breakfast, unwisely grabbed a hot pawn against Grandmaster Mark Hebden, who started the 4NCL long before me, and may even be a 4NCL breakfast centurion. His opponent was soon, of course, toast.[7]

59. GRAVE SITUATIONS

One Tuesday lunchtime, in the last week of June 2012, I found myself in the beautiful and atmospheric Brompton Cemetery near Chelsea football ground, listening to two Lutheran priests speak in Polish about a person I had barely heard of and never met. I was there principally to pay homage to the person who had helped to restore his resting place, my friend Grandmaster Stuart Conquest.

Stuart invited me to attend a 'rededication' of the grave of Johannes Zukertort (1842–1888), who challenged Wilhelm Steinitz for the first official World Championship Match in 1886. Zukertort was Polish, but spent the last ten years of his life in London.

On one of his many wayfaring adventures, Stuart had noticed that Zukertort was listed as a 'notable person' buried in the cemetery, but when he approached the plot he saw only grass, and gradually took it upon himself to restore the grave out of respect for a great chess player from the past. However, I think it would be wrong to see the motivation as completely earnest, and there is some ludic charm in this story about the unexpected ways in which we are asked to demonstrate who we are, by showing what we care about.

I can imagine many chess players thinking it would be good if someone sorted out the grave, but Stuart took the responsibility upon himself to follow up with the relevant authorities, including the people responsible for the cemetery, and at one point he literally dug out the gravestone that had slowly been subsumed by the ground. He also astutely contacted the Polish Heritage Society, who helped to raise funds for a stunning new white gravestone.

Some find the atmosphere in cemeteries to be grave, but personally I rather like it. The silent durability of the stones is complemented by the quiet pulse of the natural surroundings, which allows us to experience peace, while paying respect to life. Being surrounded by epitaphs is also a sharp reminder that we won't be here for ever, which brings the mind back to the present, where it tends to function best.

However, that Tuesday I had been running a little late and actually got lost in the cemetery. On his mobile phone Stuart said I had better hurry because the priests were approaching the grave and it would all be over soon. Thankfully I had seen them, clad in purple and gold regalia, so he advised me to 'Follow the priests!' I was soon huddled together with thirty or so attendees who understood why they were there; not so much to pay homage to Zukertort, but by doing so to reaffirm our deep love and respect for the game and the people who play it.

In his short speech Stuart mentioned that Zukertort was probably the best player in the world for a year or two, and made a passing reference to 'Qb4! against Blackburne that chess players here will know.' At that moment I felt embarrassed not to know, but I checked the game reference as soon as I went home, and the game was indeed familiar; it features an impressive and unusual tactical flourish to finish, based on a queen sacrifice to deflect the opponent's queen from the defence of her king. The chess world already has a game considered 'The Immortal Game', between Adolf Andersen and Lionel Kieseritzky, a game that never loses its vitality. After the rededication of his grave, perhaps we should call Zukertort's famous win against Blackburne the mortal game; a game that reminds us of the need for dignity in death.[8]

60. COURAGE

Winston Churchill said that courage was the one virtue that made possible all the others, and I think he was right, but it is easier to valorise courage than it is to understand it, and we often don't recognise courage in ourselves and others.

It is widely quoted that courage is not the absence of fear but the judgment that there's something more important than fear. That sounds helpful, but there's a great deal of complexity in how judgment relates to fear that gets lost in our main cultural symbols of courage – for instance soldiers valiantly risking their lives to safeguard the wounded, firefighters braving the flames to rescue the trapped.

Most images of courage relate to people doing something where fear for safety might advise us to do otherwise. In addition to such heroic courage there is also a different kind of courage based on trust, and that may be even more important.

In the Candidates tournament taking place in Khanty-Mansiysk in Russia in March 2014, Vishy Anand continued his return to form after losing his world title by achieving a winning position against the young Russian Grandmaster Dmitry Andreikin. Victory was a tantalising prospect, since it would virtually guarantee tournament victory and a rematch for the world title with Carlsen.

Watching with the commentators and online analysis engine, chess players around the world could see that objectively there were many ways Vishy could convert the advantage, but none of the solutions were entirely straightforward, and most would require enduring risk and demonstrating vigilance before victory was assured.

In the end, feeling tired and with too many moving parts in the position to feel it was wise to proceed, Vishy took the available draw by repetition. With a clear point lead and two games to go, he was still heavy favourite, so many people understood the decision, but there was also disappointment. If Vishy really wanted to win the event, why did he not take this precious chance? Should he not have shown the courage of his conviction that he was winning, by converting like a true champion? Surely this is what the new world champion, Magnus Carlsen, would have done?

But then I was reminded of the saying of Mary Anne Radmacher: 'Courage does not always roar. Sometimes courage is the quiet voice at the end of the day saying, "I will try again tomorrow."'

Vishy showed great courage after all. To pursue tournament victory at significant risk in that particular position would in fact have betrayed a lack of courage, as if he doubted his abilities, and desperately had to grab his chance while it was there, rather than trust that he could hold his nerve for the last two games, which he duly did, and he went on to challenge for the World Title once more.[9]

61. THE EXISTENCE OF GOD

It may seem indecent to speak about God in a book about chess, but I'm sure she won't mind. I doubt there is any strong relationship between chess and religious disposition, but I find that when I am focused on a tournament, and offer myself up to the slings and arrows of competition, I invariably feel that I am not alone. The experience is not so much of assistance but of benign and ineffable company, and if I allow myself to be receptive, it seems every bit as present whether I win or lose.

In February 2012 I spent an intensely absorbing hour watching a live telecast from Oxford's Sheldonian Theatre, featuring a debate between the iconoclastic atheist Richard Dawkins and the reassuringly hairy Archbishop of Canterbury, Rowan Williams. The discussion was highly convivial, typically Oxonian, and curiously English. Had they adjourned for high tea with fruit scones and crustless cucumber sandwiches, it would have felt entirely appropriate.

There were no decisive arguments, but quite a few magic moments. Williams described God as 'love and mathematics' in his singularly affable and slightly mischievous manner. And I enjoyed his question: 'If consciousness is an illusion, what isn't?' which brilliantly highlighted that the idea of an illusion presupposes consciousness.

Dawkins had no answer to that, conceding that consciousness is a mystery, and he was impressive more generally too. I am not a big fan of his brand of messianic rationalism, but in this debate he was charming, witty, lucid and respectful, and I loved his description of Planet Earth as 'a celestial Polynesia' – from the perspective of stars and galaxies and vast reaches of outer space, this planet with human life looks like it arose more by accident than design.

Dawkins also seemed more philosophically nimble and intellectually imaginative than usual, which is where he tends to underachieve. Of course it helped that his interlocutor was self-possessed and non-defensive, such that Dawkins, an instinctive intellectual predator, did not seem inclined to attack.

The most revealing moment was when Dawkins shared his love at the beauty of scientific explanations, and Williams seemed to be agreeing, leading a slightly bewildered Dawkins to ask: 'But why would you want to clutter up such a world view with something so messy as a God?' Williams replied that he did not view God in that way, as an extra thing to be shoehorned into an explanation, and that God was not clutter for him at all.

At this point, I almost felt sympathy for Dawkins, who clearly wanted to probe further. He seems troubled when brilliant minds share his scientific world view but still sense God within it. Here was a chance for Williams to explain why his God was not a 'God of the gaps', filling in temporary spaces in scientific explanations, but something, richer, deeper and subtler. Alas, at precisely this fertile point, the discussion moved on.

The most important moment in any debate is when you begin to agree about exactly what you disagree about. Once you get away from assuming that the other side lacks knowledge, scruples or insight, and start to see things from their perspective, thinking becomes productive. We rarely see this in politics, where each side tends to assume the worst of the other, and 'my-side bias', where we selectively attend to evidence, prevails.

The main thing that separates Grandmasters from weaker players is that we habitually test the quality of our ideas against the best moves of the opponent. I think the educational value of chess is too precious to be stated generically, but one quality of mind I would hope that chess cultivates is a capacity to see both (or more) sides of an argument, even if our emotional attachment to winning sometimes gets in the way. Whether we are thinking about the existence of God or whether to attack on the kingside or the queenside of the chessboard, we simply can't succeed consistently unless we are willing to respect opposing and alternative ideas as much as our own.

62. THE MEANING OF SACRIFICE

In the Christian tradition, the time between Good Friday when Christ was crucified and his resurrection on Easter Sunday is a moment of repose between despair and hope. That struggle with despair and hope defines the human condition, and Easter Saturday can therefore be seen as a microcosm of our whole lives. Perhaps the reason we don't hear much about Easter Saturday is that we live it every day.

It saddens me that people in public life have become so chary about speaking about spiritual matters, by which I mean questions about the ultimate nature, meaning and purpose of existence. Much of the population are now in an uncomfortable spiritual place, feeling neither religious nor particularly anti-religious, and seeking a spiritual perspective that is intellectually robust and personally meaningful, but not knowing how to get there.

If the reader is wondering by this point in the book whether I 'believe in God', I am fond of Jonathan Safran Foer's response: 'I am not only agnostic about the answer, I am agnostic about the question.' When it comes to the entirety of your world view, your spiritual sensibility and your cosmological framework, 'belief' is every bit as loaded and ambiguous and unhelpful a term as God. So if somebody put a gun to my head and asked: 'Do you believe in God, yes or no?', I would first say: 'Please define your terms.' Then if they began to pull back the trigger and said: 'Last chance!' I would say: 'OK, yes! But can we please talk about it afterwards?'

This kind of spiritual equivocation might now be the position of the silent majority of the population. Like many in a globalised and technologically advanced world, my spiritual outlook is varied because my life has been varied. I would say I am culturally

Christian, intellectually Buddhist, temperamentally sceptical and domestically Hindu. Emotionally and aesthetically I *feel* Christian because I grew up thinking that the individual is sacred, people are flawed and churches are beautiful. Psychologically and philosophically I *think* Buddhist because I recognise the contingent and interdependent nature of life and think living well means gradually transforming delusion into wisdom by finding and forging the right path. Through seven years of higher education I have learned to *assess* ideas sceptically and rationally, so I am not particularly credulous. There is a lot of narcissistic nonsense out there masquerading as spiritual insight, and the atheist often makes the most sense. And partly because I'm married to Siva, partly because the iconography is so charming and partly because my meditation practice is Vedantic, I *am* partly Hindu. For instance sometimes I find myself lighting incense near Indian deities, and occasionally chanting their names, but not because I believe in them as such.

I was thinking a lot about these matters in the Easter of 2014, and not just because I was working on public understandings of spirituality in a professional capacity in my day job at the RSA. I was also becoming increasingly irritated, perhaps even mildly enraged, by Easter looking like a time of friendly bunny rabbits and colourfully wrapped chocolate eggs. That year the whole shebang just seemed unbearably hollow and shallow and I was pining for fullness and depth.

Eggs and bunnies colonised Easter because its defining story gradually became an explanatory vacuum. The idea that Jesus 'died for our sins', often stated as a self-evident truth, makes absolutely no sense at first blush, and then the idea that there is hope for us because he was resurrected does not appear to clarify matters. Even if you trust the historical record enough to establish the where and the when of the event, the other big questions do not have easy answers – Who? What? How? Why?

I struggle with the who. The idea that Jesus was not just a Palestinian Jew with radical politics who told good stories but a cosmic linchpin who was uniquely placed to connect human beings to the divine seems a stretch. Only in recent years have I realised that you need to grasp the what to understand the who, and the how to understand the what, and the why to understand the how.

The 'what' of the Easter story is sacrifice, a notion that every strong chess player knows intimately. We sacrifice regularly, sometimes several times in one game. We give up our pawns and pieces and even queens for the sake of greater goals, sometimes short term, and sometimes long. A true sacrifice in chess happens when you cannot be sure if you will ever regain the material you have given away, but trust in the dynamic qualities of your position to compensate for the loss. Chess teaches you that a sacrifice is not simply about giving something up, and nor is it a simple trade of one kind of value for another. You can feel it at the board when you have sacrificed something. You are in a liminal space that is unstable and will soon change, characterised by a state of self-conscious anticipation as you await some kind of transformation.

Just as I believe chess can be seen as a meta-metaphor, i.e. a metaphor that contains many metaphors, and through which the meaning and significance of metaphor (rather than just chess) is revealed, the Easter sacrifice can be seen as a meta-sacrifice, illuminating the role of sacrifice more generally. The story is dark and difficult because when Jesus purportedly rises from the dead he is still wounded. This is not a story about everything being OK in the end. The agonising death and abject humiliation of the crucifixion was not a grand cosmic gimmick or part of a theological set piece. In this sense the story represents the ultimate sacrifice, to undergo agonising pain and feel utterly dejected and forsaken, all for the sake of others; in this case for the sake of all others.

If the what of the Easter story is sacrifice, the 'how' is something about what sacrifice does.

Sacrifice literally means to make sacred, and while sacred things are not necessarily morally good they do operate as touchstones of value that are considered absolute, and not instrumental (for instance, in Nazi Germany the swastika may not have been described as sacred, but it functioned as a sacred symbol). In chess

that might mean giving away pieces to get at the opponent's king –
the ultimate prize. Just as the king is of infinite value, things that
are held sacred are not for sale; they are qualitatively different,
and that is partly why the idea of sacrifice is culturally muted in
a consumerist society, where the emphasis is on one kind of value
and the default aim is to consume more stuff.

Sacrifice, by contrast, is more about emptying than filling, and
more about giving oneself away rather than holding on to who we
are and what we have. The literary theorist Terry Eagleton describes
sacrifice as the transition from weakness to power, in which self-
dispossession is a condition for self-fulfilment. The Easter story is
the epitome of this idea of sacrifice, namely that we have to empty
ourselves to be filled with something else; to lose our lives as we
know them to live in a qualitatively different way, and perhaps even
suffer in the process. Sacrifice is meaningful, but it is not about
happiness.[10]

The what and the how of the story mean nothing without the
why, which I confess I don't fully understand, but it no longer feels
completely absurd. When sin is understood in Francis Spufford's
sense of 'the human propensity to fuck things up', the idea of
being saved from our sins becomes more psychological than
metaphysical; it's about being at peace with our struggle to be good,
rather than sitting on the wrong side of the scales of cosmic justice.
And then when we consider the human inclination to scapegoat
others to shield ourselves from our knowledge of our propensity to
fuck things up, rather than accept that we are deeply flawed, the
idea that a sacrifice might be a necessary source of renewal seems
plausible. And if that's so, the idea that one particular sacrifice
could be cosmically significant enough to readjust our relationship
to the divine seems merely elaborate rather than incoherent. And
then when we consider our tendency to self-justify, to rationalise
and explain away the mistakes we have made, the notion that we
may not have to do this comes as a blessed relief. The why of the
Easter story, encapsulated in a line by Rowan Williams, is therefore
this: 'Something has happened that makes self-justification
unnecessary.'[11]

I am far from sure what to make of all that, but I learned from chess that we need to take sacrifices seriously, no matter where they lead.

Another aspect of the Easter story that I see as a chess player is the importance of seeing one move further. On the Easter Saturday, it looked as if a putative God had struggled to be just, and that in light of parental neglect of celestial proportions, the terrestrial bad guys had got away with torturing and killing his only son. Whether or not it is true, the story of the resurrection says that we should always try to look deeper, and see further.

That experience of reaching beyond one's grasp and feeling oneself grow in the process is a beautiful moment for any chess player. Just as Thoreau once wrote that men go fishing all their lives without realising that it's not fish they are after, many chess players play chess all their lives without realising that it's not checkmate they are after. The time we invest in the game is a sacrifice in aid of those moments of self-forgetting and self-realisation that are most deeply fulfilling.[12]

63. FEELING YOUR AGE

At a press conference during their first world championship match in 2013, world champion Viswanathan Anand (forty-three) and his challenger, Magnus Carlsen (twenty-two), had just completed a fairly uneventful draw, and were waiting for the usual onslaught of banal questions. To spice things up in front of the home crowd, one journalist asked the Indian sporting legend: 'Are you feeling your age?'

When you take the question literally, it seems strange, and perhaps ever so slightly salacious. The reigning champion answered with customary tact and diplomacy, but I felt an opportunity was lost. In a comparable moment in the 1984 presidential election, President Reagan was already seventy-three, campaigning for a second four-year term against Walter Mondale, who was fifty-six. During the first televised presidential debate a moderator asked Reagan the question on everybody's mind, which, to paraphrase, was 'Are you not too old to be president?' Reagan paused and smiled in a completely relaxed manner, before saying: 'I want you to know I will not make age an issue of this campaign. I am not going to exploit for political purposes my opponent's youth and inexperience.' He completely turned the issue on its head. Some feel this moment was pivotal, and he went on to win by a landslide.

Age has an objective quality of minutes, hours and days going by, but what it means is always somewhat relative. When he was four, Kailash was already fascinated by numbers and sizes, but could not yet grasp the concept of relativity. Almost every day he would ask me: 'Is four really big, Daddy?' I knew I should just say 'Yes', which is probably the answer he was seeking, but instead I kept trying to convey that four is big relative to two and three, but small relative to five and six. His face would turn pensive, and I would think we might be getting somewhere, but then he would ask me: 'So is six really big, Daddy?' And so it went on. With hindsight I should have quoted the former French President Charles de Gaulle: 'Age is not important, unless you are a cheese.' That would have kept him quiet for a while.

De Gaulle was of course wrong. Age is important for all sorts of reasons, not least our appetite for competition. There is no optimal age to play chess well, but it appears to be somewhere between twenty-five and thirty-five, due to the necessary combination of energy and experience, but it is dropping all the time because technology speeds up the process of improvement. The main reason age matters in chess is not cognitive; it's not that your understanding diminishes as you get older – if anything the opposite. The main issue is that reserves of energy diminish, so while we can play at full capacity in one game, we might struggle to do so over eleven days of the same event. The related issue is motivation. It is hard to care quite so intensely about the details of each move and the result of each game because the mattering ceases to be self-evident – we have to work harder on ourselves to care.

We often think of our age as if our time was sand in an hourglass that was slowly running out, but we can also think of age as the layers of a tree that is enriching and becoming ever more deeply rooted in the earth. Every year is an additional layer of meaning, in which we grow more real, not less; ever closer to our finale, and ever further from the naivety of our genesis. Our lives literally realise themselves. Ideally our sense of time passing and our sense of becoming more real should be like gracefully moving in step with a subtle rhythm, but this is a world where some dance better than others and some cannot hear the music at all. It is a world full of joyful becoming, yes, but also full of accidents, tragedy and war. Perhaps when our finite time runs out we become infinitely real, but we are likely to disappear in the process.

I am intrigued by the idea that there is a unique sensation felt by everyone at the precise moment of our life when we move into our second half, and that if only we could sense it, we would mark it with some kind of ritual or party. I am not sure whether I have felt that sensation yet, but my fortieth birthday party came close. What I do know is that as my early thirties became mid-thirties, I started to realise that my thirty thousand or so days would eventually run out. Perhaps the beginning of the end of our youth is when we start to feel our age, in the sense of noticing an embodied sense of finitude.

In one of Samuel Beckett's plays – *Krapp's Last Tape* – themes of memory, loss, regret and hope are explored through a sixty-nine-year-old listening to a tape of himself as a thirty-nine-year-old man, who in turn speaks about himself in his twenties. Krapp is a bizarre character who eats far too many bananas, but Beckett's singular skill was to use some specific sense of absurdity to speak to universals of the human condition. Krapp rewinds and fast-forwards the spool of the cassette trying to capture and relive precious moments, and repudiate his involvement with other moments. The play is tragicomic, and includes many poignant lines. My favourite is when the sixty-nine-year-old Krapp listens ruefully to his thirty-nine-year-old self saying: 'Perhaps my best years are gone. When there was a chance of happiness. But I wouldn't want them back. Not with the fire in me now.'

64. FACING UP TO DEATH

Near the beginning of Ingmar Bergman's film *The Seventh Seal*, the character Death appears before a medieval knight, Antonius Block, to claim his life. Antonius looks disappointed. He is not ready to go and says he would like to do something significant before he dies. Death replies that everyone says that.

Antonius challenges Death to a chess match, and thereby prolongs his life, a life that he describes in negative terms, consoling himself with the thought that most lives are like his, and that he will use his reprieve for 'one meaningful deed'.

Ultimately his defences could not hold, but this extra time allowed him to live with the understanding that although his days were numbered, he could do some good in that time. Death announces mate in one, and the knight concedes. Death asks if he enjoyed his reprieve, and Block replies that he did.

Once you look into what Ernest Becker called 'the denial of death' you begin to see it everywhere, not least chess, where that denial is very clearly sublimated. Every decisive game ends in the prospective death of a king with whom we projectively identify, and every game is a new life and a new story. That chess offers this particular kind of reprieve should be part of its charm rather than a dark secret, but we struggle to speak of death so openly.

In 2014 I hosted a public event on the subject of death while working at the RSA, with a panel including the writer Will Self, who said this:

'I face up to death but then I flip back into denial. Surely that's what it's like? I lie in bed in the small hours of the morning, absolutely terrified by the apprehension of my own dissolution ... And then I go to sleep and wake up in the morning and make toast.'

That is what it's like. We both know and don't know that we are going to die. We are often told that we should live each day as though it is our last, but we rarely succeed in doing so. Most of us accept abstractly that we will not be here for ever, but very few grasp at a visceral level that we are all living on borrowed time.

In August 2009, a chess story reminded me of Death's question to Antonius, and reaffirmed that we should all think seriously about how to 'enjoy our reprieve'.

The 2009 Acropolis Open in Greece was overshadowed by the death of a respected Greek player, Nikolaos Karapanos, who had a heart attack just before executing a winning move in his first-round game. His opponent, Israeli Grandmaster Dan Zoler, who happens to be a doctor, tried to revive him, but Karapanos stopped breathing before the ambulance arrived.

This story indicates just how stress-inducing chess can be, but the deeper point is that we never know when our time will come. All the major spiritual traditions speak about the importance of being ready for the unthinkable, and the importance of dying at peace, without undue regret.

It seems profane to point out that Zoler resigned the game, but he also withdrew from the event, stating that he no longer felt like playing chess in the circumstances. You can hardly blame him. Chess sometimes seems singularly charming and vitally important, but a brief reflection on our mortality has to lead to some searching questions: Is this it? Pushing these pieces around? Is this what I am supposed to be doing?[13]

The writer Oliver Burkeman observes that: 'For a civilisation so fixated on achieving happiness, we seem to be remarkably incompetent at the task.' No wonder. Our incompetence is baked into our objective, because nothing is less likely to make you happy than trying to pursue it. It is a relief to realise that happiness is not the most important thing in life.

So what is? I hesitate to say, partly because I don't know, and partly because the same fixation process is likely to arise, and the search for 'the most important thing' may keep us from living in ways that allow us to experience it. That said, the straightforward answer is joy, particularly as defined by C. S. Lewis in his autobiography, where he describes joy as 'an unsatisfied desire which is itself more desirable than any other satisfaction'.

That kind of joy is at the heart of the chess experience, characterised as it is by a sense of constant craving in an atmosphere of intellectual beauty, competitive resistance and inevitable mistakes. Lewis suggests that anyone who has experienced joy of this kind will want it again, and he doubts whether anyone who has tasted it would ever exchange it for all the pleasures in the world; that is certainly true of many chess players. Lewis adds that joy is not in our power, and that may be right, though it makes me wonder if he ever played chess.

Joy is mysterious because we seek it out as pleasure but cannot find it without pain. The subtlest and most enduring gift that chess gave me is the awareness that we can feel gratitude for life regardless of the happiness it offers at any given moment. Losing is painful but deeply meaningful. While we don't like to lose, we are most alive in those arenas where winning and losing make sense. By simulating the struggle for truth, beauty and goodness through competition, chess illuminates life as a whole, returning us to the perennial questions contained in any position: What is happening here? What am I trying to do? What's my next move?

Moving On

I cannot imagine ever saying farewell to chess, but I have been saying 'See you later' for so long that I am starting to doubt myself. I have not studied the intricacies of the game seriously or played with real competitive intent for over a decade. It is hard to imagine personal and professional circumstances where chess might again be part of the main curriculum of my life.

For the last few years chess has been an early December activity. I have been strong enough, on rating at least, to be invited to high-level Grandmaster events at the London Chess Classic in Kensington Olympia. I cared about my performance and I tried to play well. I did not have time or mental energy to channel my desire, but I turned up hoping for the best.

In 2013, for instance, I was selected as a wild-card entry to the elite rapid-play tournament of the London Chess Classic and was paired against former world champion Vladimir Kramnik. To play Kramnik head-to-head would be a dream come true for most chess players, even in a rapid game, and it's a rare honour for Grandmasters to play world champions. Alas, my lived experience was more like witnessing myself in a dream, unable to exert any control on events. The game started at 2 p.m., and that should have meant laser-like focus on the challenge ahead in the morning including both opening preparation and fortifying the psyche in various ways, for instance through meditation, walking or speaking with loved ones. In fact, I was too busy working for the RSA, my employer at the time.

I remember sitting in a Hilton hotel room in Kensington with my Chessbase program open on my laptop, but I had to finish a policy report on the complexity of climate-change denial based on a national survey that was due for publication a few days later. I was ostensibly 'working from home', and colleagues were calling to ask about media strategy while I was trying to figure out whether I had any viable answer to Kramnik's likely first move. My climate report featured in *The Times* newspaper a few days later; but I lost my chess game without a fight. I am no match for Kramnik, even on a good day, but I felt bemused by the way my life had turned out, knowing that I could not even *try* to give my best. At the highest levels the game demands levels of energy, focus and discipline that preclude other major interests. As the American Grandmaster Yasser Seirawan puts it, 'Chess is a jealous lover.'

Two years later in the VIP room at the same event I got talking to Danish Grandmaster Peter Heine Nielsen – principal trainer to two world champions, Carlsen and Anand – about the challenge of finding fulfilment in chess when you are no longer professional. I was struck when he remarked that in his view I was 'never really a chess player'. I know from working alongside Peter in Anand's team that he is a kind and discerning soul who respects my chess ability, so I didn't take offence. The point is that serious professional players tend to be extremely focused on the game relative to other aspects of life and focused on the competitive aspects of the game relative to the more aesthetic, educational or philosophical aspects. I have a weakness for both forms of diversion. It has taken me a while to accept it, but I think I always felt truer to myself when I was reflecting on what chess means for life as a whole than when I was trying to win tournaments.

On 1 December 2017, I showed up in Kensington again, this time at the UK Knockout. I had not played since the same event the previous year, so there was a déjà vu sensation. I invested a few stray hours before the event to remind myself how to think about the game, including some training games with Luke McShane, who went on to win the event. I even visited an acupuncturist friend, asking him to find the magic meridian points to help release whatever latent fighting spirit I had. He said he would attempt to release the energy trapped in my solar plexus, and I was grateful for the effort. I also remember his look of sympathetic disbelief, because I had been in the same predicament in previous years and it had never really worked. Here I was again, in a triumph of hope over experience, asking not for an ailment to be fixed, but for an old identity to be resurrected.

Concentration and willpower cannot be summoned quite so easily or quickly. Nor could I muster any appetite for opening theory. In fact I found the idea of diligently preparing openings obtuse, perhaps distasteful – it felt like wasting precious time. This experience was new.

I was hankering after lost competence and unable to let go of desire. Amidst these mixed emotions, I did something on the morning of the game that I do when I am trying to feel a complex moment of life more deeply – I consulted the *I Ching*, the ancient Chinese oracle of change; we sort a set of sticks or throw coins that can be interpreted as six straight or broken lines that are stacked on top of each other to for m hexagrams, corresponding to a commentary in the book.[1] I cannot completely disavow the possibility of divination from a source outside of my own psyche, but nor can I make sense of it. On those rare occasions when I throw the coins and draw the lines I am not seeking to know the future, because I don't believe the future can be foretold in this way. What I seek and value are additional perspectives on the present, alternative ways of sensing what is happening, and an oblique vantage point that feels helpfully *other*. The philosopher Alan Watts describes the *I Ching* as a sixty-four-sided coin toss, and the parallel with chess's sixty-four squares is noteworthy, though perhaps not more than that.

A few hours later I would be playing competitive chess again, after 365 days away. It was a knockout event over two games on the same day, leading to a rapid and then blitz play-off in the event of a tie (faster and faster we play, until somebody figuratively dies). I was up against Grandmaster Matthew Sadler, who is also no longer professional but still takes the game very seriously and studies the game for, he says, 'at least fifteen minutes every day'. In any case, the psychological challenge of playing chess as such was much greater for me than the competitive challenge of any particular opponent.

I asked the oracle: 'How can I optimise my chances of enjoying today's games?'

I received the following answer:

33: Retiring

———————————
———————————
———————————
———————————
——————— ———————
——————— ———————

Withdraw, conceal yourself, retreat; pull back in order to advance later.

The commentary included lines like 'This is a time to hide yourself ... In seclusion, you can prepare for a better time ... Decline involvements, refuse connections ... You cannot stay where you are ... Immerse yourself in this situation and endure. Knowing when to retire is a very great thing.'

My reading contained a transforming line at the fifth point: 'The way opens. As you retire, excellence comes with you.' Then the transformed hexagram was:

56: Sojourning

———————————
——————— ———————
———————————
———————————
——————— ———————
——————— ———————

> This is a time of wandering, seeking and living apart. You are a stranger in a strange land, whose identity comes from a distant centre ... You are alone, outside the social network, with few connections, on a quest of your own. Consider things carefully. Make clear decisions even if they are painful. Limit and stabilise your desires when you are with others. By doing these things, you discover what you are seeking. In this way, the time of sojourning is truly great.

Sojourning means to be somewhere temporarily, and that felt apt. Before the game I tried to adapt the reading for competitive purposes, but I already knew what it meant. I did not belong to competitive chess and had not belonged for several years. That part of my life was over. Superficially, it might seem like self-sabotage to invite an apparently negative reading and then play as if it were true, but that's not how it works psychologically. All of the sentiments conveyed by the oracle were already felt, and those feelings were enduring by their nature and had been with me for years. I could not shake them off with positive thinking or better preparation. This was not a prophecy of the future but a redescription of the present in which I recognised myself. Although I had strength, I could not access it. Although the chess world remained deeply familiar, I had become an outsider. It may never be time to retire, but it was time to let go.

I gave my available best and tried to fight, but I achieved bad positions very quickly in both games. In fact, my play in the first game was so poor that I could not recognise my former strength at all. It was like looking at myself through the mirror of the game and not recognising my own face. The issue was not just that I lost, but that my moves had no power, elegance or coherence. My pieces were so badly coordinated that I felt sad to have betrayed my own chess education and understanding.

But I was also relieved. I had finally lost it, and 'it' was what I had been trying to shake off for a decade. No doubt I could play well again one day, perhaps any day, but there was no need to pretend to be that hero, no need to be a skilled and ferocious competitor with a hunger for victory. I was going home to my family, and back to the work on bigger-than-self issues that I love the next day. It always felt too grandiose to announce my retirement from chess, as if anybody would really care, but this was the first time I felt I could say goodbye inwardly to the part of me that had craved competitive validation for so long.

I miss many things about playing chess regularly and seriously. I miss believing that each move in each game really matters. I miss the sense of strength and power and dignity that comes with playing well. I miss the felt sense of honour and self-overcoming when you make better decisions because you have learned your lessons well. I miss the clarity of purpose experienced at each moment of each game, the lucky escapes from defeat and the thrill of the chase towards victory.

And yet, I like what has become possible because I am no longer living through and for the game. I feel liberated from the centripetal pull of chess; it is easier now for my thoughts and feelings to move outwards rather than inwards. I love being a father to two playful, enquiring, exhausting young sons, and the endless challenge of becoming a grown-up. I find fulfilment in the complexity of research and the flow of writing. I feel socially and intellectually stretched while grappling with wicked policy problems and being a distinctive part of public debate. I enjoy ever-deepening conversations with friends and colleagues all the more for knowing that they are not at risk of dissipating into chess variations.

Other people play the game of chess, and I feel like one of them now, as if the part of me that plays chess is an autonomous region of my psyche, rather than the sovereign part of my identity. My mind is still charmed by the game, but my soul feels free of it.

I still play fast chess online occasionally. Hundreds of thousands of such games happen every day, and the years roll by for all of us. My older son Kailash is nine at the time of writing and he has discovered a love of chess without any particular help from me. I enjoy volunteering as a chess teacher at his school first thing on Friday mornings. Through Twitter I sometimes become aware of a great game between elite players or solve a tactical puzzle for fun. Every so often I enjoy confusing my followers by tweeting about climate change, spirituality or democracy one minute, and chess positions the next; as if they are all somehow the same thing. Perhaps they are.

I sometimes imagine that when my sons are older and my professional life has moved on I will find the time, will and energy to play chess again, and perhaps be proud of my play. My heart indulges me with this thought, but I know it is unlikely to happen. It is more likely that I will see the fullness of life every day through eyes fashioned by chess, and know the game as a precious metaphor for the world we make together. Chess is worth fighting for partly because it reveals what fighting for something feels like, and means. By saying goodbye to chess I know what I have lost and what I have found. I am grateful for the moves that have made me, and all the moves I have yet to make.

And yet, that sense of closure feels unfair to the reader. To suggest that it all makes sense now is a form of gentle hubris that lacks beauty because it is not the whole truth. Neither chess nor life is easy, and there is no reason why the relationship between them, however rich, should be clear or comforting. I remain a person who did not always exist and I will not be here for long. In a beautiful but capricious world of infinite games and many opponents, the final move is not mine to make. I prefer to end with the disarming thoughts of the fourteenth-century Persian poet Hafiz:

Tripping Over Joy

What is the difference
Between your experience of Existence
And that of a saint?

The saint knows
That the spiritual path
Is a sublime chess game with God

And that the Beloved
Has just made such a Fantastic Move
That the saint is now continually

Tripping over Joy
And bursting out in Laughter
And saying, 'I Surrender!'

Whereas, my dear,
I am afraid you still think
You have a thousand serious moves.

Acknowledgements

This book is a personal story, an expert guide to the chess world, and a philosophy of life in general. Each of these themes reflects my appreciation for others who help along the way.

The memoir is about chess infatuation maturing into love of life, which could only happen because of family, close friends and key professional allies. Grandad Rae was *in loco parentis* around the time my passion for chess became most intense, and his love has stayed with me. My two Uncle Michaels were among my first opponents and kept a fragile flame burning. I remember Uncle Philip remarking mischievously that everyone *likes to think* they're good at chess, including himself; he was certainly good at life. Fiona, Ray, Hazel, Bob, Angela, Alison, Sonia and Beverley: you were all part of the setting too, filial glue in the background that holds the psyche together.

Mark, you set the standard. I remember the first time I drew against you, after years of trying, because it felt like I had won Olympic gold. With bare kings remaining, I screeched upstairs to tell Mum. My chess journey would never have happened without you, and I wish I could have made a move along the way that would have improved your position. Thank you.

Dad, when I write here that we get to truth through beauty, I have your sensibility in mind. Mum, only now that I am a parent do I understand just how much you did for me, including all the things you wisely refrained from doing. Thank you both.

Kailash brought depth to my life by making me a father, and soul to this book as a character in his own right. Vishnu laughs in the face of chess rules; he is joyfully subversive and prefers to keep me in check with the garden hose. I'm proud to dedicate the book to my sons.

For helping me develop and direct a professional life away from chess, I am grateful to many friends, teachers, advisers and colleagues: Nick Fair, Guy Claxton, Steve Broome and Tomas Bjorkman were particularly important.

The second main theme here is a guided tour of a subculture, for which I am indebted to the people who comprised my 'chess world'. The early stewards were Mr Burns and Stan Murray at Skene Square Primary School, Richard James at Richmond Junior Chess Club, and Mr Wilson at Aberdeen Grammar School. I am particularly grateful to Luke, Mark and Daphne Russell for making me part of their chess family and expanding horizons.

Bon Accord Chess Club was a kind of incubator. To club regulars who nurtured the excess energy of youth, who looked at us with warmth, played with us or taught us, I remember you, and thank you. I'm thinking of Jim McKendrick's jokes, John Clifford's laughter, Ross Brenan's pawn grabbing, David Russell's opening theory, John Ewan's insouciance, Gordon Duthie's strange love of losing on time, Bob Daniel's look of surprise, and Mike Shepherd, who lent me chess magazines and computer software and played H.G. Wells' *War of the Worlds* in his car.

As local victories led to national challenges and international opportunities, John Glendinning was an invaluable source of support, arranging tournaments and training. And in my mind Alex McFarlane represents the kind of heroic volunteer who makes chess life possible and isn't thanked enough.

Donald Holmes taught me to love the experience of *learning* how play chess better – nothing was more important to my chess development. Close, however, was Mark Condie's charisma, energy and zeal; his belief in me around 1992–96 gave me reserves of confidence and strength for years afterwards. Paul Motwani's inspiration has been mentioned in the text, and I look forward to throwing a chocolate bar his way at the first available opportunity.

There are too many chess friends, rivals, colleagues, teachers and students to mention, but let me at least note the positive influences of John Shaw, Alan Minnican, Douglas Griffin, Adam Raoof, Luke McShane, Peter Wells, Julian Hodgson and Jon Speelman. I am also grateful to those who helped a poor chess player financially: the observer, the adviser, and the man of the cloth.

The third and perhaps main theme of the book is a series of philosophical perspectives on how to play the game of life better. For helping to develop and refine that case I am indebted to editors, friends and colleagues who pushed me to connect my chess experience to life as a whole.

The *Herald* newspaper let me write freely for a general audience with only oblique references to chess on a weekly basis from 2006–13, for which I thank the initiative of Damien Henderson and Melanie Reid, and the editorial support of many, including Simon Stuart. While the material has metamorphosed beyond recognition, those columns forged the spirit of enquiry that characterise this book.

For discerning advice and feedback along the way, I thank Mark Vernon, Mairi Ryan, Sarah Stein Lubrano, Joy Whyte, Anthea Lawson, David Rook and Sameer Singh. Marina Benjamin's input was particularly helpful in bringing out the heart and soul of the material, without losing its mind. For help with research, thanks to Olimpiu G. Urcan, Malcolm Pein, Brent Cooper and generous strangers on Twitter.

I am grateful to my agent Toby Mundy for posh fry-ups, bringing the manuscript into focus, and pitching with panache. At Bloomsbury, Michael Fishwick and Ben Hyman's early appreciation and excitement put me at ease, and I am grateful for their editorial acumen and responsiveness over several months of revisions. And since you have to finish a book about twenty times before it's actually finished, thanks to Kate Quarry for shepherding it towards publication.

Finally, Siva, love of my life. Thank you for rescuing me from chess without alienating me from it. You brought me the life and perspective that made this book possible. I could not have written it without you.

London, 1 August 2019

Appendix: Algebraic Notation

Algebraic notation is the standard method for recording and describing the moves in a game of chess. It is based on a system of coordinates to uniquely identify each square on the chessboard, with files measured with A–H (left to right) and ranks 1–8 (from White's first row of pieces to Black's). A single letter is used to represent which of the pieces is moving. This form of notation is now standard among all chess organisations and most books, magazines and newspapers. Kings are represented by K, queens by Q, rooks by R, bishops by B, knights by N. Pawns are not represented by a letter, but by the square they are moving to. The square a piece or pawn is moving from is only mentioned when it is necessary to resolve ambiguity, and captures are signified with an 'x'. The castling move is represented by o-o for kingside castling and o-o-o for queenside castling.

So if White moves the pawn two squares in front of his king on the first move, that would be 1.e4. If Black responds by bringing his king's knight out towards the centre, that would be 1...Nf6. If White protected the pawn on e4 with his queen's knight, that would be 2.Nc3. If Black then moved the pawn in front of his queen two squares, that would be 2...d5. If White captures the pawn on d5 with his pawn on e4 that would be 3.ed and if Black captured that pawn with his knight that would be 3...Nxd5.

Chess notation includes '+' for check, and symbols to convey the quality of moves: ! = good, !! = excellent, ? = bad, ?? = blunder, !? = interesting, and ?! = dubious. The scoring system is conveyed by 1–10 for a White victory, 0–1 for a Black victory and 1/2—1/2 for a draw.

Notes

INTRODUCTION

1 George Steiner, 'Fields of Force', *New Yorker*, 28 October 1972.
2 George Lakoff and Mark Johnson, *Metaphors We Live By*, University of Chicago Press, 2003; Mary Catherine Bateson, *In Our Own Metaphor*, Smithsonian Institute Press, 1991.
3 There are a range of books about the relationship between chess and life written for a general audience. Some of the better recent studies include Robert Desjarlais, *Counterplay*, University of California Press, 2012; Stephen Moss, *The Rookie*, Bloomsbury, 2016; David Shenk, *The Immortal Game*, Souvenir Press, 2008; Paul Hoffman, *The King's Gambit*, Hyperion, 2007; Jennifer Shahade, *Chess Bitch*, Siles Press, 2005; and Jan Hein Donner, *The King – Chess Pieces*, New in Chess, 2007.
4 Diego Rasskin-Gutman, *Chess Metaphors*, MIT Press, 2009.
5 David Tacey, *Religion as Metaphor*, Transaction Publishers, 2015.
6 In addition to reflecting on the cultural resonance of chess, part of my understanding of metaphor was shaped while working at the Royal Society of Arts with the philosopher and psychiatrist Iain McGilchrist. I endeavoured to make sense of the practical and policy relevance of his work on hemispheric lateralisation, the differences between how our right and left hemispheres perceive and understand the world; not so much *what* they do, but *how* they *are*, i.e. what they are like, and how those differences shape our history and culture. It is an audacious thesis, but brilliantly and thoroughly argued and it has been critically acclaimed. Many critics are keen to suggest that the relationship between hemispheric imbalances and cultural change is merely

metaphorical, but the more deeply you consider the relationship between brain and world, the harder it becomes to separate metaphors of reality and metaphors that are reality. For further details, see Iain McGilchrist, *The Master and his Emissary*, Yale University Press, 2009. Also see Jonathan Rowson and Iain McGilchrist, 'Divided Brain, Divided World: Why the best part of us struggles to be heard', RSA, 2013. Available at https://www.thersa.org/globalassets/pdfs/blogs/rsa-divided-brain-divided-world.pdf

7 Robert Epstein, 'The Empty Brain', *Aeon Magazine*, 18 May 2016. See: https://aeon.co/essays/your-brain-does-not-process-information-and-it-is-not-a-computer

8 The comparison here is between permutations and elements, and there are mathematical formulas to approximate the numbers in each case. The Shannon number, named after American mathematician Claude Shannon, is the number of possible chess games, thought to be roughly 10 to the power of 120, while atoms in the *known* universe are thought be roughly 10 to the power of 80. When numbers get that high, our inability to travel faster than the speed of light becomes a relevant constraint for measuring atoms in the universe, just as the threefold repetition and fifty-move rule are constraints on the number of possible chess games. It appears to be unlikely that there are more possible chess games than atoms in the universe that is *unknown*, which is estimated to be 250 times bigger than the observable universe, but this cannot be known for sure. I am grateful to Daniel Johnston, a US chess player and mathematician, for helping me understand this issue.

9 I owe this idea that creating and restoring order is a kind of compassion to David Brazier. 'When we are self-preoccupied we quite literally do not see most of what is around us. Therapy does not have to reinforce obsessional inward questioning. The client can simply be asked to observe things around them. In due course, they can be encouraged to start noticing what the situations around them need. The plants need watering. A room needs to be tidied. Clothes need mending. These are all acts of compassion, even though the recipient is not necessarily an animate being. The more the client opens their eyes to their surroundings, the less trapped in aversive feelings they will be. The more they can give themselves to constructive activity, the less dominance ephemeral feelings will have.' See David Brazier, *Zen Therapy*, Robinson, 2001, p. 197.

10 Ellen Langer, *Counter Clockwise: Mindful Health and the Power of Possibility*, Ballantine Books, 2009, ch.1.

11 Diego Rasskin-Gutman, *Chess Metaphors: Artificial Intelligence and the Human Mind*, MIT Press, 2009.

12 Bruno Bettelheim, *The Uses of Enchantment*, Penguin Books, 1976, p. 18.

13 Matthew Lipman, Ann Margaret Sharp and Frederick S. Oscanyan, *Philosophy in the Classroom*, 2nd edition, Temple Press, 1980, p. 13.

14 Jerome Bruner, *Making Stories: Law, Literature, Life*, Harvard University Press, 2002, p. 51.

ONE: THINKING AND FEELING

1 Mihaly Csikszentmihalyi, *Finding Flow: The Psychology of Engagement with Everyday Life*, Basic Books, 1998.

2 'Great Waves', from Nyogen Senzaki and Paul Reps, *Zen Flesh, Zen Bones*, Penguin, 2000.

3 Matthew Crawford, *The World Beyond Your Head: How to Flourish in an Age of Distraction*, Penguin, London, 2016.

4 Guy Claxton, *Intelligence in the Flesh: Why Your Mind Needs Your Body Much More Than It Thinks*, Yale University Press, London, 2015.

5 Mihaly Csikszentmihalyi and Kevin Rathunde, 'The Development of the Person: An Experiential Perspective on the Ontogenesis of Psychological Complexity' in *Applications of Flow in Human Development and Education, The Collected Works of Mihaly Csikszentmihalyi*, Springer, 2014.

6 Francis Spufford, *Unapologetic*, Faber & Faber, London, 2013.

7 Jonathan Rowson, *The Seven Deadly Chess Sins*, Gambit, London, 2001.

8 Jonathan Rowson, *Transforming Behaviour Change: Beyond Nudge and Neuromania*, RSA, 2011. Available at https://www.thersa.org/discover/publications-and-articles/reports/transforming-behaviour-change

9 This idea originally came from former world champion Gary Kasparov, who spoke of material, time and quality as the three dimensions of chess in an article in *New in Chess* magazine. I helped to develop the idea in my book *Chess for Zebras* (Gambit, 2005), where I also add the fourth dimension of clock time, or 'ticking'.

10 Bullet chess is frantic because we have only one minute each per game. This version of chess is rarely used in tournament contexts and looks like a hyper-accelerated no-contact martial art where we

appear to be angry with the clock, which we have to bang to start the opponent's timer; the main test is how quickly we can make legal moves without knocking anything over. Blitz chess – three to five minutes each per game – is also an adrenaline rush, but feels closer to sanity, and it is often played recreationally; blitz chess is more blitz than chess, because speed typically trumps skill. Rapid play is taken much more seriously; it ranges from 15 to 30 minutes each per game and can feel like a real game of chess, just a relatively brisk one; most of the time you have to take decisions much faster than you want to, and often resent it. Classical games are 'real chess' in which you either have to play a certain number of moves (e.g. 40) within a time allocation (e.g. 2 hours) and then either have another time control (e.g. 20 moves in an additional hour) and/or receive additional time (e.g. 30 minutes) to complete the game. Chess players became tired of running inexorably out of time at the end of what could be 7-hour games, so when the technology of digital clocks made it possible, we introduced shorter time allocations (e.g. 90 minutes) with no move limit, and an increment (e.g. 30 seconds), such that you receive additional time every time you press the clock, and are therefore sure of some merciful amount of time for each move, rather than maybe playing brilliantly for several hours, but then suddenly having to make, say, 10 moves in 8 seconds.

11 The previous English winner had been Julian Hodgson in 2000. In 2001 Joe Gallagher formally represented Switzerland, in 2002 Ramachandran Ramesh represented India, as did Abijit Kunte in 2003. Between 2004 and 2006 I represented Scotland and in 2007 the winner was Jacob Aagaard from Denmark, who lived in Scotland.

12 *Stuart Conquest vs Keith Arkell, British Championship Second Play-off Game, Liverpool*
1.e4 c6 2.d4 d5 3.Nd2 dxe4 4.Nxe4 Nd7 5.Nf3 Ngf6 6.Ng3 c5 7.Be2 cxd4?! This gives White a free hand. **8.Qxd4! e6 9.0–0 Bc5 10.Qh4! 0–0 11.Bd3 Be7 12.Bg5 g6?!** (12...Re8) **13.Rad1** Black is already under serious pressure. **13...Re8 14.Bb5! a6 15.Bxd7 Nxd7 16.Ne4 f6 17.Rxd7!** Splat! The dark squares cave in. **17...Bxd7 18.Nxf6+ Bxf6 19.Bxf6 Qc7 20.Be5 Qd8 21.Bf6 Qc7 22.Ne5! Bc6** (22...Bb5 23.c4) **23.Nxg6! Bd5 24.Qg5 Kf7 25.Be5** (25.Nh8+ is quicker) **25... Qd8 26.Qh6 Re7 27.Qxh7+ Ke8** White could keep the tension,

but Stuart was practical and went for a winning endgame. **28.Nxe7 Qxe7 29.Qh8+ Qf8 30.Qxf8+ Kxf8 31.b3** And 1–0 in 46.

13 David Bohm, *Thought As a System*, Routledge, Oxford, 1992.

14 This thought is part of what inspired me to create my organisation Perspectiva, where we attempt to analyse complex global challenges from the perspectives of systems, souls and society. See www.systems-souls-society.com

15 Rita Felski and Susan Fraiman, 'Introduction', *New Literary History*, 43 (2012), p.vi. http://doi.org/vzm; quoted in https://www.lwbooks. co.uk/sites/default/files/nf82_02ahmed.pdf

16 Matthew Radcliff, *Why Mood Matters*, Philosophy of Depression WordPress site, 2012. https://philosophyofdepression.files.wordpress. com/2012/02/heidegger-on-mood23rdsep2010.pdf

17 Charles Guignon, 'Moods in Heidegger's Being and Time', in Cheshire Calhoun and Robert C. Solomon (eds), *What Is an Emotion? Classic Reading in Philosophical Psychology*, Oxford University Press, New York, 1984, p. 237.

TWO: WINNING AND LOSING

1 Simon Barnes, *The Meaning of Sport*, Short Books, 2006.

2 See Edward Slingerland, *Trying Not to Try*, Canongate, 2014 and Michael Puett and Christine Gross-Loh, *The Path*, Viking 2017.

3 *Jonathan Rowson vs Magnus Carlsen, Dresden Olympiad, round 10, 23 November 2008*
1. d4 d5 2. c4 c6 3. Nf3 e6 4. e3 Bd6 5. b3 f5 6. Be2 Nf67. 0-0 Qe7 8. Bb2 b6 9. Qc1 Bb7 10. Ba3 Nbd7 11. Qb2 c5!?12. Nc3 a6 13. Rfd1 0-0 14. cxd5 exd5 15. g3 Rac8 16. Rac1 Kh817. Qb1 Ne4 18. dxc5 Nxc3 19. Rxc3 bxc5 20. Bf1! Nf6 21. Bg2Ne4 22. Rc2 a5 The position is dynamically balanced, but I remember feeling quite comfortable at the time. **23. Bb2 Rf7 24. Ba1?!** This idea is connected with my thirtieth move, and the whole idea is probably not wise. **24...Re8 25. Qc1 h6 26. Ne1! Kh727. Nd3 Rc8 28. Nf4 Bxf4 29. exf4 Qf8 30. Qa3?!** Even if this works out, it is impractical and I began to take too much time here trying to avoid losing my queen. The intuitive 30.Be5! was simplest. Black will follow up with ...d4 and Nc3 but then I can sacrifice the exchange without any real fear of losing and might even be better. At least that was Magnus's assessment at the time. **30...d4 31. Qxa5 Rd732. Qb5 Qd6 33. Qd3 Ba6 34. Qf3 d3 35. Rcc1 d2 36.**

Rc2 Qg6! This move was a mystery to me at the time, but Magnus had already seen what was coming. **37. Bf1 Bb7 38. Qe3 Re8 39. Be5 Rxe5! 40. fxe5 f4!** Winning. **41. Qe2 Ng5 42. Rc3 Qc6 43. f3 Nxf3+ 44. Kf2 Ng5 45. e6 Ne4+ 46. Qxe4+ Qxe4 47. exd7 Qd4+ 48. Ke2 Ba6+ 0–1**

4 See Franc J. G. M. Klaassen and Jan R. Magnus, 'Are Points in Tennis Independent and Identically Distributed? Evidence from a Dynamic Binary Panel Data Model', *Journal of the American Statistical Association*, vol. 96, no. 454 (June 2001), pp. 500–09, and Jose Apesteguia and Ignacio Palacios-Huerta, 'Psychological Pressure in Competitive Environments: Evidence from a Randomized Natural Experiment', *American Economic Review*, September 2009.

5 *Vishy Anand vs Levon Aronian, 2014 Candidates Khanty-Mansiysk, Russia, round 1*

1.e4 e5 2.Nf3 Nc6 3.Bb5 a6 4.Ba4 Nf6 5.0–0 Be7 6.Re1 b5 7.Bb3 0–0 8.h3 Bb7 9.d3 d5 10.exd5 Nxd5 11.Nbd2!? Qd7?! A questionable novelty, but move 18 was the real culprit. **12.Nxe5 Nxe5 13.Rxe5 Nf6 14.Re1!** There is a joy in such simple, tidy moves, like putting your socks back in the drawer. **14...Rae8 15.Nf3 Bd6 16.Be3 Re7** (16...Nd5!?) **17.d4 Rfe8 18.c3 h6?!** (18...Nd5! 19.Bd2 Rxe1 20.Nxe1 and now maybe 20...Nb6 and White is some way from getting his rook out.) **19.Ne5!** The key to White's strategy, simplifying to an endgame with the bishop pair and the b5 pawn as a hook to further open the position. **19...Bxe5 20.dxe5 Rxe5 21.Qxd7 Nxd7 22.Red1 Nf6?** (22...Nc5! 23.Bxc5 Rxc5 24.Rd7 Re2! gives holding chances) **23.c4! c6 24.Rac1 R5e7 25.a4! bxc4 26.Bxc4 Nd5 27.Bc5 Re4 28.f3 R4e5 29.Kf2 Bc8 30.Bf1 R5e6 31.Rd3 Nf4 32.Rb3! Rd8 33.Be3 Nd5 34.Bd2 Nf6 35.Ba5 Rde8 36.Rb6 Re5 37.Bc3 Nd5 38.Bxe5 Nxb6 39.Bd4 Nxa4 40.Rxc6 Rd8 41.Rc4!** And the knight is trapped. The last few moves are study-like. **41...Bd7 42.b3 Bb5 43.Rb4 Nb2 44.Bxb5 axb5 45.Ke3!** (45.Ke2 Nc4!) **45...Re8+** (After 45...Nd1+ 46.Ke2 the knight has nowhere to go.) **46.Kd2 Rd8 47.Kc3!** (not 47.Kc2 Nc4!) If 47...Nd1 Kc2 (finally!) wins the knight. **1–0**

6 *Magnus Carlsen vs Sergey Karjakin, Tata Steel Group A, 20 January 2013*
Black was tantalisingly close to equality for the whole game, but eventually succumbed to the pressure. **1.Nf3 Nf6 2.g3 d5 3.Bg2 c6**

4.0-0 Bg4 5.c4 e6 6.d3 Nbd7 7.cxd5exd5 8.Qc2 Be7 9.Nc3 Bxf3
10.Bxf3 d4 11.Ne4 O-O 12.Nxf6+ Nxf613.Bd2 a5 14.a3 Nd5 15.Rab1
Qd7 16.Rfc1 Rfe8 17.Qc4 Nc7 18.h4a4 19.Bb4 Nb5 20.Kg2 h6
21.Bc5 g6 22.Qb4 Bf6 23.Qd2 Kg7 24.Rc4Ra6 25.Qd1 b6 26.Bb4
c5 27.Bd2 Nc7 28.Rcc1 Nd5 29.Qh1 Be730.Kg1 Rd8 31.Rc2 Qe6
32.Qg2 Ra7 33.Re1 Rad7 34.Kh2 Rc8 35.Qh3Qxh3+ 36.Kxh3
h5 37.Rb1 Ra8 38.Kg2 Ra6 39.b3 axb3 40.Rxb3 Bf641.Rc4 Rd6
42.Kf1 Kf8 43.a4 Nc3 44.Bf4 Re6 45.e3 Nxa4 46.Bd5Re7 47.Bd6
b5 48.Bxe7+ Bxe7 49.Rxb5 Nb6 50.e4 Nxc4 51.Rb8+ Kg752.Bxc4
Ra7 53.f4 After some tactical skirmishing, the position has stabilised
in White's favour. The stability of the bishop on c4 means that Black
is effectively a pawn down, and f7 is a clear long-term target. At this
stage it is probably not objectively winning, but Magnus maximises
his opportunities to cause problems. 53…Bd6 54.Re8 Rb7 55.Ra8
Be7 56.Kg2 Rb1 57.e5Re1 58.Kf2 Rb1 59.Re8 Bf8 60.Rc8 Be7
61.Ra8 Rb2+ 62.Kf3 Rb163.Bd5 Re1 64.Kf2 Rd1 65.Re8 Bf8
66.Bc4 Rb1 67.g4!? hxg4 68.h5!?Rh1 69.hxg6 fxg6 70.Re6! Kh6
71.Bd5 Rh2+ 72.Kg3 Rh3+ 73.Kxg4Rxd3 74.f5 Re3 75.Rxg6+ Kh7
76.Bg8+ Kh8 77.Kf4 Rc3 78.f6 d379.Ke3 c4 80.Be6 Kh7 81.Bf5
Rc2 82.Rg2+ Kh6 83.Rxc2 dxc284.Bxc2 Kg5 85.Kd4 Ba3 86.Kxc4
Bb2 87.Kd5 Kf4 88.f7 Ba3 89.e6Kg5 90.Kc6 Kf6 If the Black king
was on f8, the position would be drawn, but he is one move too slow.
91.Kd7 Kg7 92.e7 1-0

7 Julian Barnes, 'Trap. Dominate. Fuck', *Granta Magazine*, 1 March
1994. Available at https://granta.com/trap-dominate-fuck/

8 Robert Kegan, *The Evolving Self*, Harvard University Press, 1988.

9 The following decisive game of the match marked the end of an era,
and Carlsen is still world champion at the time of writing in mid-2019.
*Viswanathan Anand vs Magnus Carlsen, World Championship Match
2013, Chennai*, round 9. 1.d4 Greeted by a round of applause by the
audience. Nobody wants another Berlin Endgame, a relatively sedate
line that risked arising from 1.e4 played earlier in the match. 1…Nf6
2.c4 e6 3.Nc3 Bb4 4.f3 d5 5.a3 Bxc3+ 6.bxc3 c5 7.cxd5 exd5 8.e3
c4 Very committal. 9.Ne2 Nc6 10.g4! 0-0 11.Bg2 Na5 12.0-0 Nb3
13.Ra2 b5 14.Ng3 a5 15.g5 Ne8 16.e4 Nxc1 17.Qxc1 Ra6 18.e5! Nc7
19.f4 b4 20.axb4?! White gains time, but loses attacking resources
and invites future counterplay. 20…axb4 21.Rxa6 Nxa6 22.f5 b3
23.Qf4 (23.h4 Nc7 24.Qa3!?) 23…Nc7 24.f6 Nervous. (24.Nh5!?)

24...g6 25.Qh4 Ne8 26.Qh6 b2 27.Rf4 b1Q+ 28.Nf1?? (28.Bf1! Qd1 29.Rh4 Qh5 30.Nxh5 gxh5 31.Rxh5 Bf5 32.g6!? (32.Bh3 Bg6 33.e6 Nxf6 appears OK for Black.) 32...Bxg6 33.Rg5 Qa5 34.Rg3! intending h4-h5 and the game is alive.) **28...Qe1!** Simply planning to take the rook on h4. **0–1**

10 *Boris Spassky vs Gary Kasparov, Reykjavik World Cup, 1988*, round 12. **1.e4 c5 2.Nc3 Nc6 3.Bb5 Nd4 4.Bc4 e6 5.Nf3 Ne7 6.0-0 Nec6 7.d3 g6 8.Nxd4 cxd4 9.Ne2 Bg7 10.Bd2 0-0 11.b4** Spassky has a comfortable position and offered a draw. **11...b6 12.b5 Ne7?!** Too passive. After 12...Na5 the position seems about equal. **13.Bb4 d6 14.a4 a5 15.Ba3 Bb7 16.Bb3 d5 17.f3! Qc7 18.Qe1 Rad8 19.Qh4 1/2-1/2** Black's position lacks purpose and his bishop on b7 and knight on e7 have few prospects. White has a range of ideas including some combination of Ng3, Rae1 and f4, and he might also consider Bc1-h6.

11 Interview from 2003, archived 17 December 2005 at the Wayback Machine, https://archive.org/web/, originally published in the *Scotsman*, 25 June 2003, under the headline 'Scotland's Oldest Man turns 107' by John Innes.

12 If two players really want to make a draw, the rules of the game make it very hard to stop them. In 1996, two teenage American girls, close friends, were paired against each other in the world U-16 championship. They did not want to compete with each other so prearranged a completely absurd yet cheering conceit in the form of an established hyper-accelerated stalemate, with all the pieces remaining on the board. No doubt there were a few smiles along the way.

Jennie Frenklakh vs Jennifer Shahade, World U–16 Championship 1996 **1.h3 f5 2.d4 e5 3.Qd3 f4** So far, so weird, but prepare to be shocked. **4.Qg3!** The exclamation mark is for audacity. **4...e4!** Resisting the temptation to call off the deal and take the queen. **5.Qh2 Be7 6.a4 a5 7.Ra3** Intending to swing the rook to the kingside. **7...Bh4!?** A prophylactic move, but not one you'll find in the Dvoretsky/ Yusupov literature. **8.Rg3 e3 9.f3 Qe7 10.c4 Qb4+ 11.Nd2 d6 12.c5** The beginning of a desperado counter-attack, urgently giving away legal moves. **12...Be6 13.c6 Bb3!? 14.d5 b6!?** And there we have it. No draw offer, not even a threefold repetition, but a hyper-accelerated stalemate, after just 14 tailor-made moves.

13 *Jonathan Parker vs Jonathan Rowson, British Championship, Swansea 2006, round 11*

1.d4 Nf6 2.c4 e6 3.Nc3 Bb4 4.Nf3 b6 5.Bg5 h6 6.Bh4 Bb7 7.e3 Bxc3+ 8.bxc3 d6 9.Nd2 Nbd7 10.f3 Qe7 11.e4 g5 12.Bf2 c5 13.Qa4 Nh5 14.h4 White's last move introduced a dangerous threat of opening the h-file, which is difficult to handle without connecting my rooks. However, it looks like if I castle queenside the White queen will take my a7 pawn and compromise my king's safety. **14...0–0–0!! 15.Qxa7 Kc7!** This crucial detail had been foreseen when I played my thirteenth move. I threaten to trap Black's queen with Ra8 and gain time to start a counter-attack in the centre. Careful analysis suggests that the lost pawn is not significant and my king was never in danger. **16.Qa4 f5 17.Qc2 g4 18.fxg4 Nhf6!** Perhaps the most elegant move of the game. Paradoxically I am opening the position to close it and White's g-pawn is an additional structural target on the open g-file. **19.Bd3?! Nxg4 20.Bg1 f4! 21.Nf3 e5 22.h5 Qf7 23.Nh4 Qxh5 24.Rh3 Rhe8 25.Nf5 Qg5 26.d5 h5 27.Qb2 Ra8 28.Be2 Ra6 29.Bf3 Rea8 30.Qb3 Ra3 31.Qb2 R8a4 32.Bd1 Ra8 33.Bf3 R3a5 34.Rh1 R8a6 35.Rh3 Bc8 36.Rh1 Nf8 37.Nh4 Nh7 38.Qd2 Bd7 39.Kf1 Nhf6 40.Ke2 Ra4 0–1** This vignette is an adapted version of my first-ever newspaper column for *The Herald*, published on 16 September 2006.

THREE: LEARNING AND UNLEARNING

1 Steven Pinker, *The Stuff of Thought*, Penguin 2008.

2 Felix Guattari, *The Three Ecologies*, Continuum, London, 2008. Guattari's mental ecology is about the way we think; the social ecology is about how we relate and act together, and his environmental ecology is the world we are dependent on. Thinking ecologically means factoring in at least these three levels and trying to understand how they are connected.

3 I am grateful to Bonnitta Roy for the conversation that gave rise to this paragraph. Her equine expertise and enthusiasm for the knight's role in chess was unforgettable.

4 Gregory Bateson's most celebrated books include *Mind and Nature*, Hampton Press, 2002 (new edition), and *Steps to an Ecology of Mind*, University of Chicago Press, 2000.

5 Genna Sosonko, *Evil Doer: Half a Century with Victor Korchnoi*, Elk and Ruby Publishing, 2018.

6 Edward J. Dale, *Completing Piaget's Project*, Paragon House, Minnesota, 2014.

7 See for instance, Margaret Donaldson, *Children's Minds*, Harper Perennial, 1986.

8 Robert Kegan, *The Evolving Self*, Harvard University Press, p. 29.

9 John Jerrim, Lindsey Macmillan, John Micklewright, Mary Sawtell and Meg Wiggins (independent evaluators), *Chess in Schools evaluation report and executive summary*, Education Endowment Foundation, July 2016. Available at https://educationendowmentfoundation.org .uk/public/files/Projects/Evaluation_Reports/EEF_Project_Report_ Chess_in_Schools.pdf

10 *Anatoly Karpov vs Artur Yusupov, Candidates Match, London, Round 8, 17 October 1989*
1.d4 Nf6 2.c4 e6 3.Nf3 d5 4.Nc3 Be7 5.Bg5 OO 6.e3 h6 7.Bh4 Ne4 8.Bxe7 Qxe7 9.Rc1 c6 10.Bd3 Nxc3 11.Rxc3 dxc4 12.Bxc4 Nd7 13.O-O e5 14.Bb3 exd4 15.exd4 Nf6 16.Re1 Qd6 17.Ne5 Nd5 18.Rg3! Here we can feel the difference between the pawn being on h6 or h7. The bishop is not stable on g6, so White has a direct target of attack on g7 that forces Black to make major structural concessions. **18…Bf5 19.Qh5 Bh7 20.Qg4! g5 21.h4 f6 22.hxg5 hxg5 23.f4! Rae8 24.fxg5! fxe5 25.g6 Bxg6 26.dxe5 Qe6 27.Bxd5 cxd5 28.Qxg6+ Qxg6 29.Rxg6+ Kh7 30.Rd6 Rc8 31.Re3 Rc2 32.Rd7+ Kg6 33.Rxb7 Re8 34.a3 d4 35.Rd3 Rxe5 36.Rxd4 Rg5 37.Rd6+ Kh5 38.Rh7+ Kg4 39.Rd4+ Kf5 40.Rd5+ Kg6 41.Rg7+ Kxg7 42.Rxg5+ Kf6 43.Rb5 a6 44.Rb6+ Ke7 45.Kh2 Kd7 46.Kh3 Kc7 47.Rb3 Kd6 48.g4 Ke5 49.Kh4 Kf6 50.Rb6+ Kg7 51.Kh5 a5 52.Rb7 +Kg8 53.a4 1-0**

11 Zachary Stein, *Education in a Time Between Worlds*, Bright Alliance, 2019, p. 73.

12 To take an example from the world at large, our current economic system includes various elements like businesses, governments, money supply, profit motive, ecological resources, land, property rights and paid and unpaid labour. These elements exist in feedback relationships with each other; for instance when there is too much money in the system for the available goods and services we get price inflation, or when we pursue indefinite economic growth with

carbon-intensive energy we get climate change, which leads to calls to change economic priorities. However, deciding on which elements to include in the economic system and what the overall purpose of the system should be are philosophical and ethical questions that the political system, in theory, should consider and resolve, ideally as part of a spirited public conversation. For instance, we might agree that the purpose of the economic system should be prosperity, but that could mean simply speed and volume of economic output, or it could be an improvement in some fundamental qualities of life, like levels of social trust, ecological health, cultural depth and vitality, and emotional wellbeing.

13 There are disagreements about terminology, but a system is typically defined as complex, as opposed to complicated, when it is not just hard to understand but hard to predict, due to emergent properties like non-linear causality, in which the effect of a cause recreates the cause through a feedback loop, or spontaneous order, where stable equilibriums arise without any design. A system is defined as adaptive rather than deterministic when it is inherently unpredictable, often due to unpredictable social actors. Even when we have perfect knowledge about a complex system, the relationship between elements can create mutations that organise themselves in ways that could not have been foreseen. The weather is a complex system, while the economy is a complex adaptive system. A chess *position* is a complicated and deterministic system in that even when it includes a near-infinite number of possibilities it is still, in principle, possible to determine the correct outcome with correct play. However, a chess *game* is a complex adaptive system because it cannot be predicted due to unpredictable human systems. One of the best resources to make sense of systems is *The Systems View of Life: A Unifying Vision* by Fritjof Capra and Pier Luigi Luisi, Cambridge University Press, 2016.

14 I am grateful to Bob Kegan for this description of the experience of teaching, outlined in the prologue to his book *In Over our Heads*, Harvard University Press, 2002.

15 John Berger, *Ways of Seeing*, Penguin Modern Classics, 2008.

16 There is a teaching story called 'Learning from the Experts', told in the first person, which reinforces this point. The story describes someone who decides to invest in jade, having been advised that this is the quickest way to become rich. He finds a renowned expert, who

says he will teach him for an hour a day, for five days, to recognise the finest-quality jade. The total cost is £5,000. The student is a little sceptical, but knows this is the world expert, so agrees to the contract. On the first day the master invites him to sit looking at a large piece of green stone. After an hour looking in silence, the lesson is over. On the next three days, as the student grows silently angrier and angrier, he is presented with a new piece of jade, and an hour's silent study.

Expecting something different on the last day, he is shocked to be presented with another piece of jade. 'I looked at the jade with urgent anticipation of the wisdom that was shortly to be delivered. After ten minutes I could stand it no longer, my patience had finally run out. I turned to the master and shouted at him: "I have spent £4,000 so far and another £1,000 today, and so far you have not taught me anything, only left me to look at different pieces of jade. What is even worse, today you have not even had the courtesy to provide me with a piece of genuine jade." '

17 Edgar Morin, *Seven Complex Lessons for Education*, Unesco, 1999, p. 27. Available at http://www.unesco.org/education/tlsf/mods/theme_a/img/03_sevenlessons.pdf

18 Jonathan Rowson, *Transforming Behaviour Change*, RSA, London, 2011.

19 Jonathan Rowson, *Spiritualise: Cultivating Spiritual Sensibility to Address 21st Century Challenges*, RSA/Perspectiva, London, 2017.

20 I wrote about my experience of learning TM and some of its personal and educational benefits almost a decade after learning it: Jonathan Rowson, 'Oddness for old hippies or a better way of life?', *The Herald*, 27 September 2007. (I did not choose the title.) Available at https://www.pressreader.com/uk/the-herald/20070423/282235186218623

21 Adam Philips, *Missing Out: In Praise of the Unlived Life*, Penguin, 2003, p. xv.

FOUR: CULTURES AND COUNTER-CULTURES

1 I have changed some details here, including names, to protect privacy as far as possible.

2 Orphans are not fictional, though. There are approximately 153 million orphans in the world, and every day an estimated 5,700 more children become orphans. These 2018 figures from UNICEF

(the United Nations Children's Emergency Fund) are staggering, and that's partly because they use the official UN definition of orphan, which refers to losing one parent. The figure for losing both parents is closer to 15 million, which is still shockingly high.

3 C. G. Jung, *Symbols of Transformation*, Princeton University Press, 1912.

4 The paper in question is J. A. Joireman, C. S. Fick and J. W. Anderson, 'Sensation-Seeking and Involvement in Chess' (2002), published in *Personality and Individual Differences*, 32, pp. 509–15.

Chess players score highly on psychological tests designed to measure sensation-seeking: 'a trait defined by the seeking of varied, novel, complex, and intense sensations and experiences and the willingness to take physical, social, legal and financial risks for the sake of such experiences'. The list of activities associated with sensation seeking typically refers to bungee jumping, sky diving, paragliding, scuba diving and mountaineering. Furthermore, during a chess game there is an accompanying testosterone rush, typically of the same order of magnitude as that experienced by people involved in one of those risky undertakings.

5 *Peter Griffin vs John Healy, Maurice Club Match, 1974*
1.e4 e5 2.Nf3 Nc6 3.d4 exd4 4.Nxd4 Bc5 5.Nxc6 Qf6 6.Qf3 Qxf3 7.gxf3 bxc6 8.Bf4 a5 9.Nd2 Nf6 10.Bxc7 0–0 11.0–0–0 d5 12.Nb3 Bxf2 13.Nxa5 ('It's always dangerous to open up lines against your own king.' – Healy) **13...dxe4 14.fxe4 Nxe4 15.Nxc6 Be3+ 16.Kb1 Be6 17.Nb4 Nd2+ 18.Ka1** (18.Rxd2 Bxd2 19.c3 was necessary.) **18... Bxa2!** Threatening a discovered check. **19.Nxa2** (19.b3 Bd4+; 19.Rxd2 Be6+ 20.Kb1 Bxd2) **19...Rxa2+! 20.Kxa2 Ra8+ 0–1.** Anastasia's Mate. A knight's pawn entombs, and the knight controls the king's exit.

6 *Jonathan Rowson vs Tony Kosten, 4NCL, Barcelo Hotel, Hinckley Island, 15 January 2012*
1.d4 Nf6 2.c4 e6 3.Nf3 Bb4+ 4.Nbd2 b6 5.a3 Bxd2+ 6.Bxd2 The star of the game, this bishop goes on quite a journey. 6.Qxd2, b4 and Bb2 is standard. **6...Bb7 7.Bf4!? d6 8.e3 Nbd7 9.Be2 Qe7 10.h3 a5 11.0–0 0–0 12.Bh2!?** It's stressful to contemplate …e5 on every move. This uncontested bishop exerts pressure on the centre, while adding a defensive unit for the king. **12...Ne4 13.Qc2 a4** I used to be terrified of my pawns being crippled like this, whereby one unit holds up two, but experience has made me less prejudiced, and the pawn is also a

liability. **14.Rad1 f5 15.Ne1 e5 16.Nd3 Ng5?!** With pseudo-threats of Nxh3+ and Qg5 (16...c5!? looks positionally correct to me.) **17.c5! bxc5 18.dxe5** (18.dxc5!? doesn't force the issue, but might have been more accurate.) **18...dxe5?** (18...d5! I underestimated this. White has to play well to avoid being worse.) **19.b4! Ba6** (19...axb3 20.Qxb3+ wins the bishop) **20.bxc5 Ne4 21.c6 Nb6 22.Rc1 Rad8 23.Rfd1 Qxa3** Strategic capitulation, but he had run out of delaying tactics. **24.Bxe5 Qe7 25.Bd4 Rb8 26.Nf4 Bxe2 27.Qxe2 Nf6?** Cracking under pressure. 27...Qf7 is more tenacious. **28.Bc5! Qf7 29.Bxf8 Rxf8 30.Qb5 g5 31.Nd3 Ne4 32.Nc5 g4 33.Nxe4 fxe4 34.Qg5+ Kh8 35.Qe5+ 1–0**

7   Caroline Criado Perez, *Invisible Women: Exposing Data Bias in a World Designed for Men*, Chatto & Windus, 2019.

8   There are various ways of searching to confirm this on the rating section of the FIDE website, https://ratings.fide.com/

9   See for instance the online debate between Cohen and Fine in the letters pages of *The Psychologist* in 2011. https://thepsychologist.bps .org.uk/volume-24/edition-2/letters

10 A good example of this kind of rethinking can be found in Kate Raworth, *Doughnut Economics*, Random House, 2017.

11 See for example Joseph Barberio, 'This Comic Perfectly Explains the Mental Load Working Mothers Bear', 24 May 2017. https:// www.workingmother.com/this-comic-perfectly-explains-mental-load-working-mothers-bear#page-13; and Susan Maushart, *Wifework: What Marriage Really Means for Women*, Bloomsbury, 2003.

12 Nicholas Humphreys, *Soul Dust*, Quercus, 2011.

13 Another relevant finding, albeit a contested one, is that boys are generally slightly more inclined to prefer things to people, which chimes with anecdotal claims, admittedly mostly made by male teachers, that in school chess clubs boys are more likely to see chess as an opportunity to compete, girls to socialise.

14 A good overview of recent research by Professor David Schmidt is 'Differences in Brain and Behaviour: Eight Counterpoints Disagreements and Agreements on the Origins of Human Sex Differences', *Psychology Today*, 8 Apr 2019, https://www. psychologytoday.com/gb/blog/sexual-personalities/201904/sex-differences-in-brain-and-behavior-eight-counterpoints. In essence, men and women can and do think differently in certain ways and in certain contexts to some extent, but conventional wisdom today

is that the issue is less about the potential aptitude of a single person and more about how powerful social expectations are in shaping the likelihood of that aptitude being realised.

15 Lise Eliot, *Pink Brain, Blue Brain: How Small Differences Grow into Troublesome Gaps – And What We Can Do About It*, One World Publications, 2012.

16 Merim Bilalić, Kieran Smallbone, Peter McLeod and Fernand Gobet, 'Why are (the best) women so good at chess? Participation rates and gender differences in intellectual domains', Proceedings of the Royal Society, 3 December 2008, https://royalsocietypublishing.org/doi/abs/10.1098/rspb.2008.1576

17 I have been unable to find the original source of this quotation, but this line has been widely quoted, for instance in Paul Hoffman's book *King's Gambit*, Hyperion, 2007. It is also quoted in *Players and Pawns: How Chess Builds Community and Culture* by Gary Alan Fine, University of Chicago Press, 2015, which is a book, alas, I only became aware of just before this one went to press.

18 To give one example of how much it could matter to shift expectations, of all the interventions that may give us a chance to reduce carbon emissions at the requisite scale and speed to minimise harmful effects from climate change, some believe the education of girls in the developing world would have the greatest impact; it's not just that the more education women have the fewer children they have and the fewer resources we then need, multiplied by several hundred million. The point is also that our chances of living differently and better depend on the kinds of shift in culture and perception that are only likely to arise from a better integration of masculine and feminine understanding in the world at large. See Homi Kharas, 'Climate Change, Fertility and Girls' Education', Brookings Report, 2016. Available at https://www.brookings.edu/blog/future-development/2016/02/16/climate-change-fertility-and-girls-education/

19 In Richard Tarnas, *The Passion of The Western Mind* (pimlico, 2010), he ends the book with an epilogue about possible futures, and writes about 'the return of the feminine' and what it might mean, for instance: 'To achieve this reintegration of the repressed feminine, the masculine must undergo a sacrifice, an ego death. The Western mind must be willing to open itself to a reality the nature of which could shatter its most established beliefs about itself and about the world. This is where the real act of heroism is going to be...'

FIVE: CYBORGS AND CIVILIANS

1 In March 2015, the online academic journal *Integral Review* summarised my Ph.D. thesis on wisdom. It can be viewed at: https://integral-review.org/issues/vol_11_no_2_mar_2015_full_issue.pdf, pp. 75–78.

2 *Deep Fritz vs Vladimir Kramnik, Bonn, Germany, 2006*
1.d4 d5 2.c4 dxc4 3.e4 b5 4.a4 c6 5.Nc3 b4 6.Na2 Nf6 7.e5 Nd5 8.Bxc4 e6 9.Nf3 a5 10.Bg5 Qb6 11.Nc1 Ba6 12.Qe2 h6 13.Be3 Bxc4 14.Qxc4 Nd7 15.Nb3 Be7 16.Rc1 0–0 17.0–0 Rfc8 18.Qe2 c5 19.Nfd2 Qc6 20.Qh5 Qxa4 21.Nxc5 Nxc5 22.dxc5 Nxe3 23.fxe3 Bxc5 24.Qxf7+ Kh8 25.Qf3 Rf8 26.Qe4 Qd7 27.Nb3 Bb6 28.Rfd1 Qf7 29.Rf1 Qa7 30.Rxf8+ Rxf8 31.Nd4 a4 32.Nxe6 Bxe3+ 33.Kh1 Bxc1 34.Nxf8 When you see this position for the first time you might notice that White threatens to bring the queen next to the king on h7, where it will deliver checkmate, supported by the backward-glancing steed on f8. Once you see this threat, preventing it is top priority and 34...Kg8 would follow, with a likely draw by perpetual check after 35.Ng6 Bxb2 36.Qd5+ Kh7 37.Nf8+ Kh8 38.Ng6+ etc. But why would you see it? Well it's just there, except it isn't. **34...Qe3??** It's a pity the computer has no facial expressions. **35. Qh7 checkmate**

3 *Levon Aronian vs Viswanathan Anand, Wijk aan Zee, Round Four. Netherlands, 2013*
1.d4 d5 2.c4 c6 3.Nf3 Nf6 4.Nc3 e6 5.e3 Nbd7 6.Bd3 dxc4 7.Bxc4 b5 8.Bd3 Bd6 9.0–0 0–0 10.Qc2 Bb7 11.a3 Rc8 12.Ng5 (12.b4 c5! leads to a theoretical draw.) **12...c5** (12...Bxh2+ 13.Kxh2 Ng4+ 14.Kg1 Qxg5 15.f3 gives White excellent compensation) **13.Nxh7** (13.Bxh7+!?) **13...Ng4! 14.f4** (14.h3 Bh2+ 15.Kh1 Qh4 16.d5 looks interesting, but I'm sure Vishy had it covered.) **14...cxd4 15.exd4 Bc5!! 16.Be2** (16. dxc5 Nxc5 is good for Black, who wins back material in all lines.) **16...Nde5!!** A painful predicament for the hapless d-pawn who wants to take a piece but will soon be taken himself. **17.Bxg4** (17. dxc5 Qd4+ 18.Kh1 Nf2+ 19.Rxf2 Qxf2; 17.fxe5 Qxd4+ 18.Kh1 Qg1+! 19.Rxg1 Nf2 Mate!) **17...Bxd4+ 18.Kh1 Nxg4 19.Nxf8 f5!** This quiet move controlling e4 is key, found at the board, although perhaps also found at home and forgotten! (19...Qh4 20.Qh7+! avoids the worst) **20.Ng6 Qf6!** Admirably patient. **21.h3 Qxg6 22.Qe2 Qh5 23.Qd3** (23.Rf3 and grovelling in a lost ending was better, but Lev appreciates

chess beauty, and allows a pleasing finish.) **23...Be3!** (23...Be3 24.Bxe3 Qxh3+ 25.Kg1 Qxg2 mate) **0–1**

4 The full Hassabis–Ellers game in question from 1992 can be seen on page two of the following link: http://www.glorneycupchess.org/prev_reports/1992/GlorneyFaber1992Rounds2and3of5.pdf

5 I reviewed Gary Kasparov's book on chess and artificial intelligence in *New in Chess* magazine in a review article called 'Deep Thinking?', September 2017. Available at http://www.kasparov.com/wp-content/uploads/2017/10/Deep-Thinking-1.pdf

6 *Rowson vs Mac, London, March 2007*

1.d4 Nf6 2.c4 e6 3.Nc3 Bb4 4.Qc2 Nc6 5.Nf3 d5 6.cxd5 exd5 7.Bg5 Be6 8.e3 h6 9.Bxf6 Qxf6 10.Bb5! When playing computers, it used to be important to avoid unnecessary tactics, but in so far as you have any chance at all, you need a certain amount of positional complexity to capitalise on human judgment. **10...0–0 11.Bxc6 bxc6 12.0–0 Bf5 13.Qd2 Rfb8 14.Rfc1 Bd6 15.Ne5!** A strong positional sacrifice. In return for the pawn I gain complete control of the position. **15...Bxe5 16.dxe5 Qxe5 17.Na4! Kf8 18.b3 Bd7 19.Nc5 Bf5 20.Rc3 a5 21.Rac1 Qd6 22.Na4 Bd7 23.Rc5 Rb4 24.Nb2 Rb5 25.Nd3 a4 26.b4 Rxc5** 26...a3 would be played by Grandmasters, because it is psychologically disturbing and makes it harder for White to keep control. **27.Nxc5 Bf5 28.a3!** The a4 pawn is a long-term weakness, tying down the Black rook. **28...Qg6 29.Kf1 Qf6 30.Qc3 Qd6 31.Kg1 Qg6 32.Qe5 Bh3 33.Qg3! Qxg3 34.hxg3 Bf5 35.f3 Ke7 36.Kf2 h5 37.Rh1 g6 38.Rc1 Bc8 39.Rc3!** An important prophylactic move, preventing Black from bringing the bishop to b5. 39.Ke1?! Ba6! 40.Nxa4 Bc4 is unclear. **39... Kd6 40.Ke1 f6 41.Kd2 Ra7 42.e4! f5 43.exd5!** Straightening the pawns, but creating new avenues for my rook. **43...cxd5 44.Re3! Bd7 45.Kc3! c6 46.Kd4 g5 47.f4! g4 48.Nd3 Be6 49.Ne5 Rc7 50.Rc3 Bc8 51.Rc5 Bb7 52.Ra5 Rh7 53.Ra7 Rc7** 53...Kc7 54.Kc5 Rh6 was more tenacious. **54.Nd3 Re7 55.Nc5 Bc8 56.Rxe7 Kxe7 57.Ke5! Bd7 58.Nxa4 Kd8 59.Nc5 Be8 60.Kxf5 1–0** (87) The Mac allowed me to take all its pawns and make a queen, and I promoted another pawn to a bishop just to check the under-promotion function. Oh what fun!

7 Yuval Noah Harari, *Homo Deus: A Brief History of Tomorrow*, Penguin Random House, 2015, p. 97.

8 *Magnus Carlsen vs Gata Kamsky, Sinquefield Cup, Saint Louis, USA,* round 1 **1.Nf3 Nf6 2.c4 c6 3.d4 d5 4.Nc3 a6 5.e3 Bf5 6.Bd3 Bxd3**

7.Qxd3 e6 8.0–0 Bb4 9.Bd2 Bxc3 Looks premature, but Black has to be careful, e.g. 9...Nbd7? 10.Nxd5! **10.Bxc3 0–0 11.a4 Nbd7 12.a5** Giving a permanent space advantage on the queenside. **12... Ne4 13.Bb4 Re8 14.Rac1 h5 15.Ne5 Qc7 16.Nxd7 Qxd7 17.Qe2** It's interesting that Magnus refrained from f3 for so long. **17...Nf6 18.Rfd1 Qc7 19.h3 Rad8 20.b3 Rd7 21.Rc2 Qd8 22.Rcc1** There is no grand plan, but equally no hurry. Kamsky is the first to lose patience. **22...h4** Not a disaster, but this is a target now. **23.Be1! Ne4 24.Qg4 g5 25.cxd5 f5 26.Qf3 cxd5 27.Rc2 Rg7 28.Rdc1 Nf6** (28... g4! looks consistent and playable.) **29.Qd1 g4 30.f3!** Superficially playing with fire, but actually taking control. **30...gxh3 31.Bxh4! Kf7 32.Qe1!? hxg2 33.Rc7+ Re7 34.Bxf6 Kxf6 35.Rc8 Qd6 36.Qh4+ Kf7 37.Qh5+ Rg6 38.f4 Qa3 39.Qh8 Rg7 40.Qh5+ Rg6 41.Qh8 Rg7 42.Qf8+ Kg6 43.Kxg2 Rgf7 44.Qd8 Rh7 45.Rg1 Qa2+ 46.Kf3+ Kf6 47.Qg8 Rh3+ 48.Rg3 Rxg3+ 49.Qxg3** 1–0

9   Jonathan Haidt, *The Happiness Hypothesis*, Arrow, 2007.

10 *Shakhriyar Mamedyarov vs Igor Kurnosov, Aeroflot Open, 2009,* round 6. **1.d4 Nf6 2.c4 g6 3.f3 d5 4.cxd5 Nxd5 5.e4 Nb6 6.Nc3 Bg7 7.Be3 0–0 8.Qd2 Nc6 9.0–0–0 f5** As recommended in my first book, *Understanding the Grünfeld*, published by Gambit in 1999. **10. h4 fxe4 11.h5 gxh5! 12.d5 Ne5 13.Bh6 Nec4 14.Qg5 Rf7 15.Bxc4 Nxc4 16.Rd4?** Qd6 (16...Nxb2! is even stronger and the first move indicated by my Rybka analysis engine. 17.Kxb2 c5!) **17.Bxg7 Rxg7 18.Qxh5 Qf4+ 19.Kb1 Bf5 20.fxe4 Bg4 21.Nge2** Both queens are attacked, but Black gets better value…**21...Qd2!** (22.Rxd2 Nxd2+ 23.Kc2 Bxh5 24.Rxh5 Nf1 wins easily.) 0–1

SIX: POWER AND LOVE

1 Michael Marmot, *Status Syndrome*, Bloomsbury Paperbacks, London, 2005.

2 The following middlegame looked like apartheid, with a clear separation of White and Black forces, until 29…e5!! brought about a new political order.
Alexander Ipatov vs Vladimir Kramnik, World Teams 2013, Turkey
1.d4 Nf6 2.Nf3 e6 3.Bg5 h6 4.Bh4 d6 5.e3 g5 6.Bg3 Nh5 7.Bd3 Bg7 8.Nbd2 Qe7 9.c3 Nd7 10.Qc2 a6 11.0–0–0 b5 12.Nb3 Rb8 13.Kb1 0–0 14.Nfd2 f5 15.f3 Nxg3 16.hxg3 c5 17.Na5 Rb6 18.f4 d5 19.b4 c4!? 20.Be2 Nf6 21.Rdf1 Bd7 22.Qd1 g4!? 23.Kb2 Rf7 24.Qc1

Bf8 25.Kc2 Rh7 26.Rh2 Be8 27.Rfh1 Nd7 28.Qb2 h5 29.Kc1 e5‼
30.dxe5 Nxe5 31.fxe5 Qxe5 White's pawns are weak, and the knight
on a5 is out of play. 32.Nf1 Bg7 33.a3 Qxc3+ 34.Qxc3 Bxc3 35.Bd1
Re6 36.Bc2 Bg6 37.Nd2 Rxe3 38.Rd1 Bf6 39.Rhh1 d4 40.Rde1
Rhe7 41.Rxe3 Rxe3 0–1

3 Francis Spufford, *Unapologetic*, Faber and Faber, London, 2013.

SEVEN: TRUTH AND BEAUTY

1 *Donald Byrne vs Robert James Fischer, Rosenwald New York, 1956*
   1.Nf3 Nf6 2.c4 g6 3.Nc3 Bg7 4.d4 0-0 5.Bf4. 5...d5 6.Qb3 dxc4
   7.Qxc4 c6 8.e4 Nbd7 9.Rd1 Nb6 10.Qc5 Bg4 11.Bg5?! Na4‼ One
   of the single most powerful chess moves of all time. 12.Qa3 Nxc3.
   13.bxc3 Nxe4! 14.Bxe7 Qb6! 15.Bc4 Nxc3! 16.Bc5 Rfe8+ 17.Kf1
   Be6‼ Another outstanding move that brought the thirteen-year-old
   worldwide fame. 18.Bxb6 Bxc4+ An aesthetically pleasing king hunt
   now follows. 19.Kg1 Ne2+ 20.Kf1 Nxd4+ 21.Kg1 Ne2+ 22.Kf1 Nc3+
   23.Kg1 axb6 24.Qb4 Ra4! 25.Qxb6 Nxd1. 26.h3 Rxa2 27.Kh2
   Nxf2. 28.Re1 Rxe1 29.Qd8+ Bf8 30.Nxe1 Bd5 31.Nf3 Ne4 32.Qb8
   b5 33.h4 h5. 34.Ne5 Kg7 35.Kg1 Bc5+ 36.Kf1 Ng3+ 37.Ke1 Bb4+.
   38.Kd1 Bb3+ 39.Kc1 Ne2+ 40.Kb1 Nc3+ 41.Kc1 Rc2 Checkmate!

2 There is a related line from the surrealist French poet Paul
   Éluard: 'There is another world, but it is in this one.' Changing
   the 'but' to an 'and' alters the meaning significantly, leaving the
   provenance and nature of the other world relatively uncertain.

3 The notion in question applies to philosophical idealism more
   generally, and can also be thought of as Pythagorean. Plato can also
   be read in a variety of ways, and some believe he has been widely
   misunderstood. For a profound discussion of related matters see
   Pierre Hadot, *What is Ancient Philosophy?* Harvard University Press,
   2004 (new edition), and Mark Vernon, *A Secret History of Christianity*,
   John Hunt Publishing, 2019.

4 Isaiah Berlin, quoted by I. McGilchrist (March 2014), 'What is the Soul
   and Why does it Matter?' [transcript]. RSA. Retrieved from https://
   www.thersa.org/globalassets/pdfs/events-transcripts/rsa---what-
   happened-to-the-soul-iain-mcgilchrist.pdf

5 Vladimir Korolkov, first prize, Lelo, 1951. Starting position with
   White to move:
   White: **Ka1, Bc1, Nf5, pf6**

Black: **Kh8, Rg6, Bc8.**
1.f7 Ra6+! 2.Ba3! (2.Kb2 Rf6!) **2...Rxa3+ 3.Kb2 Ra2+** (3...Rb3+
4.Ka2!) When I tried to solve this study, I went too far too fast, and
forgot the king could simply go back, which is why Ra2 is necessary.
4.Kc1!! This move is also precise and necessary. **4.Kc3 Rc2+ 5.Kb4**
(5.Kd4 Rd2+ 6.Ke5 Rd8) **5...Rb2+ 6.Kc5 Rc2+ 7.Kb6** (7.Kd6 Rd2+
8.Ke7 Rd7+) **7...Rb2+ 8.Kc7 Rb7+**
4...Ra1+ (4...Rc2+ 5.Kd1) **5.Kd2 Ra2+ 6.Ke3 Ra3+ 7.Kf4 Ra4+ 8.Kg5
Rg4+! 9.Kh6! Rg8!** (9...Rg6+ 10.Kxg6 Bxf5+ 11.Kf6) **10.Ne7! Be6**
And now it looks like it must be a draw because White cannot prevent
Black's main trick, after 11.Ng6+ Rxg6+ 12.Kxg6 Bxf7+ However, there
is a twist: **11.fxg8Q+ Bxg8 12.Ng6** Mate!
6 Somebody who has acquired outstanding chess judgment is Ukraine's
Vassily Ivanchuk, who celebrated his thity-ninth birthday in 2008
by sacrificing his queen for just two pawns, winning in beautiful
style.
Vassily Ivanchuk vs Sergey Karjakin, Amber Rapid France, round 4.
**1.e4 c5 2.Nf3 d6 3.d4 cxd4 4.Nxd4 Nf6 5.Nc3 a6 6.Bc4 e6 7.Bb3 b5
8.Bg5 Be7 9.Qf3 Qc7 10.e5 Bb7 11.exd6 Bxd6 12.Qe3 Bc5 13.0-0-0
Nc6 14. Qxe6+!!!** An astonishing move that will be remembered
for decades. It seems that this theoretical novelty is not 'objectively'
dangerous for Black, but it easily deserves three exclamation marks
nonetheless. It is curious that all the key variations now involve
Black trying to offer his own queen to defuse White's attack. Normal
is 14.Bxf6 gxf6 15.Ne4 Bxd4 16.Rxd4 Nxd4 17.Nxf6+ Kf8 18.Qxd4
Rd8 19.Qh4 with dynamic equality. **14...fxe6 15.Nxe6 Qe5?! 15...
Qe7! 16.Nd5 Nxd5 17.Bxe7 Ncxe7 18.Nxc5 0-0-0** and White
probably has enough activity to draw **16.Nxg7+! Kf8 17.Ne6+
Kf7 18.Rhe1 Qxe1? 18...Qxg5+! is better. 19.Nxc5+! Kg6 20.Rxe1
Kxg5 21.Nxb7** White now has three pawns for the exchange. Black
fought grimly, but the result was never in doubt and White won in
49 moves. **1–0**
7 Frank Pasquale, *The Black Box Society: The Secret Algorithms That
Control Money and Information*, Harvard University Press, 2015.
8 Dirk Philipsen, *The Little Big Number, How GDP Came to Rule the
World*, Princeton University Press, 2015.
9 See 'The Global Crisis of Measurement', Chapter 3 of Zachary Stein,
Education in a Time Between Worlds, Bright Alliance, 2019.

10 In the following game, against a strong IM who always seems to cause me problems, I felt I was extremely lucky to win, but I was also proud of the way I created the luck.

Jonathan Rowson vs Michael Hennigan, 4NCL, 2006

1.d4 Nf6 2.c4 g6 3.Nc3 Bg7 4.e4 d6 5.f3 0–0 6.Be3 c5 7.dxc5 dxc5 8.Qxd8 Rxd8 9.Bxc5 Nc6 10.Ba3 a5 11.Rd1 Be6 12.Rxd8+!? Rxd8 13.Nd5 Nb4? 14.Nxb4 axb4 15.Bxb4 Nd7 16.f4? 16.b3 seems obvious in hindsight, but I didn't see that after 16...Ne5, apparently losing further time with 17.Bd2! keeps control. **16...Bxb2 17.Nf3 Ra8 18.Bd3 Rxa2** Here I had a long think, and realised I had to fight for survival. **19.Bb1!** When I played 16.f4, 19.0–0 was my idea, counting on the attack on e7 and threat of f5, but (unluckily?) he has **19...Ba3! 20.Bb1 Ra1 21.Bc3 Bc5+! 22.Kh1 Ra3** and Black wins. I cannot give a full analysis of the moves that follow, but I managed to keep some pressure on my opponent, even though he retained some advantage until quite close to the end. **19...Ra1 20.Kd2! Nb6 21.Rd1! Nxc4+ 22.Ke2 Nd6 23.e5 Nc8 24.Rd8+ Kg7 25.Bc2 Ba3 26.Bxa3 Rxa3 27.Nd4!** Michael had three minutes left to play 13 moves, so I offered a draw. White has ample compensation, so the draw offer was mainly a winning attempt, knowing from experience that he would probably start playing too ambitiously to justify declining the offer, which is exactly what happened. **27...Bg4+ 28.Kf2 Nb6 29.Be4 Bc8?! 30.Bf3!? Rc3 31.Re8! e6 32.Rd8 Threatening Nb5-d6. 32...Rc5 33.Nb3 Rc3 34.Nd2! Nd5?! 35.Ne4 Rc2+ 36.Kg3 b5 37.Nd6 Nb6 38.Ne8+ Kh6 39.Nf6 g5? 40.Rg8! gxf4+ 41.Kh4 1–0 Ng4** Mate is unstoppable.

11 An hour spent making sense of the following game is a good therapy. There is nothing explicit about the healing, but deep down we know that life is full of moments like 22...Bh3!! and we need to be ready for them.

Maxim Matlakov vs Pavel Eljanov, Chigorin Memorial, Russia 2013

1.d4 Nf6 2.c4 e6 3.Nc3 Bb4 4.Qc2 d5 5.cxd5 exd5 6.Bg5 c5 7.dxc5 h6 8.Bh4 0–0 9.e3 Be6 10.Nf3 Nbd7 11.Be2 Rc8 12.0–0 Rxc5 13.Nd4 Qc8 14.Ndb5 Bxc3 15.Nxc3 Ne4 16.Be7 Nxc3 17.bxc3 Rxc3 18.Qa4 Re8 19.Bb4 Rc2 20.Bd3 Rc7 21.Qxa7 At this point it feels like White should be better due to the bishop pair and better structure. **21...Ne5 22.Bb5?** An understandable mistake because everybody likes to put bishops together, but the White king is now completely alone. (**22.Be2!** is better.)

22...Bh3!! Suddenly, Black is completely winning – it's four against none on the kingside. **23.Qd4** If White takes the bishop he gets mated: 23.gxh3 Qxh3 24.f4 Rc2! 25.Rf2 Nf3+ 26.Kh1 Qxh2+! **27. Rxh2 Rxh2#; Or 23.Bxe8? Qg4** and mate follows.
23...Nf3+! 24.gxf3 Re4! Fuel for an unstoppable fire. **25.Qxd5 Rxb4 26.Rfd1 Rxb5 27.Qxb5 Rc5! 28.Rd8+ Qxd8 29.Qxc5 Qf6!** A brutally quiet final move with a decisive double threat (mate and the rook). **0–1**

12 The best introduction to Buddhism I know is Steve Hagen, *Buddhism Plain and Simple*, Penguin Books, 1999.

13 Friedrich Schiller, *On the Aesthetic Education of Man*, Dover Edition, 2004, p. 52.

EIGHT: LIFE AND DEATH

1 Adam Phillips, *Missing Out: In Praise of the Unlived Life*, Penguin, 2013.

2 Emily Esfahani Smith, *The Power of Meaning: Finding Fulfillment in a World Obsessed with Happiness*, Broadway Books, 2017.

3 David Loy, *Studies in Lack: A Buddhist History of the West*, SUNY Press, 2002.

4 Mark Gafni, The Radical Kabbalah (books 1 & 2), pp. liii–liv, Integral Publishers, 2012.

5 See John Welwood, *The Psychology of Awakening*, Shambhala, 2002. Welwood discusses the risk of 'spiritual bypassing' in which we attempt to deal with emotional problems through spiritual practices rather than working on them with psychological methods.

6 *Levon Aronian vs Luke McShane, Tal Memorial 2012 Moscow*, round 3. **1.d4 d5 2.Nf3 Nf6 3.c4 c6 4.Nc3 a6 5.Bg5!? dxc4 6.a4 h6 7.Bh4 b5!** An over-the-board novelty, but a familiar idea. **8.axb5 cxb5 9.Nxb5 axb5 10.Rxa8 Bb7 11.Ra1 g5 12.Bg3 e6** There's no good way of meeting Bb4+ so White will have to forgo castling. **13.e3 Bb4+ 14.Ke2 Nc6 15.Ne1** By no means forced. I would be looking to avoid putting my rook on a2, so 15.Qb1!? Na5 16.Qa2 Nb3 17.Rd1, or perhaps 15.Qc2 here. **15...Na5 16.Be5 0-0 17.h4 g4 18.Nc2 Be7 19.Ke1 Nb3 20.Ra2 h5 21.Be2** 21.f3 gxf3 22.gxf3 Ng4! is no better. **21...Bd6!** Very strong and restrained. **22.f3?** 22.Ra7 is given by Ramirez 22...Bxg2 (22...Be4!? may be better.) 23.Rg1 Be4 24.Bxg4 Nxg4 25.Rxg4+ hxg4 26.Qxg4+ Bg6 27.h5 Bxe5 28.hxg6 Bg7 29.Qh3 draws. **22...Nd5** (22...Bxe5! 23.dxe5 Nd5) **23.fxg4?** (23.Ra7! Bc6 24.f4! was the last

chance to stay in the game.) **23...Bxe5 24.dxe5 Qb6 25.Bf3 Nxe3 26.Nxe3 Qxe3+ 27.Qe2 Qc1+ 28.Qd1 Qe3+ 29.Qe2 Qc1+ 30.Qd1 Bxf3** In hindsight it's obvious that Black is now winning, but given that Luke was on 0/2 against the world number two, I am impressed he avoided the repetition by perpetual check, which must have felt at least a little tempting at the time. **31.gxf3 Qe3+ 32.Qe2 Qc1+ 33.Qd1 Qe3+ 34.Qe2 Qf4** White can only wait helplessly for the Black rook to decisively enter on d2. **35.Qh2 Qxf3 36.Rf1 Qe4+ 37.Kf2 Nd2 38.Rg1 Qf3+** (39.Ke1 Qe3+ 40.Kd1 Nb3 and mate will follow shortly after White's spite check.) **0–1**

7 *Mark Hebden vs Graham Morrison, 4NCL, 2012, Sunningdale*
1.d4 Nf6 2.Nf3 e6 3.e3 b6 4.Bd3 Bb7 5.0–0 c5 6.c4 Be7 7.Nc3 cxd4 8.exd4 d5 9.cxd5 Nxd5 10.Ne5 0–0 11.Qg4 Nf6 12.Qh4 Ne4 13.Qh3 Qxd4 14.Bf4 Nf6 15.Ne2 Qa4 16.Rfc1 Na6 17.Rc4 Qe8 18.Ng4 g6 19.Nh6+ Kg7 20.Be5 Nc5 21.Rh4?! (21.Rxc5! bxc5 22.Nf4 planning some combination of Qh4, Ng4 or Nh5+ is winning.) **21...Rh8 22.Nf4 Nxd3 23.Qxd3 Rd8 24.Qe3 Qc6** (24... Kf8!) **25.Rc1 Qd7 26.h3?!** (26.Nh5+! gxh5 27.Rd4 wins.) **26...Kf8 27.Rc7 Qd1+ 28.Kh2 Nd5 29.Nxd5** (29.Bg7+! Kxg7 30.Qe5+ mates in 3!) **29...Qxd5 30.Rxb7 Qxb7 31.Rf4 f5 32.Bxh8 Bg5 33.Rxf5+! exf5 34.Qxg5 Rd6 35.Be5 Re6 36.Qd8+ 1–0**

8 *Johannes Zukertort vs Joseph Blackburne, London, 1883*
1.c4 e6 2.e3 Nf6 3.Nf3 b6 4.Be2 Bb7 5.0–0 d5 6.d4 Bd6 7.Nc3 0–0 8.b3 Nbd7 9.Bb2 Qe7 10.Nb5 Ne4 11.Nxd6 cxd6 12.Nd2 Ndf6 13.f3 The esteemed Russian chess trainer Mark Dvoretsky considers the knight on e4 to be 'superfluous' and 13.Nb1!? intending f3 and Nc3 is recommended. **13...Nxd2 14.Qxd2 dxc4 15.Bxc4 d5 16.Bd3 Rfc8 17.Rae1 Rc7 18.e4 Rac8 19.e5 Ne8 20.f4 g6 21.Re3 f5 22.exf6 Nxf6 23.f5 Ne4 24.Bxe4 dxe4 25.fxg6 Rc2 26.gxh7+ Kh8 27.d5+ e528.Qb4! R8c5** (28...Qxb4 29.Bxe5+ Kxh7 30.Rh3+ Kg6 31.Rg3+ Kh6 32.Rf6+ Kh5 33.Rf5+ Kh6 34.Bf4+ Kh7 35.Rh5 mate) **29.Rf8+! Kxh7 30.Qxe4+ Kg7 31.Bxe5+ Kxf8 32.Bg7+ Kg8 33.Qxe7 1–0**

9 *Viswanath Anand vs Dmitry Andreikin, FIDE Candidates Tournament 2014, Khanty-Mansiysk*, round 12 **1.e4 c6 2.d4 d5 3.Nc3 dxe4 4.Nxe4 Bf5 5.Ng3 Bg6 6.h4 h6 7.Nf3 e6 8.Ne5 Bh7 9.Bd3 Bxd3 10.Qxd3 Nd7 11.f4 Bb4+ 12.c3 Be7 13.Bd2 Ngf6 14.0–0–0 0–0 15.Qf3 Qc7 16.c4 a5!? 17.Kb1 Rad8 18.Bc1 a4 19.Rhe1 a3 20.b3 Bb4 21.Re3 c5 22.d5! exd5 23.cxd5 Nb6 24.Red3 Qc8?! 25.d6 Rfe8 26.Nh5! Re6**

27.Nxf6+?! (27.d7!) **27...Rxf6 28.d7** (28.Ng4!) **28...Qc7 29.Qg4 c4!
30.Rg3! g6 31.h5! cxb3 32.Rxb3! Na4! 33.hxg6 fxg6 34.Rxb4! Nc3+
35.Kc2! b5!** Posing problems by controlling c4. **36.Kb3 Na4 37.Qf3**
(37.Bd2! 37...Nc5+ 38.Kxa3 Ra6+ 39.Kb2 Qa5 40.a4! Nxa4+ 41.Kc1!
Qc7+ 42.Kb1 but that's a fairly inhuman line) **37...Nc5+ 38.Kc2
Na4+ 39.Kb3 Nc5+ 40.Kc2 Na4+41.Kb3** (41.Kd2!? Qd6+ 42.Nd3
Rf7! Keeps the material but feels risky. I was hoping for 41.Rc4! bxc4
42.Bxa3 when White threatens Be7 and appears to be winning, but it's
hardly courageous to sacrifice other people's rooks and risk everything
on their behalf.**1/2—1/2**

10 BBC Radio 4, *Thinking Allowed*, 'Sacrifice', 26 March 2018. https://
    www.bbc.co.uk/sounds/play/b09w10b7

11 Rowan Williams, *Choose Life*, Bloomsbury Publishing, 2013.

12 In the following game, my opponent sacrificed a pawn, and before
    taking it I had to be very sure of the path ahead. Before the final
    move it looks like all is lost, but my unexpected and decisive knight
    retreat to its starting square was a little Easter surprise.
    Jonathan Rowson vs Alex Yermolinsky, 30th World Open, Philadelphia,
    round 4, 2002. **1.e4 c5 2.Nf3 Nc6 3.Bb5 d6 4.0–0 Bd7 5.Re1
    Nf6 6.h3 Rc8 7.c3 Ne5 8.Bxd7+ Qxd7 9.d4 cxd4 10.cxd4
    Rxc1!? 11.Qxc1 Nd3 12.Qe3 Nxe1 13.Qxe1 e6 14.Nc3 Be7 15.Rd1
    0–0 16.e5 Nd5 17.Nxd5 exd5 18.Qa5 Qc6 19.Qxa7!** A difficult
    decision requiring careful calculation. **19...Qc2 20.Rd2 Qc1+
    21.Kh2 Bg5!?** I had seen this coming: **22.Re2 Bf4+ 23.g3 Qd1
    24.Ng1!** Without this move I would be losing material, but now
    Black has to retreat and his position falls apart. Seeing this well
    concealed move was a vivid illustration to me that I had grown in
    strength as a player, largely through my recent efforts to improve
    my calculation. **1–0**

13 Karapanos's final game suggests he had a creative mind. Although
    he was outplayed in the first phase of the following game, he shows
    considerable flair once the middlegame begins.
    Nikolaos Karapanos vs Dan Zoler, 24th ICT, Acropolis, Chalkida, 2009
    **1.d4 Nf6 2.c4 e6 3.g3 Bb4+ 4.Bd2 c5 5.Bxb4 cxb4 6.Bg2 0–0 7.Nf3
    d6 8.0–0 a5 9.a3 Na6 10.Nbd2 Qc7 11.h3 Rd8 12.e4 e5 13.Qe2 b6
    14.a4!? Bb7 15.b3 Re8 16.Rad1** Closing the position with 16.d5 was
    probably best. **16...Rad8 17.Rfe1 exd4 18.Nxd4 Nc5 19.f3 Nh5** (19...
    Ba6!? White's queen is not totally comfortable.; 19...d5 also looks
    playable) **20.Nf1 d5 21.cxd5?!** (21.f4! Nf6 22.e5 Nfe4 23.cxd5 Nc3

24.Qg4 Nxd1 25.Rxd1 with excellent compensation, e.g. 25...Bxd5? 26.Bxd5 Rxd5 27.Nf5) **21...Bxd5 22.exd5!?** Practically quite strong, but theoretically suspect. **22...Rxe2 23.Rxe2 g6** 23...g5!? looks radical, but by stopping f4 it makes d5 much harder to protect. **24.f4 Nf6 25.Nc6 Rd7 26.Ne5 Rd8 27.Nc6 Rd7 28.Ne5 Nxb3!?** Had Black played 28...Rd8 and agreed to a draw, would the heart attack have been prevented? **29.Nxd7 Nxd7** 29...Qxd7! 30.d6 Qxa4! winning the a-pawn is a big deal. **30.d6 Qc5+ 31.Kh2 Kg7 32.Re7 Qc8 33.Ne3 Nf6 34.d7 Qd8 35.Ng4 Kf8 36.Ne5! Nc5** 36...Nc5 37.Rxf7+ Kg8 38.Rxf6 wins easily. **1–0**

MOVING ON

1 This particular reading came from Stephen Karcher, *How to Use the I CHING*, Element Books, 1997.

Index

A Note on the Author

Jonathan Rowson is a writer, philosopher and chess Grandmaster who was British Chess Champion 2004–6. He holds degrees from Oxford, Bristol and Harvard universities and was formerly director of the Social Brain Centre at the RSA and an Open Society Fellow. In 2016 he became co-founder of Perspectiva, where he leads research on the interplay of systems, souls and society.

A Note on the Type

The text of this book is set Adobe Garamond. It is one of several versions of Garamond based on the designs of Claude Garamond. It is thought that Garamond based his font on Bembo, cut in 1495 by Francesco Griffo in collaboration with the Italian printer Aldus Manutius. Garamond types were first used in books printed in Paris around 1532. Many of the present-day versions of this type are based on the Typi Academiae of Jean Jannon cut in Sedan in 1615.

Claude Garamond was born in Paris in 1480. He learned how to cut type from his father and by the age of fifteen he was able to fashion steel punches the size of a pica with great precision. At the age of sixty he was commissioned by King Francis I to design a Greek alphabet, and for this he was given the honourable title of royal type founder. He died in 1561.

H. 11/19
C 5/20
O 11/20
W 5/21